T0360430

WHEN
ENTREPRENEURS
MEET

The Collective Governance
of New Ideas

WHEN
ENTREPRENEURS
MEET
The Collective Governance
of New Ideas

Darcy W.E. Allen

RMIT University, Australia

World Scientific

W JERSEY · LONDON · SINGAPORE · BEIJING · SHANGHAI · HONG KONG · TAIPEI · CHENNAI · TOKYO

Published by

World Scientific Publishing Europe Ltd.

57 Shelton Street, Covent Garden, London WC2H 9HE

Head office: 5 Toh Tuck Link, Singapore 596224

USA office: 27 Warren Street, Suite 401-402, Hackensack, NJ 07601

Library of Congress Cataloging-in-Publication Data
Names: Allen, Darcy W. E., author.
Title: When entrepreneurs meet : the collective governance of new ideas /
   Darcy W.E. Allen, RMIT University, Australia.
Description: New Jersey : World Scientific, [2021] | Includes bibliographical references and index.
Identifiers: LCCN 2020044316 | ISBN 9781786349187 (hardcover) |
   ISBN 9781786349194 (ebook) | ISBN 9781786349200 (ebook other)
Subjects: LCSH: Entrepreneurship. | Research, Industrial. | Technological innovations. |
   New products. | Knowledge management.
Classification: LCC HB615 .A663 2021 | DDC 338/.04--dc23
LC record available at https://lccn.loc.gov/2020044316

British Library Cataloguing-in-Publication Data
A catalogue record for this book is available from the British Library.

Copyright © 2021 by World Scientific Publishing Europe Ltd.

All rights reserved. This book, or parts thereof, may not be reproduced in any form or by any means, electronic or mechanical, including photocopying, recording or any information storage and retrieval system now known or to be invented, without written permission from the Publisher.

For photocopying of material in this volume, please pay a copying fee through the Copyright Clearance Center, Inc., 222 Rosewood Drive, Danvers, MA 01923, USA. In this case permission to photocopy is not required from the publisher.

For any available supplementary material, please visit
https://www.worldscientific.com/worldscibooks/10.1142/Q0269#t=suppl

Desk Editors: Aanand Jayaraman/Michael Beale/Shi Ying Koe

Typeset by Stallion Press
Email: enquiries@stallionpress.com

Printed in Singapore

About the Author

Dr. Darcy W.E. Allen (Twitter: @DrDarcyAllen) is a Research Fellow at the RMIT Blockchain Innovation Hub. He is an economist and writer working on the economics of new technologies. Dr. Allen has published journal articles across popular economics and law journals including *Research Policy* and *Harvard Negotiation Law Review*. His recent books include: *Crypto-democracy: How Blockchain Can Radically Expand Democratic Choice* (Lexington Books, 2019) and *Unfreeze: How to Create a High Growth Economy After the Pandemic* (American Institute for Economic Research, 2020). Dr. Allen has appeared as an expert witness before Australian national and state parliamentary inquiries, his commentary and writing has appeared widely across the electronic and print media, and he sits on the editorial board of several blockchain journals.

Acknowledgments

This book is an edited and updated version of my doctoral dissertation, *The Private Governance of Entrepreneurship: An Institutional Approach to Entrepreneurial Discovery*. I wrote that dissertation as a doctoral student at the RMIT College of Business in Melbourne under the guidance of Jason Potts and Sinclair Davidson. My motivation was to better understand how entrepreneurs discover market opportunities for new technologies. At a time of rapid economic and political change, understanding entrepreneurial discovery and growth remains an incredibly important question.

The complex interplay between entrepreneurship, technology and regulation continue to frame my research today—albeit with a more specific focus on blockchain technology. While these ideas were developed as a doctoral student at RMIT, they led to the development of the RMIT Blockchain Innovation Hub, the world's first social science research center dedicated to blockchain technology. I am deeply grateful to the team and for the culture that has developed. This culture is not just one of intellectual curiosity, but a shared understanding that ideas are best developed collectively.

Many people have directly influenced the ideas in this book. Jason Potts, including in his recent book *Innovation Commons: The Origin of Economic Growth*, entrepreneurially connected commons and innovation. Sinclair Davidson, Chris Berg and Aaron M. Lane have been remarkably fruitful sources of questioning, mentoring and guidance. My other fellow candidates and colleagues are also greatly appreciated, including Prateek Goorha, Peter Gregory and Trent J. MacDonald. I would also like to thank

Richard E. Wagner (George Mason University) and Anthony Endres (The University of Auckland) as examiners, as well as co-authors of other publications, including Angela Daly (now University of Strathclyde), Ramon Lobato (now RMIT), and Jarkko Moilanen.

There are many reviewers and conference participants to thank. Some of the core contributions of the book have been outlined in the *International Journal of the Commons* (2016), *Journal of Entrepreneurship and Public Policy* (2019), *New Perspectives on Political Economy* (2017) and the *Journal of Peer Production* (2014). I have also published related book chapters in *Banking Beyond Banks and Money* (Springer, 2016) and *Blockchain Economics* (World Scientific, 2019). I would also like to thank conference attendees at the Southern Economic Association Conference (2016), International Association for the Study of the Commons (2015), RMIT Entrepreneurship and Innovation Seminar (2018), Sydney Blockchain Workshops (2015) and the PhD Conference in Business and Economics at the University of Queensland (2015).

Most of all, I would like to thank my family for encouraging me to write. I am forever grateful. To my wife, Klara, this book is dedicated to you—for your love and patience.

Contents

Chapter 1

Governing Entrepreneurial Discovery

1.1 Introduction

Understanding where growth comes from is the core of economics.[1] Since the seventeenth century, many countries have experienced over two centuries of remarkably enduring economic growth. But was luck, geography, or culture responsible for this prosperity? Economists have converged on at least two interrelated answers to this question of where growth comes from: (1) innovation and technological change; (2) effective institutions and governance.[2] This book lies at the intersection of these two drivers. The common thread throughout the book is the development of a better understanding of the institutional conditions of entrepreneurial discovery of market opportunities. What happens when entrepreneurs meet? What governance structures do entrepreneurs use to collectively develop ideas?

---

[1] This is true since at least when Adam Smith (1976 [1776]) enquired into the wealth of nations.

[2] Modern economic growth theory has endogenously integrated innovation into its growth models. It has emphasized that the significant contributing factors to economic growth (including innovation and investments in human capital) are endogenous. The field focuses on the externalities and spillovers within an economic system. Drawing on the work of Adam Smith (1976 [1776]) and David Ricardo (1821), modern economic growth theory expanded from the work of Arrow (1962a). It more recently included Aghion and Howitt (1990), Griliches (1991), Grossman and Helpman (1991), Lucas (2009), and Romer (1986, 1990). This demonstrates the increasing understanding of the importance of innovation and technical change within the process of economic growth. Also, see McCloskey (1981) on institutions and innovation.

The core aim of the book is to better understand the governance structures in the earliest stages of entrepreneurial discovery, where entrepreneurs are seeking to apply technologies in novel ways. The process of entrepreneurial discovery does not happen in an institutional vacuum. Entrepreneurs create and utilize governance structures to share ideas and to reveal new ones. This book develops a new institutional approach to understanding entrepreneurial discovery, applies this understanding to frontier technologies, and outlines a new approach to economic and innovation policy. My two guiding concepts are entrepreneurship and institutions.

Entrepreneurship is the process of discovering new ways to organize our lives, businesses and societies to meet human needs. This entrepreneurial process propels economies. The speed of technological change in the twenty-first century is palpable. Economist Ludwig von Mises even argued that *all* human action is entrepreneurial.[3] Therefore, while this book focuses on entrepreneurship over new technologies, such as 3D printers, artificial intelligence and blockchains, its contributions are also generalizable across many areas of entrepreneurial discovery, many of which may not initially be understood as being entrepreneurial. If we can better understand the process and context of entrepreneurship, we can better understand the process of economic growth and prosperity.

Entrepreneurship occurs within an institutional context of firms, markets, governments, and, as this book argues, private self-governance. *Institutions* are the informal and formal rules of the game within which individuals act, shaping the way they coordinate, cooperate and compete.[4] Growth is constrained within, and facilitated by, institutions.[5] Recent economic histories have shed light on the importance of institutions. Deirdre McCloskey, for instance, has argued that institutional decentralization following the Enlightenment enabled people to "have a go" and act

---

[3] See Mises (1949).

[4] The structure of institutions also incentivizes the direction of entrepreneurial activity. See Baumol (1990).

[5] A strand of the new institutional economics has focused on the importance of institutional structures, both formal and informal, to the process of economic growth and development. See, e.g., Acemoglu and Robinson (2012), Allen (2011), Easterly (2006), Hodgson (1993), North (1990), and Olson (2008). For new development economics, see Boettke *et al.* (2008).

entrepreneurially.[6] Joel Mokyr attributes growth to the emergence of a "culture of growth," where societies began to discover and apply useful prescriptive knowledge in industry.[7]

We can take this understanding that institutions matter and apply it to the earliest stages of entrepreneurial discovery. What are the governance structures within which entrepreneurs make discoveries? More deeply, what is the foundational economic problem that entrepreneurs face? Is there a role for government in facilitating the governance of entrepreneurial discovery? The answers to these questions lie on the boundaries of institutional economics, entrepreneurial theory and political economy. They all speak to the "innovation problem" in economics.

In theory, we can pinpoint an "innovation problem"—where too little innovation is created—that arises both from the prosperity-generating benefits of economic growth and the public good characteristics of producing new ideas. In economics, the approach to the "innovation problem" involves a choice-theoretic (c.f. contract-theoretic) analysis.[8] This choice-theoretic analysis emphasizes how investment and resources for innovation are allocated: how much investment is directed toward inventing and innovating? Innovation policy subsequently seeks to remedy this lack of investment through direct subsidies (e.g., public funding) or shifting incentives (e.g., intellectual property).

Rather than a choice-theoretic focus on investment in innovative activities, a contract-theoretic approach directs attention to the institutions, contracts, and governance of the entrepreneurial process. This new institutional approach looks at how entrepreneurs discover market opportunities by coordinating information with others through governance structures. A contract-theoretic lens to entrepreneurship suggests that the core innovation problem for the early-stage entrepreneur lies in coordinating information about market opportunities with others under radical

---

[6] See McCloskey (2010, 2016).

[7] See Mokyr (2009, 2016).

[8] James Buchanan (1975, 1979b) distinguished between the "lens of choice" of economic thought—focused on the allocation and investment of scarce resources—and the "lens of contract" of economic thought—with its focus on the institutional "rules of the game." For the former, see Robbins (1932). For the latter, see North (1990). On how voluntary exchange occurs within these rules see, e.g., Coase (1937), Ostrom (2010), and Williamson (2005). One of the primary contributions of this book is to shift the thinking about entrepreneurship and the innovation problem towards a "lens of contract."

uncertainty, with non-zero transaction costs. The "innovation problem" is not an aggregate allocation of resources problem, but an entrepreneurial institutional governance problem.

The governance choices available to an entrepreneur are not a simple dichotomy between firms and markets. In this book, I suggest that the earliest stages of the innovation process might be best governed through unique hybrid governance structures, including innovation commons. An innovation commons is a self-governance structure that uses mechanisms, such as reputation to pool entrepreneurial resources for opportunity discovery. Innovation commons are dynamic polycentric structures that have characteristics of both firms and markets. The existence of the innovation commons has deep implications for how we remedy the innovation problem through innovation policy.

The three main contributions of this book are as follows:

(1) The first contribution is to define the economic problem facing the entrepreneur in the earliest stages of their discovery process using both entrepreneurial theory and transaction cost economics (Chapter 2).[9] The entrepreneurial problem is a governance problem—a choice of which institutions economize on the transaction costs of undertaking non-price coordination with others under uncertainty. By examining the transaction costs of the entrepreneurial problem—informed by Oliver Williamson's transaction cost economics framework—we can better understand what governance solutions to the innovation problem might best economize on those costs.

(2) The second contribution is to introduce a potential hybrid self-governance solution: the innovation commons (Chapter 3).[10] An innovation commons is a rule-governed space where non-price distributed entrepreneurial resources are coordinated under collectively governed polycentric rules.[11] An innovation commons is only temporarily effective and is best understood as a complement rather than a substitute to other institutions of innovation. We reveal some examples of such private governance mechanisms (e.g., social ostracism) by focusing on hackerspaces (Chapter 4) and the burgeoning blockchain industry

---

[9]See, e.g., Williamson (1975, 1979, 1985a).
[10]See, e.g., Ostrom (1990, 2005, 2010).
[11]The theory of the innovation commons is outlined in Allen and Potts (2016) and Potts (2018, 2019).

(Chapter 5). A focus on the blockchain industry reveals the potentially higher-order need for coordinating institutions, such as innovation commons for institutional technologies.

(3) The third contribution is to develop and apply a new subjective political economy framework, drawing on new comparative economics, in order to analyze the entrepreneurial choice over the institutions of innovation (Chapter 6).[12] The Institutional Possibility Frontier (IPF) from new comparative economics is extended to incorporate the Austrian notion of subjective costs.[13] This new subjective political economy framework is applied to understand how private self-governance of entrepreneurial discovery relates to modern innovation policy, providing several implications for the political economy of the institutions of innovation.

1.2 How to Understand the Innovation Problem

The way in which we conceive the innovation problem matters because it throws light on large amounts of innovation policy and government intervention. In economics, the precise diagnoses of what this innovation problem is (and how it is to be remedied) remain contested. Here, we outline two of those perspectives on the innovation problem: market failure and systems failure. These approaches are both primarily choice-theoretic in that their analytical foreground is on the sub-optimal allocation of investment that can be remedied through state intervention. They are obscure about the entrepreneurial process and the institutions within that process takes place. Understanding these conventional perspectives provides a contrasting background for the approach to the innovation problem developed in this book.

In the mid-twentieth century, Richard Nelson and Kenneth Arrow outlined the economic problem of innovation as a *market failure*.[14] From this perspective, new ideas have special characteristics, including indivisibilities, non-convexities, and uncertainties. As it is also potentially highly costly to produce these ideas and technologies (and there is uncertainty over later recouping those costs), free, frictionless and competitive

---

[12]See, e.g., Djankov *et al.* (2003) and Shleifer (2005).
[13]The subjective political economy framework is outlined in Allen and Berg (2017).
[14]Arrow (1962b) and Nelson (1959).

markets will allocate too few resources to innovation,[15] i.e., investment in the production of new knowledge suffers a market failure because the marginal cost will always be below the average cost, and whoever invests those fixed costs may be outcompeted by new entrants. This is the conventional market failure definition of the innovation problem: innovation is incompatible with perfect competition.

This market failure view frames the innovation problem as a public goods investment problem. An economy will fail to provide the optimal level of investment because weak incentives mean that the social welfare-maximizing costs of innovation will not be met by profit-maximizing firms. But these incentives can be shaped by intervention, i.e., innovation policy.[16] Government-led innovation policy has primarily been rationalized and proposed from this market failure view.[17] It is the polity who corrects the deficiencies of the market.

Today, innovation policies include intellectual property rights, direct or indirect subsidies to private firms, and direct public provision.[18] Governments impose innovation policy through two broad categories: market-based interventions or planning-based interventions.[19] Market-based innovation policies include private monopoly rights through intellectual property, while planning-based interventions include the creation of direct non-market organizations, such as public science institutions, which defrays the missing costs of innovation through public funding.[20] Between these extremes are hybrid mechanisms operating through both markets and governments, including Research & Development (R&D) tax credits.

---

[15]See Usher (1964). Romano (1989, p. 863) proposes there will be zero innovative activities in free, frictionless and competitive markets: "In the frictionless perfectly competitive market, with no barriers to the use of information, the market will provide no R&D investment."

[16]This gap between the private and social investments of innovation activities is a central empirical focus of the literature (Hall & Lerner, 2010).

[17]Bleda and Del Rio (2013, p. 1040) outline that the market failure and systems failure perspective (discussed here) are both rationales "used as theoretical justifications for government intervention in many innovation policy analyses." See also Martin (2016) and Martin and Scott (2000).

[18]See Jones and Williams (1998), Martin and Scott (2000), and Nelson (1993).

[19]See Bleda and Del Rio (2013).

[20]See Boldrin and Levine (2008).

The entire suite of innovation policies are state-based attempts to ameliorate the innovation market failure problem. They all attempt to resupply the missing innovation through the creation of monopoly rents, transfers or public supply. There are many different innovation policy institutions with costs and benefits at different margins.[21] Yet, all these institutions are designed in the context of a mismatch of private and social costs of innovation, aiming to artificially raise the level of resources dedicated to innovation activities by taking innovation out of perfect competition. The dominant public policy motivation of these institutional interventions is that the government can resupply the production and investment costs of the innovation process. As governments push up the level of innovation investment, the innovation problem is solved, and the engines of economic growth are propelled.[22]

The innovation problem can also be described through an *innovation systems* understanding. An innovation systems perspective views the innovation process as a highly complex evolutionary process—a system of institutions and organizations with various nonlinear feedback processes, through which technologies and knowledge flow throughout the economy.[23] Innovation systems theory stems from both evolutionary economics and old institutional economics.[24] Economist Joseph A. Schumpeter was a strong influence on both the technological change literature (which was influenced by evolutionary biology and the theory of the firm) and also the neo-Schumpeterian tradition (focusing on how novelty transforms economics in open systems through adoption and diffusion). The innovation systems approach incorporates the study of firm dynamics and dynamic capabilities, and is influenced by the theory of the firm.[25]

In the innovation systems approach, the different parts of the innovation system are open-ended, complex and evolutionary.[26] But similar to the market failure approach, the innovation system is diagnosed with

---

[21] See Davidson and Potts (2016b) and Goolsbee (1998).

[22] See Davidson and Potts (2016a). Also see Chapter 6 for a deeper discussion of policy.

[23] See Dodgson *et al.* (2011), Freeman (1995), and Lundvall (1992).

[24] See Hodgson (1993) for a review of the old and new institutional economics. The old institutional economics lacked robust methods of comparative institutional economics (see Coase, 1998).

[25] See, e.g., Penrose (1959).

[26] See Lundvall (1992), Nelson (1993), and Nelson and Winter (2009).

various failures of coordination between those parts. The innovation systems approach is in some ways more general than the market failure approach because it moves from the idea of "top-down" steering in the market failure approach to "network-steering."[27] The different mechanisms of "steering" constitute the modern systems of innovation policy.[28] This systems approach provides "greater potential for identifying where public support should go" and has "given way to the identification of new rationales for government intervention."[29]

Both the market failure and the systems failure perspectives on the innovation problem are essentially choice-theoretic analyses.[30] The foreground of both perspectives of the innovation problem examines the misallocation of material resources. A theoretical diagnosis of sub-optimal choices of innovative economic agents, compared to some optimum allocation of resources, motivates steering and correction through innovation policy. Despite the market failure roots in neoclassical welfare economics and the systems failure perspective in evolutionary economics, both ultimately aim to generate innovation by ameliorating the failures of the innovation problem through governments shifting incentives.

This book provides a contrasting, contract-theoretic, analysis of the innovation problem. My new approach is not centered on network-level or society-level steering of innovation investment and allocation, or on some level of optimal investment in innovation activities. My lens is that of the entrepreneur and the economic problems they face in discovering market opportunities. The economics of entrepreneurship has failed to take a prominent position within the two main perspectives of the

---

[27] As Bleda and Del Rio (2013, p. 1039) argue, in the innovation systems approach, "the rationale for government intervention goes beyond a market failure argument: it implies to embed policies within a broader institutional context, and a shift from top-down to network steering." Indeed, as the innovation systems literature expanded, there was a greater recognition that there were systems at lower levels than at the national level (see Kastelle *et al.*, 2009). See also Freeman (2002) for an analysis of how levels of innovation systems relate to economic growth rates.

[28] See Soete *et al.* (2010).

[29] See Woolthuis *et al.* (2005, p. 609).

[30] See Williamson (2002b, p. 172) "Economics throughout the twentieth century has been developed predominantly as a science of choice ... economists who work out of such setups emphasize how changes in relative prices and available resources influence quantities ..."

innovation problem outlined above. Developing a contract-theoretic approach to the innovation problem is not just important at the theoretical level for discovering robust characterizations of the underlying institutional mechanisms of entrepreneurial discovery and therefore economic growth. It also contributes to the political economy understanding of how innovation policies help or hinder the solution to this problem.

1.3 The Aim of This Book

The aim of this book is to develop and apply a contract-theoretic approach to the innovation problem. My aim is to examine the governance problem facing entrepreneurs as they seek to discover market opportunities, understand how a range of private ordering governance solutions emerge to solve this economic problem, and outline the implications of this to the political economy of the institutions of innovation policy.

My approach draws on what economist Peter Boettke calls the mainline of economic thought.[31] This mainline of economic thought can be traced from Adam Smith on specialization and trade, through to the epistemics of Friedrich Hayek and Ludwig von Mises, the constitutional analyses of James Buchanan, the transaction cost economics framework analyses of Oliver Williamson and the examination of collective action solutions to social dilemmas by Elinor Ostrom, among others.[32] They have all variously focused on the market as a dynamic process, comparative institutional analysis and the coordination of knowledge.[33] They have consistently emphasized and explored the "golden triangle" of property rights, transaction costs and contracts.[34] Scholars approaching economic problems from this perspective seek to understand the complexities and uncertainties of an economic system and examine how individuals exchange within those institutions. They begin from the perspective of the individual (in our case, the entrepreneur), the economic problems they face (in our case, coordinating information to reveal opportunities), and

---

[31] See Boettke (2007, 2012) and Mitchell and Boettke (2017).

[32] See Buchanan (1975), Buchanan and Tullock (1962), Hayek (1945, 1948), Mises (1949), Ostrom (1990, 2005), Smith (1976 [1776]), and Williamson (1979, 1985a).

[33] See Mitchell and Boettke (2017) for a recent overview of the mainline of economic thought.

[34] Ménard and Shirley (2014, p. 544) describe new institutional economics as operating on the "golden triangle" of property rights, transaction costs and contracts.

the institutions necessary to coordinate the information to solve this problem (in our case, private self-governance).

This book shifts the analysis of the innovation problem back to the mainline of economic thought. This places the entrepreneur within the context of a complex market economy, seeking to explain not only how existing organizations arrange their innovation activities and the incentives they have to invest in innovation activities but also how entrepreneurs first discover and then act on market opportunities under extreme uncertainty. This contrasts starkly from beginning with aggregate societal perspectives of innovation as suffering a market failure between some socially optimum level of investment and the current private allocation of investment.[35]

Entrepreneurial discovery should not be treated as an institutionally void black box. Entrepreneurs are not all-knowing. They, like all of us, suffer from bounded rationality. They must make choices under structural uncertainty about the future, and they must coordinate information to alleviate this uncertainty through comparatively effective governance structures.[36] In this way, a mainline approach to the innovation problem is analyzed from the perspective of the entrepreneur and how comparatively effective institutions reap the mutual gains from exchange.[37] Indeed, as Buchanan once claimed, "mutuality of advantage from voluntary exchange is, of course, the most fundamental of all understandings in economics."[38]

---

[35] This is a methodologically individualist approach. This should not be confused with the political philosophy of individualism or suggest that an individual operates in autarky. Indeed, see Buchanan (1990, p. 13): "Individual autonomy, as a defining quality, does not, however, imply that the individual chooses and acts as if he or she exists in isolation from and apart from the community or communities of other persons with whom he or she may be variously associated."

[36] Austrian entrepreneurial theory holds that the entrepreneur is a person who must make economic calculations and judgments about future market opportunities under uncertainty and within a complex and evolving economic system (Foss & Klein, 2012; Knight, 1921; Mises, 1949).

[37] This book draws on the logic of transaction cost economics, which holds that the structure of private orderings can be understood primarily based on transaction cost economizing (Williamson, 1975, 1979, 2005). This incorporates the potential for private orderings to be developed through collective action (Ostrom, 1990, 2005, 2010) and expands the potential for organizations to solve the innovation problem beyond firms, markets and states. See also Chapter 2.

[38] See Buchanan (2001, p. 29).

1.4 Book Structure and Summary

This book is broadly structured into three parts that roughly correspond to three questions:

(1) What is the economic problem that early-stage entrepreneurs face? Part I (Chapters 2 and 3) develops the core theory of the book and argues that it may be a transaction cost economizing for early-stage entrepreneurs (proto-entrepreneurs) to coordinate information under polycentric hybrid governance structures.
(2) How do entrepreneurs ameliorate this problem using self-governance structures? Part II (Chapters 4 and 5) focuses on two examples (hackerspaces and blockchain technology) to demonstrate that proto-entrepreneurs can collectively develop private polycentric governance solutions to the innovation problem of entrepreneurial discovery.
(3) What are the political economy implications for innovation policy? Part III (Chapter 6) develops and applies a new framework from new comparative economics—the subjective IPF—to draw implications for innovation policy.

Part I of the book builds theoretical foundations. Chapter 2 develops a contract-theoretic way to understand the economic problem facing the entrepreneur. The proto-entrepreneur is introduced as a person who operates in the earliest stages of the entrepreneurial process where they do not yet hold an actionable market opportunity. Proto-entrepreneurs must gather and interpret further non-price information about market opportunities (e.g., complementarities with other technologies, political resistance). But this information is distributed about the economy, shrouded under uncertainty, and faces non-zero transaction costs. Coordinating it requires economic governance. The proto-entrepreneurial problem is to escape innovation autarky in order to govern the exchange of information with others. This is outlined using the transaction cost economics framework of Oliver Williamson. A transaction cost analysis suggests that the transaction cost economizing governance structure in the earliest stages of the innovation problem may be different from that further along an innovation trajectory.

Chapter 3 focuses on the potential hybrid governance structures to solve the proto-entrepreneurial problem. The innovation commons are introduced as privately governed polycentric collective action governance structures within which proto-entrepreneurs coordinate the distributed and contextual non-price information that is necessary to reveal actionable market opportunities. Such structures may be economizing because of their capacity for autonomous and coordinated adaption. The polycentric nature of hybrid solutions also ameliorates the structural uncertainty of coordinating non-price proto-entrepreneurial information with *ex-ante* unknown trading partners and overcomes the hazards of opportunism due to asset specificity and the realization of any economically valuable opportunities. These solutions may constitute an efficient institutional choice for overcoming proto-entrepreneurial structural uncertainty where the gains from coordination are highest, but their effectiveness will diminish over time, thus making them a temporary and transient solution.

Part II of the book focuses on the study of these private governance solutions. Chapter 4 examines the institutional mechanisms of hackerspaces. Hackers are proto-entrepreneurs seeking to discover valuable uses for new technologies. Several private governance mechanisms in hackerspaces that help ameliorate the transaction costs identified previously are revealed, including the following:

- graduated social ostracism to exclude defectors;
- costly signaling as a form of non-price coordination to match complementary information;
- collective action democratic processes and endogenous rule formation based largely on who has contributed to the hackerspace and to help maintain governance autonomy;
- nested hierarchies of rules as clearly distinguishable sub-systems of rules which enable the spontaneous ordering of individual hackers into sub-groups or teams.

Hybrid governance structures such as hackerspaces are predicted to emerge where there are potential gains from coordinating with others, including around highly disruptive institutional technologies such as blockchain. Chapter 5 focuses not on a class of governance, such as hackerspaces, but on the coordinating institutions around blockchain. Examples of unique governance structures in the blockchain industry include blockchain hack-a-thons, conferences and online forums. These organizations differ widely, including the degree to which agents may autonomously interact and exchange, and how goals are generated.

The second part of the chapter draws on the seemingly obscure field of new development economics. Blockchain entrepreneurs are seeking to build the new institutional structures of the cryptoeconomy—those institutions that protect property rights and facilitate exchange outside of the reach of the state. We can understand this process as private economic development coordinated through blockchain innovation commons.[39]

Part III of the book focuses on the implications for innovation policy. Chapter 6 extends the IPF and applies it to understand the entrepreneurial choice over the institutions of the innovation problem. The IPF compares institutions on how they imperfectly control the dual costs of dictatorship (stemming from state power) and disorder (stemming from private appropriation).[40] But each coordination problem within the innovation process will face a different constellation of trade-offs between dictatorship and disorder. Furthermore, because of subjective costs, each individual person perceives these costs differently. Taken together, these extensions form a new "subjective political economy" framework. This framework is applied to the institutions of innovation, creating a Subjective Innovation Institutional Possibility Frontier (SIIPF) that has implications for innovation policy. The emergence of private governance solutions to the innovation problem implies that the disorder costs of private governance may have been systematically overweighted. The application of innovation policy then becomes an institutional discovery process under uncertainty, where the range of search is constrained and evolves alongside the ideas and rhetoric of the innovation problem.

---

[39]For the new development economics, see Boettke *et al.* (2008), Fine (2006), Leeson and Boettke (2009), and Rodrik (2008).
[40]See Djankov *et al.* (2003) and Shleifer (2005).

PART I

An Institutional Approach to the Innovation Problem

Chapter 2

The Early-Stage
Entrepreneurial Problem

2.1 Introduction

Friedrich Hayek argued that the economic problem is coordinating distributed and uncertain bits of information not known to anyone in its totality.[1] This very same economic problem is faced by entrepreneurs as they seek to discover market opportunities. How should entrepreneurs coordinate information to reveal opportunities?[2] At its core, discovering market opportunities—and, indeed, all human actions—is a process of gathering and combining distributed knowledge to make judgments under uncertainty.[3]

---

[1] See Hayek (1945, 1989).

[2] Throughout the socialist calculation debate in the mid-twentieth century, Hayek outlined what came to be known as the "knowledge problem" in economics: "... the knowledge of the circumstances of which we must make use never exists in concentrated or integrated form, but solely as the dispersed bits of incomplete and frequently contradictory knowledge which all the separate people possess. The economic problem of society is thus not merely a problem of how to allocate "given" resources ... it is a problem of the utilization of knowledge not given to anyone in its totality" (Hayek, 1945, p. 519). A similar perspective of the economic problem of knowledge coordination is outlined in this chapter in the context of entrepreneurial discovery of market opportunities.

[3] As outlined here, the Austrian theories of entrepreneurship focus on the coordination and the interpretation of knowledge to discover market opportunities (Kirzner, 1994; Knight, 1921; Mises, 1949).

We saw in Chapter 1 that the conventional analysis of the innovation problem is one of the choice-theoretic failures. This choice-theoretic analysis emphasizes what level of resources, and where, people invest in innovation activities and the incentives they face in making these choices. This chapter, in contrast, focuses on the foundations of a contract-theoretic approach to the innovation problem. This approach is developed by applying the logic of transaction cost economics (TCE) to our understanding of the entrepreneur.[4] From an institutional perspective, early-stage entrepreneurs (proto-entrepreneurs) face an institutional choice in solving their economic problem: will proto-entrepreneurs engage in firms, markets, clubs, networks or commons to economize on the costs of coordinating distributed information?

The TCEs framework developed by Oliver Williamson draws on earlier institutional economics scholarship.[5] From this perspective, the proper level of economic analysis is the transaction. The logic of TCEs is that the structure of an economic organization is a comparative question. It is based both on the characteristics of transactions and the characteristics of different governance structures. How do different institutions economize on the hazards of exchange? People face a problem of forming and maintaining private orderings to realize the mutual gains from exchange.[6]

To generate predictive analytical power, the TCEs framework involves three main steps: (1) characterizing the transaction costs of a given economic problem across multiple dimensions (such as the asset-specific nature of the transaction); (2) characterizing governance structures across multiple dimensions (such as adaptability); (3) predicting what economic governance might best economize on transaction costs. We begin with the former: identifying the transaction costs of the entrepreneurial problem.

To define the transaction costs of a contract-theoretic approach to the innovation problem, we first need to know what that economic problem is. What is the economic problem that the entrepreneur faces? The economics of governance and the economics of entrepreneurial discovery

---

[4]On the TCE framework, see Williamson (1975). On entrepreneurial theory, see Casson (1982), Foss and Klein (2012), Knight (1921), Mises (1949), and Williamson (1985a).
[5]See Coase (1937, 1960), Commons (1931b), and Williamson (1979, 1985a).
[6]See Williamson (2002a).

have generally focused on separate aspects of the innovation process. While innovation economics "disregards the role of entrepreneurial imagination in setting up the firm," the entrepreneurial literature "recognizes the significance of entrepreneurial imagination without making the connection to the particular institutional conditions of the firm."[7] The notion of exchange of information between entrepreneurs with non-zero transaction costs has as yet not been central to innovation economics.[8] When organizational economics is employed in the context of innovation, it generally asks where innovation activities, such as research and development, should efficiently occur.[9] Solutions tend to be constrained to the competitive market or the hierarchical firm.[10]

But the entrepreneurial process does not necessarily begin with existing firms operating in competitive markets. This institutional context obscures from the core entrepreneurial problem of coordinating information and making judgments about valuable market opportunities. This book points to the earliest stages of market opportunity discovery, i.e., where a person holds a not-yet-fully-formed entrepreneurial prospect in

---

[7]See Witt (1999, p. 108). There exists literature outlining theories of entrepreneurial teams as well as the entrepreneur within the context of the firm and firms (Alvarez, 2007; Alvarez & Barney, 2005; Bylund, 2015; Foss & Klein, 2012; Harper, 2008). However, the organizational economics literature and the literature on entrepreneurial theory have generally focused on separate problems.

[8]For an early exception on the link between transaction costs and innovation, see Teece (1996, p. 193), which begins to embrace transaction cost within the context of firm organization, after proposing that "much of the literature in economics proceeds as if the identity of the firm in which innovation is taking place is of little moment." Further literature embracing transaction costs in the economics of innovation are outlined here.

[9]For instance, Globerman (1980) seeks to explain the existence of hierarchical organization of innovation in the telecommunications industry. Also, see Auerswald (2008), Casson (2005), and Langlois (2007).

[10]See Nelson and Winter (2009), Pisano (1991), and Teece (1986). The organizational choice for innovation can also be explained in terms of dynamic transaction costs (Langlois & Robertson, 2002) or dynamic capabilities (Langlois & Foss, 1997; Teece *et al.*, 1997; Winter, 2003). There have also been transaction cost-based analyses of horizontal and vertical research joint ventures, and of relational contracting models of R&D, which have developed into network governance models of open innovation (Chesbrough, 2003; Dahlander & Gann, 2010) and user innovation (von Hippel & von Krogh, 2003). The property rights approaches have also sought to analyze R&D in an incomplete contracts framework (Aghion & Tirole, 1994; Hart & Moore, 1990).

their mind. They are not entrepreneurs yet—they are *proto*-entrepreneurs. They lack the necessary information to act upon a specific opportunity. This economic problem—the proto-entrepreneurial problem—is then analyzed within the TCEs framework. From this perspective, the entrepreneurial innovation problem is a comparative institutional governance problem of which different governance structures economize on the transaction costs of coordinating the distributed non-price information necessary to reveal an actionable opportunity in different ways. This analysis precedes the conventional starting point of the economics of innovation, enquiring directly into the knowledge coordination processes that precede acting on perceived opportunities.

I also incorporate an intertemporal dimension. The economic problem facing the entrepreneur changes through time. The entrepreneur faces different economic problems throughout an innovation trajectory as they move from a problem primarily characterized by knowledge coordination of discovering market opportunities towards a problem of production costs associated with acting on and exploiting those perceived opportunities. This distinctive intertemporal regularity is termed an "entrepreneurial fundamental transformation."[11] The implication of this entrepreneurial fundamental transformation, as we will see, is to reveal an early pre-transformation-stage economic problem with unique transaction costs (and correspondingly unique governance structures).[12]

2.2   Who is the Entrepreneur in Economics?

Different schools of economic thought approach the entrepreneur in different ways. The way they approach the entrepreneur depends on the underlying economic assumptions taken.[13] Twentieth-century mainstream neoclassical economics, for instance, generally assumed that individuals held perfect information and acted within a static equilibrated system in an attempt to constrain the complex and evolving economy into tractable economic models. These assumptions obscure the process of

---

[11] This is analogous to Oliver Williamson's "fundamental transformation."

[12] Following Harper (2008, p. 614) on entrepreneurial teams, the analytical approach here is "institution-neutral in that it does not presuppose a particular governance structure (such as a start-up firm)."

[13] See Endres and Woods (2006) for differentiation between the neoclassical, Austrian and behavioral theories of entrepreneurial decision-making.

entrepreneurial discovery. Indeed, William Baumol has referred to the entrepreneur as the "spectre who haunts our economic models" while Stanley Metcalfe reflected that the entrepreneur and standard economic theory "have never made easy travelling companions."[14] This section briefly reviews the history of the entrepreneur in economics before outlining the proto-entrepreneur and the economic problems they face.

Early theories of entrepreneurship lacked a distinct functional theory. The term "entrepreneur" traces back to the eighteenth century when Richard Cantillon rendered a direct translation from the term "undertaker."[15] Cantillon's entrepreneur was a specialized risk-taker who formed contracts with employees and insulated them against the risks of changing prices. Adam Smith's focus on the division of labor and the order of the market meant that to him entrepreneurs were individuals who translated demand into supply.[16] Jean-Baptiste Say also argued the entrepreneur brought together workers, capital and resources to actualize new knowledge into a good, using their personality of "judgment, perseverance, and a knowledge of the world, as well as business."[17] Alfred Marshall saw the entrepreneur as a natural and rare leader with the ability to foresee demand and supply, and the willingness to undertake risky ventures.[18]

Such early approaches to the entrepreneur lacked a pure theory or a critical analytical evaluation of the entrepreneur and their role in the economic system.[19] Entrepreneurs were largely indistinguishable from business managers and were regularly linked to the ownership of land, labor and capital.[20] They were not characterized by their functionality (such as having a role in the market process), but generally by their personality. Entrepreneurs were daring, witty, or even courageous.

Because of these individualist conceptions, the entrepreneur was often added as another element in the business process as a factor of production. Neoclassical production functions can add the entrepreneur—specifically, the output of the entrepreneur as embodied within technical

---

[14] See Baumol (1993, p. 197) and Metcalfe (2004, p. 157).

[15] See Cantillon (1772).

[16] See Smith (1976 [1776]).

[17] While Say (1832) focused more on knowledge than Smith, there was still little theory of the process of entrepreneurial discovery itself.

[18] See Marshall (1890).

[19] See Kirzner (1994).

[20] See Quesnay (1888).

innovations—as a fourth factor of production alongside land, labor, and capital.[21] While entrepreneurs are acknowledged as introducing novelty to an economic system, there is little focus on the process of entrepreneurial discovery itself. William Baumol even went as far as to say that in the neoclassical model, the "theoretical firm is entrepreneurless—the Prince of Denmark has been expunged from the discussion of Hamlet."[22]

There are several economic assumptions that make an economy theoretically entrepreneurless. Assuming perfect knowledge leaves no room for meaningful choice. Perfect knowledge implies no possibility of entrepreneurial skill or judgment or alertness associated with foresight, expectation or prediction of an uncertain future. For the entrepreneur to be incorporated into an economic system, this system must be complex, evolving and contain uncertainty. There must be opportunity costs associated with making choices over different courses of action, and this process must occur through the passage of time (i.e., dynamically).[23]

Entrepreneurs are also meaningless if an economy is always in equilibrium. Indeed, entrepreneurship is tightly linked to the notion of disequilibrium. In equilibrium, all economic resources are assumed to be optimally allocated, thereby suggesting no economic opportunities. In an equilibrated system, the entrepreneur would become "purely passive."[24] Disequilibrium is critical to the conception of entrepreneurship either when the entrepreneur is assumed to move an economy towards equilibrium (such as in the Kirznerian market process approach) or when entrepreneurial discovery and disruption push the economy away from the circular flow of economic life (such as in the process of Schumpeterian creative destruction).[25]

---

[21] See Endres and Woods (2006) for a review of the modern theories of entrepreneurship.

[22] See Baumol (1968, p. 66).

[23] For instance, see Metcalfe (2004, p. 170) on market process theory and entrepreneurship: "In the Schumpeterian and Austrian perspectives, markets do not generate equilibrium; rather, they generate order, they solve a problem that of allocating resources to meet needs, but that order necessarily generates its own internal reasons to change."

[24] See Clark (1918, p. 122) and Salerno (2008).

[25] The entrepreneur may move an economic system towards equilibrium, such as in Kirzner's system of alertness, or away from equilibrium, such as in Schumpeter's system of entrepreneur, pushing the circular flow of economic life out of equilibrium. See Kirzner (1978a) for a description of the differences between these conceptions or Metcalfe (2004) for the distinction between Schumpeterian "destruction" and Kirznerian "creation."

Any useful theory of entrepreneurship requires an economic system with the coordination of information and resources under uncertainty.[26] It is therefore unsurprising that entrepreneurial theory has largely flourished within schools of economic thought that embrace uncertainty, knowledge coordination and dynamic market processes, such as the Austrian school of economics.[27] In the few passages Carl Menger dedicated to the entrepreneur, he proposed that the entrepreneur must first "obtain information about the economic situation" before making "all the various computations" of economic calculation.[28] This understanding foreshadows the broader Austrian conception of entrepreneurs as functional agents within the context of an uncertain market process, who process information to discover opportunities under uncertainty.[29] We can separate three common elements of the entrepreneur within the Austrian school (and within mainline economics more broadly):

- *Entrepreneurs choose and act under uncertainty*: Entrepreneurs propagate novelty and newness by identifying and acting on new means−ends relationships under a state of uncertainty.
- *Entrepreneurs exhibit or possess a kind of judgment, alertness, or skill in acquiring information and making economic calculations*: Entrepreneurs interpret information to discover or create profit opportunities within a catallaxy.
- *Entrepreneurs act to coordinate or allocate scarce resources*: Entrepreneurs act to exploit opportunities, and, in a market economy, receive economic rents as they undertake voluntary economic exchange with other choosing agents.[30]

---

[26] See Chiles *et al.* (2007) and Venkataraman (1997).

[27] This choice, imagination and creativity are "lacking in standard neoclassical analyses" (Jakee & Spong, 2003b, p. 126). See Dekker (2016) for an analysis of the Austrian school of economics, including the centrality of the entrepreneur. See also Hébert and Link (1988) for an analysis of the historical roots of entrepreneurial theory.

[28] See Kirzner (1978a) and Menger (1871, p. 159).

[29] See O'Driscoll *et al.* (1996). Austrian economists acknowledge macroeconomic problems, such as inflation, but diagnose these as microeconomic problems. In the context of the "innovation problem," Austrian economists acknowledge the macroeconomic effects—for instance, lower economic growth and living standards—but seek microeconomic explanations over the entrepreneur. These microeconomic explanations occur within a dynamic context of uncertainty.

[30] See Langlois (2007) and Phelan (2014).

Different conceptions of the entrepreneur—for instance those by Joseph Schumpeter compared to Israel Kirzner—weight these elements in different ways. Choosing how these elements are weighted is important for adopting a perspective conducive to the contract-theoretic analysis developed in this book.

The Schumpeterian entrepreneur has a macroeconomic functional role in the economy and is described through their personality and tendency as an economic leader.[31] Schumpeter's approach to entrepreneurship evolved.[32] His earlier scholarship focused on the psychology of the entrepreneur and their role in shaping the world around them.[33] Here, the entrepreneurial function was to disrupt the "circular flow of economic life," pushing novelty and newness into the economic system through a "gale of creative destruction" and exploitation of potential profit opportunities. Schumpeter's later scholarship focused on how large firms undertake research and development and on the political economy implications of change.[34]

Both of Schumpeter's conceptions of the entrepreneur are ineffective for our purposes because they focus on either the personality of the entrepreneur or the process of research and development within firms. In that sense, this understanding of the entrepreneur is not institution-neutral. Indeed, there is a lack of theory relating to knowledge coordination and discovery, and the economic process that precedes the founding of a firm. Other theories of the entrepreneur, outlined here, are more conducive to developing a mainline approach to the innovation problem because they focus on the economic problem entrepreneurs face in relation to uncertainty and knowledge coordination.

The theory of entrepreneurship as alertness to opportunities was developed by Israel Kirzner and remains one of the most influential contributions to entrepreneurial theory.[35] Kirzner's entrepreneur was a product of an attempt to bridge mainstream economic theory with the conception of opportunity discovery and the market process.

---

[31] See Schumpeter (1934, 1942).

[32] For analysis of the shifting of thought on the entrepreneur by Schumpeter, see Andersen (2012), Fagerberg (2012), Kirzner (1999), and Langlois (2003).

[33] For Schumpeter's early scholarship, see Schumpeter (1934). See Wieser (1914) for influence.

[34] For later scholarship, see Schumpeter (1942).

[35] See Kirzner (1978a, 1997, 1999).

Entrepreneurs are those who are alert to, and thus correctly identify, the value of resources and other market factors, and are subsequently rewarded with profit.[36] The Kirznerian entrepreneur exists within a broader conception of the market process, and while this is complementary to the Schumpeterian entrepreneur above, it reduced the entrepreneur to their purely functional form as an arbitrageur.[37]

While the Kirznerian entrepreneur has been widely applied, it abstracts from the process of knowledge coordination and discovery, characterizing an entrepreneur who is alert to a pure arbitrage opportunity.[38] This shortcoming generated substantial criticism, particularly relating to the trade-offs in connecting the Austrian and mainstream approaches to economic thought.[39]

While Kirzner's approach to entrepreneurship may be more conducive to developing an institutional approach to the entrepreneurial problem than Schumpeter's, there is a lack of focus on knowledge coordination processes from the perspective of the entrepreneur. Kirzner's alert entrepreneur acts on market opportunities without active search, despite the fact this approach is distinct from the neoclassical models of rational search.[40] Some of the lesser examined scholarships of Kirzner does emphasize more heavily the coordination processes of subjectively imagined preferences when multiple time periods are introduced—or "Kirzner Mark II."[41] Nevertheless, when the notion of coordination is

---

[36] See Kirzner (1978a).

[37] As Vaughn (1998, p. 142) notes: "in Kirzner's system, the entrepreneur functions as an arbitrageur, buying cheap and selling dear."

[38] See Shane and Eckhardt (2003).

[39] See Buchanan and Vanberg (1991), McCaffrey (2014), and Rothbard (1985). There have been various criticisms of Kirzner despite the fact he recently clarified his approach as having "*nothing* to say about the secrets of successful entrepreneurship" (Kirzner, 2009, p. 1, emphasis in original). For instance, Jakee and Spong (2003a, p. 482) outline how "the determinism inherent in his approach creates inconsistencies with any attempt to integrate a greater recognition of true uncertainty." This notion of uncertainty is elaborated further here—particularly that the entrepreneur faces radical structural uncertainty. See also Korsgaard *et al.* (2015a) for an examination of the Kirznerian entrepreneur and the distinct approaches to alertness and opportunity discovery in his work.

[40] For a model of rational search, see Stigler (1961). Also, see Korsgaard *et al.* (2015a, p. 4) on the different Kirznerian entrepreneurs.

[41] The lesser examined scholarship includes Kirzner (2013). See Korsgaard *et al.* (2015b, p. 5).

introduced into the Kirznerian framework, it is introduced from the perspective of the market process rather than from the perspective of the entrepreneur coordinating with others to discover those opportunities. A Kirznerian approach also implicitly assumes prices and markets exist, within which an alert entrepreneur acts. By focusing on entrepreneurs as having a personal characteristic of alertness in perceiving economic opportunities others do not see, the Kirznerian entrepreneur obscures from the uncertainty of discovering opportunities and therefore also obscures from the knowledge coordination processes necessary to overcome uncertainty to the point of action.

From here, we can see why subjectivism and uncertainty are critical in understanding the process of entrepreneurship. Indeed, "the entrepreneur is shorthand for uncertainty, imperfect information, and the unknown."[42] George Shackle made the distinction between an objective past and a subjective future due to the constantly moving, complex and evolving "kaleidoscope" of an economic system.[43] This understanding is often referred to as being radical because the future is effectively considered non-existent. Nevertheless, this subjective understanding underscores the reality that entrepreneurial choice and action must take place within a constantly moving economic system.

Influenced by the work of Shackle, Ludwig Lachmann also emphasized uncertainty and the social institutions necessary to reduce uncertainty.[44] Further, Lachmann examined the capital combinations necessary for opportunity discovery, holding that the entrepreneur "approach[es] capital structures like complex networks of artifacts that require continuous interpretation" and the entrepreneur finds meaningful gaps in capital structures.[45]

Lachmann stressed continuous interpretation and that entrepreneurial interpretation occurs within a complex and dynamic economic system. His work on heterogeneous capital theory ties in with the broader entrepreneurial literature that entrepreneurs must create or identify new ends-means relationships which have remained undetected or underutilized as

---

[42] See Jakee and Spong (2003a, p. 461).

[43] See Shackle (1983; 1992, p. 428).

[44] See Lachmann (1976). The Lachmannian conception of entrepreneurship in incorporated further into Chapter 5 on the complementary combination of blockchains to form the cryptoeconomy.

[45] See Endres and Harper (2013, p. 323).

ill-structured problems of search and discovery of market opportunities.[46] These interwoven concepts of uncertainty, discovery and knowledge coordination reveal the need for the interpretation of information about market opportunities. Indeed, as Don Lavoie wrote: "Profit opportunities are not so much like road signs to which we assign an automatic meaning as they are like difficult texts in need of a sustained effort of interpretation."[47]

The discovery of market opportunities under uncertainty requires some form of entrepreneurial judgment. Entrepreneurs cannot weigh all given alternatives between market opportunities, understand payoffs of each of those paths in advance, or make a choice optimally as if in an environment of probabilistic risk. In this way, the economic problem of entrepreneurial judgment is a problem of "case" rather than "class" probability.[48] Indeed, one of the primary differences between entrepreneurial and non-entrepreneurial activity is that entrepreneurship is characterized more by uncertainty rather than risk.[49]

To the extent entrepreneurship is the process of making judgments about future states of the world before creating new means-ends frameworks, the entrepreneur does not deal with probabilistic risk within a structured problem, but rather perceives solutions to unknown problems. They are unaware of the structure of the economic problem they face.[50] Entrepreneurs face *structural* uncertainty. Uncertainty does not just leave pure arbitrage opportunities, room for action and potential profits for those who are alert to them.[51] Uncertainty also requires entrepreneurs to

---

[46] For Lachmann on capital theory, see Lachmann (1956). For the broader entrepreneurial literature, see Gaglio and Katz (2001) and Shane and Eckhardt (2003).

[47] See Lavoie (1991, p. 46).

[48] See Mises (1949). Following Knight (1921), uncertainty is about unique events over which outcomes are not only unknown, but are fundamentally unknowable (Shackle, 1992). This contrasts with risk, where a probabilistic understanding of the problem can be developed. The type of uncertainty relating to entrepreneurship is explored further here.

[49] Indeed, as Alvarez and Barney (2005, p. 778) note: "There is growing agreement that one of the most important differences between nonentrepreneurial and entrepreneurial decision-making is that the former takes place under conditions of risk, whereas the latter takes place under conditions of uncertainty." See also Loasby (2002).

[50] Langlois (1994, p. 118) defines "structural uncertainty" (*c.f.* "parametric uncertainty") as "a lack of complete knowledge on the part of the economic agent about the very structure of the economic problem they face" which is exhibited clearly in the case of entrepreneurship.

[51] See Kirzner (1978b) and Rumelt (2005).

apply judgment under structural uncertainty before they can act.[52] In this view, the economic problem facing the entrepreneur is to make economic calculations or judgments over multiple courses of action. These judgments or calculations must precede acting and exploiting those opportunities.

The theory of the entrepreneur as a judgmental decision maker suggests that entrepreneurs must combine and interpret information over costs, benefits and complementary investments to reveal or crystallize an actionable market opportunity in their mind, prior to acting on that potential opportunity. This notion of entrepreneurial judgment stems back to the original conception of Cantillon and continues through the work of Frank Knight, Ludwig von Mises and, recently, Nicolai Foss and Peter Klein.[53] This understanding of entrepreneurship as judgment emphasizes knowledge coordination and interpretation given a subjective future. We now turn to defining the characteristics of the information entrepreneurs require to make those judgments.

2.3 Entrepreneurs Need Information

Inputs into entrepreneurial judgment and calculation include all resources required to discover and exploit market opportunities.[54] This includes the information necessary to define market opportunities to the point of action. In the Kirznerian tradition, the entrepreneur looks to the public information set of prices.[55] Kirzner's entrepreneur is alert to, and thus perceives, arbitrage opportunities between existing prices, before acting to earn profit. This pure entrepreneur relies largely on the institutions of

---

[52] See, for example, Busenitz (1996), Gaglio and Katz (2001), and Kaish and Gilad (1991). Uncertainty may also prevent entrepreneurial action because of their willingness to shoulder or bear that uncertainty. This understanding fits more closely with entrepreneurs' differential levels of motivation, attitude and so on (e.g., Douglas & Shepherd, 2000).

[53] To the extent that all human action occurs under uncertainty, then judgment precedes all economic choices, not just of that of entrepreneurs. Mises (1949) therefore defined a smaller set of actors as "promoters," who owns and invests capital, is a businessperson, is particularly alert, and exhibits above-average creativity and leadership. It is the "promoter" who drives the market towards innovation and improvement, and derives their profit from a superior ability to anticipate the future demand of consumers.

[54] See Shane and Venkataraman (2000).

[55] See Kirzner (1978a, 1997).

the market to perceive and act on entrepreneurial opportunities, as well as their own inherent alertness to those opportunities.

Prices can be considered a complete set of information for the Kirznerian entrepreneur because the market process that determines those prices incorporates distributed information, i.e., prices contain local knowledge of circumstances and indicate how they have changed.[56] From this perspective, the alert Kirznerian entrepreneur considers the distributed information contained within market prices.[57]

But the price system is only effective at recoordinating extant economic activity because "prices fail to provide information on how new markets could be served ... [and prices do not] accurately guide the discovery and exploitation of entrepreneurial opportunities."[58] In the Kirznerian system, markets and prices are assumed to exist as pure arbitrage opportunities which are exploited by alert entrepreneurs. For new technologies that are at the stage of invention, but that the useful applications have not been fully developed, however, markets and prices do not yet exist. It is reasonable, therefore, to suggest that market prices constitute an incomplete information set for the earliest stages of entrepreneurial discovery. Early-stage entrepreneurs require more than price information to make judgments about future opportunities.

The proto-entrepreneurial problem precedes the first phase of the Schumpeterian innovation trajectory.[59] They operate prior to the origination of an actionable opportunity. The proto-entrepreneur requires more

---

[56]As Hayek (1945, p. 519) explained, "the knowledge of the circumstances of which we must make use never exists in concentrated or integrated form but solely as the dispersed bits of incomplete and frequently contradictory knowledge which all the separate individuals possess."

[57]Entrepreneurial discovery can be viewed as operating on different levels of Williamson's institutional hierarchy (Williamson, 1998, 2000). Bylund and McCaffrey (2017) outline how the Kirznerian entrepreneur acts at the level of prices in markets, whereas the Knightian judgmental entrepreneur operates at a deeper level of, for instance, shaping public affairs and institutions. Of particular note is the claim of a higher level of entrepreneurial uncertainty when operating at deeper levels of the institutional hierarchy.

[58]See Shane and Eckhardt (2003, p. 166).

[59]See Dopfer (2006) for an outline of the innovation trajectory in the three main phases of origination, adoption, and retention. See also Dopfer and Potts (2009). The analysis of the "proto-entrepreneurial" problem in this chapter precedes the first phase, origination, because it is focused on the economic problem of coordinating information to reveal market opportunities, prior to acting on them.

than purely technical information (i.e., the information constituting a new technology), or pure price information (i.e., the information read from markets). Navigating the proto-entrepreneurial problem primarily requires *non-price, distributed,* and *uncertain* information, i.e., the information necessary to develop effective business models.

In the earliest stages of proto-entrepreneurial discovery, a cloud of uncertainty surrounds them regarding a future economic opportunity. Proto-entrepreneurs endeavor to engage in entrepreneurial action and exploitation for profit, but market prices form an insufficient or incomplete information set for them to solve their economic problem. Additional non-price information is required to perceive an entrepreneurial opportunity and therefore to engage in entrepreneurial action. In this way, the primary resource the proto-entrepreneur requires as an input into their judgment is non-price information. As Hayek argued:

> *it has become customary among economists to stress only the need of knowledge of prices, apparently because—as a consequence of the confusions between objective and subjective data—the complete knowledge of the objective facts was taken for granted.*[60]

Here, we focus on this non-price subjective and local information required to solve the proto-entrepreneurial economic problem in the early stages of new technologies.[61] While proto-entrepreneurs may hold much of the technical information of a new technology, the information that is much less clear is the non-price information relating to economic opportunities for the technology. This information includes regulatory barriers, how consumers will use it, the trajectories of other related technologies, the sourcing and security of resources for production, potential investors and scalability challenges. This information is not reasonably contained within prices.

Non-price proto-entrepreneurial information has characteristics different from the price information read in markets. The information faces *uncertainty* before it is combined with complementary information. It is *distributed* about the economy in the minds of others, and it has *uncertain value* across multiple dimensions.

---

[60] See Hayek (1937, p. 49).
[61] See Chapter 5 for a further discussion of the nature and entrepreneurial problem of one particular technology: blockchain.

The first type of uncertainty relates to the fact that future states of the world are uncertain and proto-entrepreneurs do not have perfect foresight and cannot anticipate all future contingencies of profit opportunities (i.e., entrepreneurs are boundedly rational). More deeply, however, proto-entrepreneurs face further uncertainty over the value of proto-entrepreneurial information. The value of this information is not necessarily clear before it is synthesized with other information, and its value is revealed by combining this information with other complementary heterogeneous information through a process of trial and error experimentation. The information necessary to form a market opportunity has highly uncertain value before it is combined because the value of such knowledge only emerges once it has been assembled. The value of an opportunity is unclear before all the parts are coherently synthesized, and the value of the information is only fully realized once an entrepreneur acts upon this information. Even if all proto-entrepreneurial information was obtained, the value of any opportunity would remain inherently unknowable because an economy is always in flux and thereby the viability of market opportunities is constantly shifting.

This information is also *distributed* about the economy in the minds of others. Some non-price information will be held by proto-entrepreneurs in relation to their own prior experience and education.[62] But because of radical uncertainty and bounded rationality, no entrepreneur can access or process all of the information needed to perfectly assess a market opportunity in respect of how a technology works in particular circumstances. Just as different entrepreneurs will discover different opportunities because they possess different prior knowledge, all of the pieces of knowledge that in total describe a market opportunity are distributed over many agents in an economy.[63] There is a division of knowledge.[64] The information proto-entrepreneurs require is divided and distributed about the economy in the minds of various stakeholders and consumers and within different institutional and regulatory constraints.

While no one person can fully comprehend or hold all the distributed information necessary to whittle away uncertainty over a market opportunity, this information could be coordinated with other people to partially

---

[62] See Shane (2000).
[63] On prior knowledge, see Venkataraman (1997).
[64] See Hayek (1937).

ameliorate that division of knowledge. This suggests potential gains from exchange in whittling away uncertainty so that entrepreneurial opportunities are revealed. The implication of these potential economic gains of combining distributed non-price proto-entrepreneurial information is that their economic problem is primarily a coordination or governance problem. Proto-entrepreneurship becomes a comparative institutional question over the coordination of non-price information that potentially constitutes actionable market opportunities. Indeed, this notion of non-price coordination was recently developed focusing on how market exchanges require a broader agreement on value that comes through non-price coordination mechanisms.[65]

Viewing economic problems from the perspective of coordination problems can be best seen in the work of Hayek in the context of the market price system. While Hayek did not explicitly write a theoretical account of the entrepreneur, he wrote about the institutions coordinating dispersed knowledge through prices in markets.[66] Hayek proposed that "the entrepreneur must in his activities probe beyond known uses and ends if he is to provide means for producing yet other means which in turn serve still others..."[67] He also outlined the adaptive discovery process of market-based institutional change:

Much of the knowledge of the individuals which can be so useful in bringing about particular adaptations is not ready knowledge which they could possibly list and file in advance for the use of a central planning authority when the occasion arose.[68]

---

[65] As we will see here, it is the non-price coordination that occurs between "proto-entrepreneurs" in the process of solving their economic problem that acts as a complement to later economic problems within the innovation process, including coordination between prices in markets. As Kuchař and Dekker (2017, p. 24) note: "Our thesis that exchanges typically rely not just on an overlap of interest, but on a more extensive agreement rests on a contention that the orders of worth that embed this agreement and thus shape markets are emergent phenomena, just like market prices. They are kinds of emergent non-price coordination, and complement the price coordination that takes place in markets and is widely regarded as the primary type of emergent coordination."

[66] See Ebner (2005).

[67] See Hayek (2011, p. 104).

[68] See Hayek (1973, p. 187).

We can now turn to the question of how the uncertain and distributed information necessary to coordinate market opportunities is coordinated. What are the institutions through which proto-entrepreneurs coordinate distributed non-price information about market opportunities? This question sits on the cusp of both organizational economics and entrepreneurial theory.

Several scholars have connected the economics of organization and the entrepreneur. Mark Casson, for instance, argues that the entrepreneur is a specialist in judgment over the coordination of scarce resources and that this specialization includes entrepreneurial skills, such as finding each other, communicating reciprocal wants, negotiating prices, exchanging goods, and screening quality.[69] This implies the entrepreneur must construct sets of institutions and mechanisms to overcome these obstacles, i.e., entrepreneurial discovery includes creating and maintaining institutions within which one might discover information.[70]

Nicolai Foss and Peter Klein also connect the entrepreneurial theory of judgment with heterogeneous capital theory and the theory of the firm.[71] These authors propose that entrepreneurial judgment itself is non-tradable, but that this judgment can be delegated within a firm. In this view, the firm is the organization in which entrepreneurs own and manage capital and assets: "[entrepreneurial judgment] cannot be bought and sold on the market, such that its exercise requires the entrepreneur to own and control a firm."[72] While it is unclear whether judgment can be traded, the proto-entrepreneurial inputs into that judgment may be coordinated and combined, potentially revealing complementarities in the form of actionable market opportunities. In this context, this chapter seeks to extend these connections between governance and entrepreneurial theory through the TCEs framework.

My approach to the proto-entrepreneurial problem is distinct from the above approaches. It begins where proto-entrepreneurs are shrouded in a cloud of uncertainty preventing them from entrepreneurial action. While previous scholarship acknowledges that entrepreneurial coordination and exchange are not costless—and involves the choice and development of governance structures in order to make judgments—the institutional

---

[69] See Casson (1982, 2005).
[70] See Earl and Wakeley (2005).
[71] See Foss and Klein (2012).
[72] *Ibid.*

solutions to that problem are constrained to the firm. In contrast, my approach begins from the "institution-neutral" perspective of a governance problem of escaping innovation autarky to engage and coordinate non-price information about market opportunities with others in a wide range of potential governance structures.[73] Indeed, the proto-entrepreneurial process of coordinating information to make judgments doesn't necessarily, or even efficiently, occur within the boundaries of a hierarchical firm.[74]

2.4 Escaping Entrepreneurial Autarky

The default for a proto-entrepreneur is to remain in *autarky*. Here, they have no contractual or economic organization extending from them in relation to their perceived opportunity. Remaining in autarky is familiar in innovation economics because it endures as the idea of the lone genius.[75] The lone genius forms a market opportunity in their own autarkic mind, which is then internalized within the hierarchical firm. The entrepreneur is black-boxed as a production function for new ideas, and the choice-theoretic analytical focus is then directed towards the level of effort or investment.[76] Competitive innovating firms are similar to the autarkic lone genius because they are both a single entity with little consideration of how individuals interact and coordinate dispersed and contextual non-price information. The value of the innovation is either embodied as a new

---

[73] This is similar to the difference in approach from Coase (1937) to Williamson (1985a). While specifically Coase sought to examine the relationship between markets and firms, Williamson developed a more general framework which does not begin in one particular organizational form or another, i.e., Williamson's TCE framework is institution-neutral.

[74] Broadening the suite of potential governance structures to economize on judgment has important implications for the remainder of this book, which focuses on hybrid polycentric institutions at the beginning of the entrepreneurial problem.

[75] Indeed, as Cooney (2005, p. 226) outlines in relation to entrepreneurial teams: "One of the great myths of entrepreneurship has been the notion of the entrepreneur as a lone hero, battling against the storms of economic, government, social, and other environmental forces before anchoring in the harbour of success."

[76] Modern innovation economics operationalizes this approach by observing the microincentives constraining or displacing this process and indeed attempts to correct them through innovation policy.

technology or a commodity or is exchanged once property rights are attached to the idea. This autarkic vision assumes the transaction costs of entrepreneurial coordination are zero—there is therefore no meaningful exchange or coordination occurring at the level of entrepreneurial discovery of market opportunities. As is the case with all economic problems, however, undertaking the economic problem of innovation in autarky is not necessarily, or even likely to be, the most efficient path for solving the innovation problem. We know that specialization and trade can bring mutual gains, why not with entrepreneurial ideas?

It seems unlikely that entrepreneurial discovery will best happen alone. Economists have long understood that autarky tends to be a poor solution to economic problems. The process of entrepreneurial judgment and discovery of market opportunites, as with all economic activities, requires interacting, exchanging and specializing with others. Whittling away uncertainty about potential market opportunities first requires bringing other ideas together, before applying judgment, and later acting on and exploiting those ideas. Before acting, proto-entrepreneurs must first coordinate uncertain and dispersed non-price information, and, because this information is distributed about the economy and is of uncertain value, entrepreneurial discovery involves coordinating and cooperating with others. An alternative path for the proto-entrepreneur has therefore come into view: escape autarky.

While the outputs of both the autarky and contracting views of entrepreneurship are the same—new knowledge embodied in the form of a market opportunity—the former focuses on production costs and investment in a choice-theoretic analysis, whereas the latter focuses on how governance structures economize on transaction costs of contracting with others. Developing a contract-theoretic understanding of entrepreneurial judgment and discovery returns the analytic unit of analysis to the transaction and proceeds to examine the costs and hazards experienced by proto-entrepreneurs as they interact and exchange with others.

In some respects, the innovation problem remains an investment problem, but it is not one of incentivizing an optimal level of investment. Rather, it is one of how private ordering governance structures can facilitate and incentivize exchange of entrepreneurial information that economizes on the transaction costs of coordinating this information. From here, it is clear why proto-entrepreneurs must "escape" autarky—because in coordinating with others, they face hazards of transaction costs. The contract-theoretic innovation problem is a question of creating governance mechanisms to induce mutual investment and subsequent cooperation to realize gains from the coordination of proto-entrepreneurial information with others.

A major conceptual implication of the contract-theoretic institutional approach to the proto-entrepreneurial phase of the innovation problem is that it redefines the innovation problem in terms of comparative governance. From a contract-theoretic perspective, the proto-entrepreneurial problem is to acquire the distributed bits of contextual information about potentially exploitable opportunities by organizing in groups under non-zero transaction costs. Those groups might include communities, clubs, teams, departments, firms, networks, clusters, or commons.

This is a new foreground of the innovation problem, as compared to the choice-theoretic conception outlined previously. This approach is built around an entrepreneurially centered account of economic action, in which transactions form the unit of analysis and where different orders of innovation governance arise primarily in the service of transaction cost economization.

The division of knowledge, and potential gains from trade from coordinating this knowledge with others, incentivizes proto-entrepreneurs to develop governance structures to economize on transaction costs, i.e., there are potential gains from trade from coordinating non-price entrepreneurial information, that coordination faces non-zero transaction costs, and private orderings will comparatively economize on those costs.[77] The proto-entrepreneur must decide whether to proceed alone to develop their potential market opportunity to act on it, or whether to, and how to, organize with one or several others to coordinate non-price information and develop the new idea into an opportunity.

The contract-theoretic view of the innovation problem contrasts with the more familiar technology-centered or production function-centered views of innovation economics. In the technology-centered view, costs are resource or factors of production costs associated with exploiting an opportunity. Focusing only or primarily on production and exploitation of an opportunity is tantamount to assuming that the transaction costs of proto-entrepreneurial judgment to discover opportunities is zero. The entrepreneurial discovery is assumed to occur seamlessly and costlessly.

---

[77]A private ordering is what Williamson (2002b, p. 172) describes as "efforts by the immediate parties to a transaction to align incentives and to craft governance structures that are better attuned to their exchange needs."

In contrast, in the contract-theoretic view, discovery requires organization, and this organization is costly. The analytical heart of this new contract-theoretic perspective is to examine how entrepreneurs chose to enter economic organization and in what form.

The way the proto-entrepreneurial problem will be solved is a function of the transaction costs facing them as they coordinate entrepreneurial information with others. Because of non-zero transaction costs, the entrepreneur faces a choice over comparatively economizing governance structures, including the choice to create new governance structures. The actual form that the organizational governance of proto-entrepreneurship takes will depend upon the microstructure of transaction costs and how proto-entrepreneurs perceive comparatively effective governance structures in economizing on those costs. This enables a comparative institutional analysis of the innovation problem through the logic of TCEs, which is covered in Section 2.5.

2.5 Coordinating Information is Costly

Understanding economic problems by taking the transaction as the analytical unit continues in a long line of institutional scholars whose works viewed economic problems in terms of coordination and governance rather than allocation and investment.[78] TCE, at its most basic level, understands three things: (1) there are gains from specialization and exchanging with others; (2) exchange relationships face non-zero production and transaction costs; (3) institutional governance structures can ameliorate some of these contracting hazards by structuring the order of exchange.[79]

Economic organization matters, and this economic organization is primarily a result of transaction cost economizing activities.[80]

---

[78] For example, see Coase (1937), Commons (1931a), and Williamson (1985a). Propositions of governance structures to economize on the costs of entrepreneurial discovery (i.e., an application of the "discriminating alignment hypothesis") are examined in Chapter 3. The aim of this chapter is to focus on the "transaction" side of Williamson's private ordering equation and therefore to outline the nature of asset specificity and uncertainty in the context of entrepreneurial judgment.

[79] See Williamson (2007) for an overview of the foundational elements of the TCE.

[80] See Tadelis and Williamson (2010).

Ronald Coase first explained the existence of firms, connecting the hazards of exchange with economic organization.[81] Institutional structures were no longer taken as given. Alternative forms of economic organization—firms versus markets—were the result of economic choices. In Coase's analysis, however, technology was the major factor determining organizational boundaries based on the idea of marginalism of the different organizational forms of firms and markets in dealing with costs.

The understanding that different governance structures deal with transaction hazards in comparatively different ways, however, still led early TCE to receive a "bad name" in economics because the concept lacked operational and predictive power.[82] Oliver Williamson later operationalized TCE into a theoretical framework, thereby making the field a microanalytic endeavor.[83] In the TCE view, different transaction costs are dealt with in different ways by different governance structures.

The logic of TCE rests on several behavioral assumptions stemming from the inherent non-trivial uncertainty about future states of the world. The behavioral assumptions outlined here are the result of the assumption that because future changes in the world may impact on the terms of the relationship, parties must seek to determine potential changes *ex ante*.

While the precise level of uncertainty varies, there is obviously some non-trivial level of underlying uncertainty associated with each transaction. Beginning from this understanding, and then relaxing other unrealistic behavioral assumptions (e.g., benevolent trading partners, and mobile and homogenous investments), we can demonstrate the hazards of exchange and thus the need for economic governance and organization. This understanding is particularly important in the context of exchanging proto-entrepreneurial non-price information, where, as we have seen, agents face structural uncertainty and radically incomplete contracts.[84]

---

[81] See Coase (1937).

[82] This implies that transaction costs were seen to be invoked in a tautological way—to "explain" differences in organization after the fact—leading the field to receive a "well-deserved bad name" (Fischer, 1977, p. 322).

[83] See Williamson (1975, 1979, 1985a, 2002a).

[84] Incomplete contacting theory holds that contracts cannot specify in advance the entire suite of contingencies, which leads to transaction hazards such as hold-up problems (Grossman & Hart, 1986; Hart & Moore, 1990). Contracts for the coordination of "proto-entrepreneurial" information are necessarily incomplete contracts, as we see here

Proto-entrepreneurs—like all people—face the constraint of bounded rationality.[85] To write any completely contingent contract requires *ex ante* determination of all potential future changes in the world. The computational capacity to achieve this far exceeds the human mind. Bounded rationality means that proto-entrepreneurs cannot devise and articulate an entire decision tree of contingencies for a market opportunity in advance. Even assuming uncertainty, if proto-entrepreneurs exhibited perfect rationality, then exchange hazards could be overcome by *planning* for future contingencies.[86] Relaxing the assumption of perfect rationality, however, implies that effectively planning a decision tree is impossible.

Even despite the unavoidable incompleteness of contracts stemming from bounded rationality, perfectly benevolent proto-entrepreneurs could simply *promise* each other to renegotiate any unforeseen contracting difficulties in good faith as they arise, for instance, whether or not an actionable opportunity is perceived. This would include writing in general clause contracts and adapting later through renegotiation.[87]

But people can also act *opportunistically*. When some trading partners can take economic advantage of situations of asymmetric information, i.e., acting opportunistically, and particularly in the face of asset specificity outlined here, the efficacy of promise falls down because even some opportunistic agents who self-interest seek with guile make contract

---

in relation to the inherent uncertainty over trading partners and the value of "proto-entrepreneurial" resources before they are combined.

[85]The literature on bounded rationality is traced back to Simon (1957), in which boundedly rational agents are compared to classical models of perfect rationality. Simon incorporated the notion of heuristics—of rules to make decisions rather than strict optimization—which now forms a basis for behavioral economics. Proto-entrepreneurs, like all economic agents, are boundedly rational.

[86]In this circumstance, writing a completely contingent contract would be possible but prohibitively costly (see Bajari & Tadelis, 2001). Similarly, the incomplete contracting literature assumes that due to incompleteness, the cost of writing completely contingent contracts is prohibitively expensive. This implied contracting process is closely associated with the mechanism design literature (Hurwicz, 1973; Myerson, 1979).

[87]One of the central problems of economic organization, and economics more broadly, is that people are boundedly rational and cannot anticipate all potential future contingencies. This implies that all contracts are incomplete. The incomplete contacting literature is closely connected with the theory of the firm (Grossman & Hart, 1986). For a review of the literature on incomplete contracting, see Aghion and Holden (2011) and Tirole (1999).

Table 2.1:   Implied contracting processes given different assumptions.

Behavioral Assumption			
Bounded Rationality	Opportunism	Asset Specificity	Implied Contracting Process
−	+	+	Plan
+	−	+	Promise
+	+	−	Compete
+	+	+	Governance (private ordering)

Notes: Present in significant degree = +; presumed to be absent = −.

Source: Adapted from Williamson's *The Economic Institutions of Capitalism*.

adaptation and renegotiation hazardous.[88] The potential for opportunism is hazardous because it is impossible to determine whether *ex ante* a trading partner will act opportunistically.[89]

Even if we take these problems of bounded rationality and opportunism, the market process still theoretically enables parties who have contracted with defectors to easily turn to others to write new contracts through *competition*. Such a competitive process, however, requires mobile and homogenous investments so that people can employ discrete market contracts and resolve disputes in court.

The investments in entrepreneurial process may not be fully mobile, i.e., they can be *asset-specific*. The identities of trading partners can generate hazards and hold-ups in future time periods.[90] In the presence of asset-specific investments, discrete market contracts may be hazardous because of the rise of asymmetric bargaining power and therefore potential hold-up problems and threats (this is despite the fact that it is of interest to both parties to continue the exchange relationship). The implications of these various behavioral assumptions are summarized in Table 2.1.

Given that the process of entrepreneurial market opportunity discovery is highly contextual, and given the heterogeneous nature of non-price information, it is reasonable to assume some level of asset specificity in entrepreneurial coordination as well as bounded rationality and the

---

[88]Maintaining opportunism while assuming perfect rationality then comprehensive contracting would still be necessary and possible.

[89]The types of entrepreneurial opportunism are explored further in Chapter 4. At present, it is sufficient to note the potential for opportunistic behavior.

[90]See Williamson (1985a).

potential for opportunism. The limited rationality of the human mind, the presence of at least some opportunistic agents, and the potential for asset-specific investments, which incur the loss of economic rents in finding new trading partners, imply more complex forms of private ordering. The proto-entrepreneur cannot simply rely on planning, promising or competing to overcome the costs of coordinating non-price information. They need *governance*.

For proto-entrepreneurs to coordinate, they must create and enforce governance structures to economize on the transaction costs inherent in the problem they face. Transaction costs include search and information costs, bargaining costs, coordinating and enacting costs, and monitoring and enforcement costs.[91] Transaction costs are analytically distinct from the costs associated with the transformation or production costs of making and producing things.[92] Douglass North proposes that these transaction costs are impacted by the factors of measurement, enforcement, ideological attitudes and perceptions, and the size of the market.[93]

To define transaction costs and therefore better understand the proto-entrepreneurial problem, we now turn to the TCE framework.[94] This approach defines transaction costs along three dimensions:

(1) type and degree of uncertainty;
(2) type and degree of asset specificity;
(3) frequency of transaction.

What level and type of uncertainty does the proto-entrepreneur face? Are the exchanges of non-price information between proto-entrepreneurs idiosyncratic? How do these dimensions change through time as groups of entrepreneurs exchange and coordinate information and define and

---

[91] See Dahlman (1979). Transaction costs can similarly be defined by what they are not, as is the case in Cheung (1990), who defines transaction costs based on those costs that are not conceivable within the Robinson Crusoe economy.

[92] The Coasean definition of a transaction cost is "the cost of using the price mechanism," whereas two distinct meanings have subsequently developed (Allen, 1999). In the neoclassical literature, transaction costs refer to "the costs resulting from the transfer of property rights," whereas in the New Institutional literature, it is "the cost of establishing and maintaining property rights."

[93] See North (1990).

[94] See Williamson (1979).

crystallize market opportunities? Answering these questions has implications for the transaction cost economizing governance structure throughout an innovation trajectory.

The presence and level of *asset specificity* matter because they suggest whether the identities of trading partners matter. When an exchange relationship creates specific investments, there is an incentive for parties to continue the contracting relationship. Continuity of the relationship is valued because the quasi-rents generated throughout exchange would be sacrificed if the relationship terminated.[95] The economic value of these quasi-rents leads to contractual asymmetries, and, in the face of opportunistic behavior, bring with them pervasive contracting consequences.

The level and type of *uncertainty* characterizing a transaction determine the extent to which the transaction will face *ex post* hazards. Higher levels of uncertainty create larger contractual gaps and increase the possible need for later adaptations.[96] Uncertainty in the TCE framework relates to how the future states of the world will impact on the possible completion of the contract as it was drafted, including both exogenous events that impact on the transaction, as well as the strategic opportunistic disclosure or non-disclosure of information from the other party.

The *frequency* of a transaction relationship determines the extent to which the cost of specialized governance structures can be recovered—the more frequent a transaction, the higher potential to recover the cost of a governance structure. The frequency of transactions is not examined here because of its "ambiguous implications" for economic organization.[97]

To what extent are these costs present in the proto-entrepreneurial problem? We begin with the type and degree of uncertainty. As outlined above, the economic problem facing proto-entrepreneurs—of discovering actionable opportunities—include various search and information costs due to the uncertainty inherent in the problem. The main difference between the production of a widget and the discovery of a market opportunity is that the latter involves the combination and coordination of

---

[95]As Klein *et al.* (1978, p. 298) note: "After a specific investment is made and such quasi rents are created, the possibility of opportunistic behavior is very real."

[96]Increasing levels of uncertainty are relatively uninteresting where there are few asset-specific investments.

[97]This follows Tadelis and Williamson (2010, p. 13).

information under structural uncertainty to produce new knowledge.[98] In the TCE framework, it is assumed that market opportunities exist where contracts have some form of known deliverable and the potential parties to an exchange are known, i.e., the parties to an exchange understand what they are transacting for and agree on the value, even if this value cannot later be verified by a third party.

The type of uncertainty facing the proto-entrepreneur is distinct from the concept of uncertainty with the TCE framework outlined above. The proto-entrepreneur faces a higher level of fundamental *structural* uncertainty than other forms of production due to its inherent novelty of making choices and coordinating information within the poorly defined problems. The type of uncertainty that the proto-entrepreneur faces, however, even extends to include the information over who their potential trading partners are. They do not know who has, or which other people have, the relevant and sufficient complementary heterogeneous information to define an opportunity. Proto-entrepreneurs face structural uncertainty on many fronts, including the following: the nature and type of information held by other proto-entrepreneurs, whether or not an opportunity will be crystallized from a given exchange, what the value of that opportunity will be if one is revealed, and indeed whether the other party is acting opportunistically in the information they exchange. This type of proto-entrepreneurial uncertainty uniquely characterizes the economic problem of initially discovering and then developing a novel idea prior to acting on an opportunity.

The type and degree of uncertainty facing the entrepreneur changes through time. As proto-entrepreneurs coordinate information, make judgments, and begin to define opportunities, the structural uncertainty they face regarding this opportunity falls. Part of this fall in uncertainty is because their complementary trading partners (at least to the extent of their perceptions) are revealed, i.e., as proto-entrepreneurs discover those who hold complementary information that helps define market opportunities, and therefore realizing some mutually beneficial exchanges of information resulting from the division of knowledge, the level of structural uncertainty shifts towards more classic uncertainty. The type

---

[98]This understanding is similar to the distinction between invention and innovation (Schumpeter, 1934), where the former includes the technical knowledge while the latter includes all of the additional information, i.e., non-price, distributed and contextual information, about how to apply that technology in useful ways.

of uncertainty begins to relate to a known problem, such as how future states of the world will impact on the exploitation of the perceived opportunity rather than an unknown problem. Indeed, the type of uncertainty starts to align more closely with uncertainty within the TCE framework.[99]

We must also consider the type and degree of asset specificity. The type of asset specificity for proto-entrepreneurs primarily refers not to physical capital but to entrepreneurial human capital as they learn about a specific market opportunity.[100] Asset-specific investments need not arise from conscious investments, but arise through the spontaneous interactions of learning by doing.[101] Proto-entrepreneurial investments are primarily investments in human capital in the process of discovering a market opportunity.

The degree of asset specificity changes over time as proto-entrepreneurs move along an innovation trajectory. In the earliest stages, there is little measurable economic value because they lack the necessary information to act on their perceived opportunity. But as they engage and exchange information, they may begin to perceive actionable market opportunities. A continuing relationship between proto-entrepreneurs theoretically comes with human capital investments as information is coordinated and articulated. This suggests asset specificity and perceived quasi-rents have been generated as the contractual relationship has developed.[102] As a contractual relationship develops between proto-entrepreneurs, the relationship is no longer faceless—a bilateral or multilateral dependency condition may have been obtained through the

---

[99] This interpretation of a decrease in uncertainty can alternatively be described as the movement from a problem primarily comprising transaction costs—of finding other "proto-entrepreneurs" and exchanging information with them about market opportunities—to one primarily of production or transformation costs—of exploiting a perceived opportunity.

[100] See Williamson (1979, p. 240) for an illustration of human capital investments: "Specialized training and learning-by-doing economies in production operations are illustrations [of human-capital investments]."

[101] See Tadelis and Williamson (2010).

[102] In the management literature (e.g., see Alvarez, 2007) a distinction is made between an entrepreneurial rent and a quasi-rent, with the former occurring under uncertainty and the latter under risk. In this chapter, I refer to perceived quasi-rents, i.e., a perceived future market opportunity in the subjective perception of the entrepreneur, which collapses the two concepts together.

generation of asset-specific investments from understanding, articulating, and defining a perceived market opportunity together.

As structural uncertainty declines about trading partners and the market opportunity, the realization of previously uncertain economic value opens the potential of asymmetric bargaining relating to this opportunity. In this way, when proto-entrepreneurs move from sharing and exchanging information with others in efforts to discover an opportunity, to the point when they perceive an opportunity and entrepreneurially act on it, there is a shift in the microstructure of transaction costs. Rather than transactions with very little actionable economic value, the proto-entrepreneurs create a new bundle of potential property rights in the form of a market opportunity. The perception of quasi-rents relates to how some economic value that has been generated during the exchange may be foregone if the relationship was severed. In Section 2.6, we characterize this shift as an "entrepreneurial fundamental transformation."

2.6 Entrepreneurial Fundamental Transformation

We can connect these intertemporal aspects of uncertainty and asset specificity described above to outline a distinctive intertemporal regularity within the innovation process—an "*entrepreneurial* fundamental transformation." In Oliver Williamson's conventional "fundamental transformation," what begins in *ex ante* competition in markets, where multiple agents bid for a contract, ends in *ex post* bilateral supply as the trading relationship develops,[103] i.e., as a trading relationship develops, there can be an intertemporal change in the economizing governance structure from a situation of large numbers competitive bidding in markets to one of small numbers bilateral supply in firms. This transformation from competition to asymmetric hazards is largely due to the increase in asset specificity, leading to asymmetric bargaining powers in later rounds of bidding. Transformation occurs because a scenario of relatively faceless contracting is supplanted with a scenario "where the pairwise identity of the parties matters."[104] A trading relationship may efficiently begin in competitive markets, but due to the build-up in asset-specific investments and the fact that quasi-rents would be foregone if the relationship was severed,

---

[103] See Williamson (1979).
[104] See Williamson (1985a, p. 62).

integration within a hierarchical firm may become the economizing governance solution. A bilateral dependency condition is obtained, which creates the need for "value-preserving governance structures—to infuse order, thereby to mitigate conflict and to realize mutual gain ..."[105] The potential for a "fundamental transformation" furnishes the need for a more complex governance structure to be developed to realize the gains from exchange. In Williamson's conception of markets and hierarchies, the potential governance solutions to a fundamental transformation range from market-based solutions (and standardization with the backdrop of the legal system) to integration within hierarchies (substitution of the legal system for internal control).

We can see a similar "entrepreneurial fundamental transformation" following our analysis of the intertemporal nature of the proto-entrepreneurial problem. As proto-entrepreneurs coordinate information with others, the microstructure of transaction costs shifts. As proto-entrepreneurs jointly discover complementarities between bits of heterogeneous non-price information about capital combinations, quasi-rents are generated. These quasi-rents are valuable and take the form of human capital investments between multiple proto-entrepreneurs. The investments in discovering and defining market opportunities in groups make it more difficult to turn to others, implying that these inputs are no longer mobile and homogenous and that economic value would be sacrificed if the relationship was severed,[106] i.e., "once [a] transaction-specific investment is made by one party, quasi-rents are created which can sometimes be appropriated by the other party."[107]

The collaborative discovery of market opportunities creates economic value which may be bargained over through opportunism. While proto-entrepreneurs may both jointly wish to fully realize the economic benefits of the market opportunity—by, for example, founding a start-up

---

[105]See Williamson (2002a, p. 176).

[106]See Klein *et al.* (1978).

[107]See Monteverde and Teece (1982, p. 322). In the absence of opportunism, the contracting difficulties relating to the "entrepreneurial fundamental transformation" would vanish because as a market opportunity with economic value is revealed, the parties would easily adapt and redraw contracts so as to divide the future benefits. However, when at least some parties in a population are opportunistic some of the time, we have a bilateral monopoly where "both buyer and seller are strategically situated to bargain over the disposition of any incremental gain whenever a proposal to adapt is made by the other party" (Williamson, 1985b, p. 63).

firm—they are also incentivized to opportunistically bargain in future periods. As economic values enter the relationship through the discovery of a market opportunity, it is reasonable to suggest that these asset-specific investments in human capital "can be realised only so long as the relationship between the buyer and seller is maintained."[108] The contractual hazards that emerge throughout a proto-entrepreneurial exchange relationship come about because the human-capital investments throughout the market opportunity discovery process would be "sacrificed if the ongoing supply relation were to be terminated" and also because the value of a specific market opportunity is realizable and actionable.[109]

The "entrepreneurial fundamental transformation" has dynamics similar to Williamson's "fundamental transformation" because both end with a bilateral dependency due to an increase in asset-specific investments and therefore the potential for vertical integration within a hierarchical firm to overcome contracting hazards. As proto-entrepreneurs coordinate dispersed contextual entrepreneurial information, they shift to a small numbers game where the continuity of the relationship is valued. This implies that different phases of the innovation process face different economic problems with different structures of transaction costs.

In the process of coordinating non-price information with others, uncertainty is whittled away not just about the opportunity itself but also about the contracting relationship between the collaborating agents. This change suggests the need for more complex centralized governance solutions to prevent opportunism. There is an increased likelihood that internal vertical integration will be an efficient governance structure. As Ménard proposes, "the more specific mutual investments are, the higher are the risks of opportunistic behavior, and the tighter are the forms of control implemented."[110] In other words, "the greater is the appropriation concern, which grows with the specificity of investments, the more centralized the coordination needs to be."[111]

---

[108] See Williamson (1985a, p. 62).

[109] See Williamson (1985a). These contractual hazards relate to the potential for "hold-up" through opportunistic renegotiation following non-verifiable specific investments. See the work on incomplete contracting theory in this regard (Grossman & Hart, 1986; Hart & Moore, 1990; Klein *et al.*, 1978; Tirole, 1999).

[110] See Ménard (2004, p. 354).

[111] See Ménard (2004, p. 354). This transformation to a centralized hierarchical governance structure, however, is not costless, as Klein *et al.* (1978, p. 298) note: "As assets become more specific and more appropriable quasi rents are created (and therefore the possible

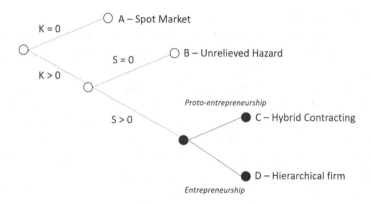

Figure 2.1:   Entrepreneurial fundamental transformation.

The centralized hierarchical firm—conventionally the organizational structure at the heart of innovative activity—is familiar as a solution once market opportunities have been perceived. But it is unclear what the pre-transformation proto-entrepreneurial transaction cost economizing governance structure is. The "entrepreneurial fundamental transformation," however, does not begin as a competitive bidding process concerned with prices and quality in markets. Proto-entrepreneurs begin with many other potential trading partners who hold potentially complementary information. Therefore, we can pinpoint two sequential economic problems that constitute the innovation problem:

(1) Gather non-price information from others and make proto-entrepreneurial judgments over viable market opportunities: This problem is the focus of this book.

(2) Act upon those perceived economic opportunities in search of profits: This is the more conventional remit of innovation economics.

This can be summarized in an adaptation and extension of Oliver Williamson's contracting schema, as outlined in Figure 2.1.[112]

Without asset specificity ($K = 0$), the proto-entrepreneur could create a spot market for the information they require to make judgments and

---

gains from opportunistic behavior increases), the costs of contracting will generally increase more than the costs of vertical integration. Hence, *ceteris paribus*, we are more likely to observe vertical integration."

[112] See Williamson (2002a, p. 183).

define a market opportunity. In the presence of asset specificity ($K > 0$), however, the proto-entrepreneur has two choices—they could employ no contractual safeguards (Node B) and risk opportunism, or create some form of governance structure (through hybrid contracting or a firm).

In this section, I have proposed the existence of an "entrepreneurial fundamental transformation" where the proto-entrepreneur begins with one economic problem with a particular microstructure of transaction costs, yet as this problem is solved, they begin to face a different microstructure of costs. This transformation can be represented as a shift in the transaction cost economizing governance structure from Node C to Node D, i.e., from hybrid governance to hierarchical governance. While this chapter has not enquired into the transaction cost economizing governance structure for Node C, prior to the entrepreneurial transformation, Chapter 3 will focus on this aspect.[113]

2.7 Conclusion

The analytical foreground of the market failure analysis of the innovation problem is a choice-theoretic analysis focusing on the investment and allocation of innovation resources. This chapter has developed the foundations for the contrasting contract-theoretic analysis, centered on the entrepreneur and the economic problems they face. My approach has drawn on the theory of the entrepreneur within mainline economic theory and outlined this understanding within the TCE framework. The proto-entrepreneur requires further uncertain, contextual and distributed non-price information to define and crystallize a market opportunity to the point of action. The non-price information proto-entrepreneurs require to whittle away uncertainty about their potential opportunity is distributed about the economy in the minds of others. Given non-zero transaction costs, the primary proto-entrepreneurial problem is to coordinate this information with others in a range of comparatively effective governance structures, such as firms, clubs, commons, or networks. While understanding they must interact with others, proto-entrepreneurs do not know

---

[113] My main claim in Chapter 3 is that the transaction cost economizing governance structure for the proto-entrepreneur, i.e., Node C, may be in a hybrid form of contracting within an innovation commons.

what governance structures are most efficient in solving this problem or even who their mutually beneficial trading partners might be. The proto-entrepreneurial problem, therefore, is a governance problem.

This new approach to the proto-entrepreneurial innovation problem was operationalized using the TCE framework by theoretically defining the type and degree of uncertainty and asset specificity that proto-entrepreneurs face as they seek to solve their economic problem. While for the earlier stages of proto-entrepreneurship, there is high structural uncertainty (including finding other collaborative agents with complementary bits of information), and low asset specificity (because there is little actionable economic value), as complementary trading partners and non-price information are exchanged and market opportunities become crystallized, the type and level of uncertainty and asset specificity shift.

The type of uncertainty moves from structural uncertainty towards more classic uncertainty. Asset specificity increases as quasi-rents build up. This suggests an "entrepreneurial fundamental transformation" where the transaction cost economizing structure shifts along an innovation trajectory as proto-entrepreneurs move from discovery of opportunities to acting on those opportunities as entrepreneurs. While the latter post-transformation analysis is familiar within the Williamson framework—vertical integration within a centralized hierarchical firm—the governance structure for the former pre-transformation proto-entrepreneurial problem is unclear and forms the primary focus of this book.

There are several implications of this new contract-theoretic approach to the innovation problem. The specific ways in which idiosyncratic investment and opportunism manifest as problems of private ordering are all consequences of the transaction costs incurred in seeking to coordinate under structural uncertainty. A focus on the proto-entrepreneurial governance choice means that the innovation problem can be viewed as one of *private ordering* before it manifests as a problem of public goods provision. The basic economics of entrepreneurial discovery now consists of entrepreneurial actions to economize on transaction costs by selecting appropriate governance structures to coordinate non-price information under uncertainty.

The solutions to the innovation problem now expand beyond firms and markets to encompass the potential for a wider range of private ordering solutions.[114] My approach goes beyond the conventional remit of organizational innovation economics, which resides in an institutional environment of firms, markets and states, to incorporate a broader range of governance structures including commons. This new perspective sets the path for understanding alternative institutions within the entrepreneurial discovery process. Examination of the transaction costs of discovering valuable market opportunities in groups suggests a unique economizing governance structure prior to the founding of an entrepreneurial firm in order to reveal market opportunities. Enquiring into the potential for polycentric collective action governance in hybrids will be the task of Chapter 3.

---

[114]My approach, following Harper (2008, p. 614) is "institution-neutral in that it does not presuppose a particular governance structure (such as a start-up firm)." Note, however, that my approach to the innovation commons outlined in Chapter 3 does not assume, as is the case in Harper (2008), that the team of entrepreneurs has a "common goal," except to the extent they face a "proto-entrepreneurial" problem. In this sense, those "common goals" must themselves be discovered.

Chapter 3

Beyond Entrepreneurial Firms and Markets

3.1 Introduction

From discovering opportunities to acting on and testing these opportunities, the innovation process is made up of many economic problems.[1] All these problems have different structures of transaction costs and therefore different economizing governance solutions. In this chapter, we shift from examining transaction costs to emphasize the governance structures that economize on those costs. We examine the early stages of the proto-entrepreneurial economic problem and propose a potential hybrid governance solution: the innovation commons. The core argument is that, rather than using hierarchical firms or distributed markets, proto-entrepreneurs might best form new hybrid governance structures—including innovation commons—to share information and reveal opportunities with others.

We once again use the TCE framework—together with the literature on common pool resources—to examine how different governance alternatives deal with the transaction costs of the proto-entrepreneurial problem. The unique transaction costs of the proto-entrepreneurial problem suggest that they need both the freedom of interacting with others to coordinate and discover complementary bits of information that are shrouded under uncertainty, while also facing threats of opportunism in this coordination process. An effective governance structure therefore needs both "autonomous" and "coordinated" adaptive characteristics.

---

[1] This chapter draws on Allen and Potts (2016).

This implies that the economizing governance structure may be a hybrid that incorporates multiple centers of decision-making (i.e., polycentrism), effective monitoring, provision for exit, and fluid contracting.

The transaction cost economizing origin for developing new technologies might not be in hierarchical firms but in self-organizing and privately governed institutional spaces called innovation commons. Innovation commons are collectively governed spaces to coordinate non-price information resources to alleviate uncertainty around market opportunities. They may be an effective governance solution for the proto-entrepreneur.[2]

In some ways, innovation commons are similar to other commons (e.g., fisheries, forests) because they are bottom-up rule-governed spaces.[3] But they also exhibit unique behavioral characteristics that stem from the underlying resource. Some of the features of innovation commons include the following: their emergence around the early stages of new technologies, industries and general purpose technologies where uncertainty and the potential gains from exchange of proto-entrepreneurial information is the highest; their role to process uncertainty rather than perpetually deal with uncertainty; and the fact that they are spatially and temporarily mobile, operating at different sizes and scales across the space of economies.

Most importantly, from the perspective of an innovation trajectory, innovation commons are likely to be *temporary* institutional phenomena. This temporary nature is because of the "entrepreneurial fundamental transformation" described in the previous chapter. The success of an innovation commons shifts the structure of transaction costs for the proto-entrepreneur and enables other institutions to outcompete it.[4] If an innovation commons governance structure is successful at revealing an entrepreneurial opportunity for the proto-entrepreneur, the best way to exploit that opportunity may be to act on that opportunity through a hierarchical firm.

---

[2]This draws on the commons literature, such as Ostrom (1990, 2005, 2010) and Poteete *et al.* (2010).

[3]Frischmann *et al.* (2014), Hess and Ostrom (2003), Madison *et al.* (2010), and McGinnis and Ostrom (1992).

[4]This shift is a result of the shifting microstructures of transaction costs as outlined in the previous chapter—as "proto-entrepreneurs" spontaneously order into complementary groups and begin to define actionable market opportunities, increasing idiosyncratic investments in this contractual relationship come with pervasive contracting consequences.

It is of course true that not all entrepreneurial discoveries of market opportunities will occur in an innovation commons. Different opportunities will be discovered under different institutional arrangements. Where those opportunities are discovered will depend on entrepreneurial institutional choices as well as other factors such as the division of knowledge. My claim here is more modest: following the logic of transaction cost economics, the governance characteristics associated with hybrids and commons regimes may best deal with the transaction costs of opportunity discovery.[5]

3.2   Firms vs. Markets in Solving Entrepreneurial Problems

Governance structures comprise the institutional rules through which exchanges are negotiated, executed, and enforced.[6] This section examines and compares the different governance structures. The logic of TCE proposes that the structure of private orderings is a result of the efforts to economize on the transaction costs of exchange in different ways.[7] Examining the characteristics of governance structures enables the application of Oliver Williamson's "discriminating alignment hypothesis."[8]

The governance characteristics of firms and markets can be understood by juxtaposing the scholarship of Friedrich Hayek and Richard Barnard. Together, Hayek's analytical focus on markets and Barnard's focus on hierarchies demonstrate the central problem of comparative economic analysis. The institutions of the market process analyzed by Hayek best describe the capacity of a governance structure to exhibit "autonomous adaptation." The institutions of the hierarchical firm analyzed by Barnard best describe the capacity of a governance structure to exhibit "coordinated adaption." Both Hayek and Barnard emphasize the

---

[5]This efficiency is only to the extent that individual proto-entrepreneurs subjectively perceive the commons to be efficient. See Chapter 6 for a further examination of the subjective costs that are the inputs into institutional choice.

[6]See Commons (1931a), North (1990), and Williamson (2005).

[7]See, e.g., Williamson (1991).

[8]The "discriminating alignment hypothesis" is where "transactions, which differ in their attributes, are aligned with governance structures, which differ in their cost and competence, so as to effect a transaction cost economizing outcome" (Williamson, 2007, p. 17).

capacity of different institutions to adapt to the inevitably changing conditions of the future.

Markets are emblematic of the governance characteristics of both autonomous adaptation and high incentive intensity. Hayek proposed that the central problem of an economic system is the adaptation to the changing circumstances of time and place.[9] This view of the economic problem implies that people must adapt to small disturbances in their economic affairs and reposition their contracts accordingly. In markets, this form of autonomous (or spontaneous) adaptation occurs through the adaptation of a constellation of independent people, each of whom hold distributed bits of competing and often contradictory information.

Markets are also effective at autonomous adaptation because the action of agents is tightly linked to their incentives, i.e., markets exhibit high incentive intensity. High-powered incentive intensity implies the net receipts of a person and their choices are closely associated with their decision-making. High incentive intensity, however, also increases the potential economic gains of opportunistic behavior and is therefore sometimes "deliberately suppressed" within firms.[10]

Firms are emblematic of the governance characteristics of coordinated adaptation and low incentive intensity. The hierarchical firm represents recourse from the market toward administrative governance mechanisms.[11] In stark contrast to market-based governance described above, the characteristics of the hierarchical firm deal well with the need for "coordinated adaptation" in a fluctuating environment. Coordinated adaptation was examined by Richard Barnard relating to administration and the ability of managers to coordinate through conscious design and direction.[12] Intentional adaptation and organization help mitigate some of

---

[9] See Hayek (1945).

[10] As Williamson (1991, p. 280) notes: "Incentive intensity is not an objective but is merely an instrument. If added incentive intensity gets in the way of bilateral adaptability, then weaker incentive intensity supported by added administrative controls (monitoring and career rewards and penalties) can be optimal."

[11] Ronald Coase (1937) first answered the question of why firms exist relating to the comparative costs of using the market mechanism (in particular, there were costs relating to uncertainty) that could be reduced by internalizing within a firm.

[12] Indeed, as Williamson (1996, p. 103) notes on coordinated adaptation and Barnard's work: "The conscious, deliberate and purposeful efforts to craft adaptive internal coordinating mechanism were those on which Barnard focused."

the contractual hazards of markets, including when asset specificity creates bilateral dependency. For this reason, Williamson proposed that the contractual hazards that arise due to the "fundamental transformation" were best solved through integration within the hierarchical firm.[13] Hierarchies reduce the opportunism relating to the incentive intensity of markets, but hierarchies also impose costs of bureaucracy associated with administrative control.[14]

Hybrids have characteristics of both firms and markets. Williamson first outlined and described hybrid organizations as exhibiting "semi-strong incentives, an intermediate degree of administration apparatus, displays semi-strong adaptations of both kinds."[15] Hybrids include a wide range of heterogeneous multilateral governance structures.[16] A hybrid structure may be transaction cost economizing compared to firms and markets for several reasons. One reason is that markets are not able to bundle and standardize the relevant resources.[17] Integration within hierarchical firms reduces flexibility and creativity.[18]

Once we accept that different governance structures economize on hazards in different ways, then it becomes clear that TCE is a comparative enquiry that "tries to explain how trading partners choose, from the set of feasible institutional alternatives, the arrangement that protects their relationship-specific investments at the least cost."[19] People choose governance structures that best solve their economic problem. People, including entrepreneurs, will choose governance structures that economize on the sum of both production costs (costs incurred in executing the contract) and transaction costs (including costs incurred in arranging, monitoring, and enforcing the contract). The characteristics of transaction costs (uncertainty, asset specificity, and frequency) and governance structures (adaptability and incentive intensity) can be aligned to theoretically

---

[13]To deter opportunistic "hold-up" problems, the complex and costly governance structures, such as the firm, may need to be built (see, e.g., Ménard, 2000; Tirole, 1999).

[14]This contractual hazard and the need for monitoring and compensation has been examined in the principle-agent literature, including Alchian and Demsetz (1972), Grossman and Hart (1983), and Hölmstrom (1979).

[15]Williamson (1991, p. 281).

[16]See Masten (1996) and Ménard (2004).

[17]See Teece and Pisano (1994).

[18]See Ménard (2004).

[19]See Klein (1998, p. 468) and Shelanski and Klein (1995).

determine the transaction cost economizing strategy. For instance, while some idiosyncratic and uncertain transactions will best occur within a hierarchical firm, other more highly standardized transactions, with many competing buyers and sellers, may best occur over a market (since the cost of setting up and internalizing the costs may be too large). We can use this TCE framework logic to ask how the proto-entrepreneur should solve their economic problem.

Markets might not be an effective solution for the unique proto-entrepreneurial problem. It is difficult, if not impossible, to write a contract for a contextual piece of entrepreneurial information before neither the value nor the holder of such information is clear. While in established markets prices can coordinate distributed information, when new markets are being created—where the structure of the future market and industry is unclear—it is difficult to price such information. The price system may be efficient in recoordinating extant economic activity, but it is ineffective for future markets because it is only *ex post* that a price may take into account the innovative value.[20] Prices in existing markets do not provide information about highly novel business models or information about failed ventures. Markets also struggle with the "information paradox" at the heart of the proto-entrepreneurial problem—non-price distributed information is incredibly difficult to price until it has been disclosed and combined with other information.[21] Coupled with the high incentive intensity of markets, the "information paradox" facing the proto-entrepreneur demonstrates an increased threat of opportunism.

Firms might also be ineffective at alleviating uncertainty around an economic opportunity. Could proto-entrepreneurs integrate coordination within the boundaries of a firm? Conventional innovation economics suggests that the innovation process begins within either a start-up or an existing firm. These governance structures, however, may be a poor way to coordinate the information necessary to solve the proto-entrepreneurial problem. A firm has a boundary that determines the agents and resources within the organization. The location of the complementary information required to discover a valuable opportunity, however, is shrouded in uncertainty. This leaves the question of whether the necessary

---

[20] See Shane and Eckhardt (2003).

[21] As Arrow (1962b, p. 615) notes: "There is a fundamental paradox in the determination of demand for information; its value for the purchaser is not known until he has the information, but then he has in effect acquired it without cost."

complementary information is within the boundaries of the firm or whether this information could be purchased over the market once a firm has been founded.

One of the primary uncertainties facing the proto-entrepreneur seeking to discover market opportunities is to determine who the other people within that firm will be. Further, as Alvarez argues: "when the economic value associated with a new market opportunity is uncertain, it is difficult to know whether or not a firm should be created, and if it is created, how any rents allocated by a firm should be allocated."[22] In this way, the structural uncertainty facing the proto-entrepreneur makes the founding of a firm difficult. Firms are characterized by hierarchical administrative controls where individuals are placed within teams or projects. It is unclear how non-price distributed information should be coordinated and combined to reveal valuable market opportunities.[23]

The shortcomings of the firm here relate primarily to the fundamental structural uncertainty of the complementarity of dispersed non-price information. Internalizing innovation activities within the firm brings organizational protection from opportunism and high incentive intensity. But the subsequent administrative control increases the possibility that complementary information necessary to define market opportunities is not contained within the boundaries of a firm or is not effectively coordinated and combined through the administrative controls of a hierarchy.[24] This is a lack of "autonomous adaptation," suggesting administrative controls may inhibit the spontaneous ordering of proto-entrepreneurial information. In this way, firms may be effectively overcoming the combined hazards of incentive intensity and asset specificity that build up throughout the innovation process, but may not economize on the other transaction costs of the proto-entrepreneurial problem that characterize the earliest stages of the innovation process.

What we can see is that the economic organization of proto-entrepreneurship is constrained from above and below in terms of transaction costs. Bounded rationality, distributed information, and structural uncertainty imply that all contracting will be necessarily and often radically incomplete. Governance solutions must deal with the need for

---

[22] Alvarez (2007, p. 428).
[23] This problem is revisited later in the context of spontaneously ordering polycentric teams within hybrid organizations in Chapter 4.
[24] See Ménard (2004).

spontaneous coordination to discover opportunities. A governance structure cannot seek to anticipate all contingencies in the proto-entrepreneurial coordination process or to administratively control this process due to bounded rationality.[25] But governance of proto-entrepreneurship cannot be completely free from coordinating mechanisms because of the threat of opportunism. They require some signaling mechanism to determine complementary trading partners with which they can reap the gains from coordination in discovering opportunities. These dual concerns suggest a complex trade-off between the governance characteristics of firms and markets. Given the need for both spontaneous and coordinated adaptation—and therefore possessing some of the governance structures of both firms and markets—one potential transaction cost economizing solution is in hybrids.

The governance options for the proto-entrepreneur are not limited to the firm–market duality.[26] Hybrid polycentric governance structures, i.e., governance structures that have many centers of decision-making and exhibit governance characteristics of both firms and markets, may economize on the transaction costs of the proto-entrepreneurial problem because they simultaneously deal with the structural uncertainty of discovering complementary trading partners, while maintaining some safeguards to protect against opportunism.[27]

The concept of a hybrid governance structure within the context of the institutions of innovation theoretically incorporates a wide range of collaborative forms of governance within the innovation and management

---

[25] These can be usefully arrayed on what Djankov *et al.* (2003) call the Institutional Possibility Frontier (IPF) as a convex function on the axes of the costs of disorder and the costs of dictatorship. This framework is extended and applied in Chapter 6.

[26] See Coase (1937). The main governance approach in the organizational economics of innovation has been to develop the Williamson make-or-buy problem in the context of *vertical integration* (Pisano, 1991; Robertson & Langlois, 1995), and more recently *open innovation* (Dahlander & Gann, 2010; Lazzarotti & Manzini, 2009). Evolutionary and Schumpeterian economists have countered through innovation competencies in the knowledge-based theories of the firm (Marengo & Dosi, 2005; Nelson & Winter, 2009; Penrose, 1959).

[27] The notion of polycentric governance structures has been developed with the Bloomington School by both Elinor and Vincent Ostrom. Their focus has been on how the polycentric governance of complex economic systems may be the most effective institutional solution for some social dilemmas.

literature, including open networks and collaborative joint ventures.[28] Much of this scholarship, however, emphasizes the links between existing firms and users, or between existing firms. The exception to this is the private collective user-led innovation literature, which tends to emphasize that the collaborative nature is due to some form of social provision.[29] In this way, the existing literature of hybrids as a solution to the innovation problem obscures from the institutional choice of proto-entrepreneurs to engage in governance as a transaction cost economizing strategy before proceeding to other phases in the innovation process.

To narrow our focus, we now turn to one form of a polycentric hybrid solution: an innovation commons. We place this proposition within the broader collective action common pool resource management literature and propose the behavioral characteristics of this new institution of innovation.

3.3 Governing Commons

The common pool resource management literature emerged during the 1980s and 1990s through the works of Elinor Ostrom and colleagues at the Bloomington School.[30] This research program sought to examine both successful and failed examples of the governance of common pool resources to understand the rules which overcome the hazards inherent in social dilemmas (largely free-rider problems stemming from the tragedy of the commons).[31] Many case studies demonstrated that individuals could govern common pool resources through collective action processes and that these may be institutionally optimal to the economic problems these people face. Therefore, this commons literature expanded the solutions to

---

[28]For open networks, see Hagerdoorn (1993), Pisano (1991), Powell *et al.* (1996), Robertson and Langlois (1995), and von Hippel (1986). For collaborative joint ventures, see Caloghirou *et al.* (2003).

[29]See von Hippel (1986), and von Hippel and von Krogh (2003).

[30]Analysis of the history of the Bloomington School can be found recently in Aligica and Boettke (2009), Aligica *et al.* (2014), Herzberg (2015), and Tarko (2016).

[31]Hardin (1968, p. 1244) introduced the concept of the "tragedy of the commons" through a thought experiment of an open access pasture and the differences between individual and group rationality, concluding that "freedom in a commons brings ruin to all." See also Feeny *et al.* (1990) for a review of the literature stemming from this original article.

social dilemmas beyond firms, markets and states.[32] Rather than suffering from a tragedy of overappropriation—to be remedied through markets or states—a wide range of cases of common pool resource management showed that collective action governance may be an optimum institutional solution to economic problems. This understanding, however, should not be confused with suggesting commons solutions are some form of panacea.[33]

The institutional and political economy analysis of commons can be split into several different categories based on the nature of the underlying resource and the methodological techniques employed in analyzing them. The first wave of commons literature emphasized shared physical natural resources, such as fisheries, grazing pastures and forests. A second wave of commons studies developed as the literature moved toward examining intangible common pool resources of information and knowledge, such as science and culture.[34] This second generation focuses on a variety of topics and resources, including open source software, roller derby, the airplane industry, and genetic information and research.[35] All of these case studies attempted to apply the ideas of collective action common pool resource management into new area, including the development of a set of design rules for long-enduring common pool resource management.[36]

The commons literature has demonstrated that commons can be understood as efficient governance models to minimize transactions costs associated with private order resolutions of collective action problems (i.e., social dilemmas) involved in contributing and pooling resources. When new commons are analyzed, they are now often based on intangible

---

[32]As Ostrom (2010, p. 432) proposes: "Thus, in some contexts, one can move beyond the presumption that rational individuals are helpless in overcoming social dilemma situations." Also see Chapter 6 for a broader outline of the sweep of the common pool resource management literature.

[33]As Ostrom *et al.* (2007, p. 15176) notes: "Practitioners and scholars who fall into panacea traps falsely assume that all problems of resource governance can be represented by a small set of simple models." Also see Ostrom (2007) for panaceas in the governance of resource problems.

[34]For science, see Boyle (2007) and Schweik and English (2012). For culture, see Frischmann *et al.* (2014) and Ostrom and Hess (2007).

[35]See Contreras (2014), Fagundes (2014), Lucchi (2013), Meyer (2014), and Schweik (2007, 2014).

[36]The eight commons design rules are outlined in Ostrom (1990).

resources, such as culture, and exist on a larger and broader scale than the original first wave of commons.[37] This transition between analyzing tangible commons, in which we can see and feel the underlying resource units of fish or trees, to the intangible commons, which are much more difficult to measure, has not been analytically smooth.[38]

Analyzing commons based on ideas rather than commons of things is more difficult for two reasons: it is difficult to understand what the resource is because such resources are often substantially more intangible and dynamic, and because there is a further actor within a knowledge commons who produces and provides the underlying resource.[39] In this context, the innovation commons defined and characterized in the following section constitute a third wave of commons that are potentially transaction cost economizing governance structures for coordinating the information necessary to define actionable market opportunities.

3.4 Entrepreneurship in the Commons

The key resource in an innovation commons is not a technology, but the distributed, uncertain and non-price information about the market opportunities for a technology. The resource is non-price proto-entrepreneurial information that facilitates the use and application of a new technology to discover value. Much of this information is experimentally acquired, often tacit, non-price, and of little value in itself, but holds potential value when combined with other heterogeneous complementary information that pieces together the puzzle of how the technology might be applied, by whom, to do what, in combination with what, and so on.

An innovation commons acts as a potential coordinating governance institution for the non-price coordination necessary to gather the information inputs into entrepreneurial judgment. They are proposed to exist in the early stages of the innovation process—and therefore in the early stages of a new technology—when a group of proto-entrepreneurs come together to coordinate and exchange information about this technology to

---

[37] See, e.g., Epstein *et al.* (2014), Hess (2008), and Ostrom *et al.* (2002).

[38] Poteete *et al.* (2010).

[39] See Cole (2014) and Madison *et al.* (2010). As Poteete *et al.* (2010) notes, this shift in the literature has required commons scholars to devise new methods and refine previous concepts about what constitutes a common pool resource and common property regime.

discover opportunities for its use and development. These unique governance structures will emerge through collective action, where proto-entrepreneurs perceive such a structure as best to solve their problem.

An innovation commons is not a "technology commons" or even a "knowledge commons." The resource is not the technology *per se*, but the information about the technology that facilitates its development. Rather, the resource is a unique form of tacit non-price proto-entrepreneurial information that exists to discover new knowledge (about opportunities).[40]

An innovation commons may be an efficient governance model for early-stage economic organization of discovery and development of an opportunity because it has both "coordinating" and "autonomous" adaptation characteristics. Because the proto-entrepreneur does not know what they are producing, how they are going to do it, or who they are going to do it with, a hybrid and flat polycentric governance structure may be transaction cost economizing.

The rules and mechanisms of an innovation commons might help guard against the hazards of opportunism while simultaneously allowing entrepreneurial discovery (and thus group formation) so that agents can interact to discover potentially actionable market opportunities.

Not all innovation commons are the same—each will be created and will evolve in relation to the local conditions of the proto-entrepreneurs and their resources. But at first the rules of an innovation commons might be similar to the basic design rules of the other commons (e.g., clearly defined boundaries).[41] But because of the unique nature of the transaction costs of the proto-entrepreneurial problem, and the underlying resource,

---

[40]The literature on knowledge commons focuses on the management of existing information sources (Cole, 2014; Frischmann *et al.*, 2014; Madison *et al.*, 2010), while an innovation commons is concerned with the coordination of non-price information to discover new information. This notion of complementarity in the coordination of the resource suggests it is a unique subcategory of common pool resource.

[41]The similarities of enduring, self-governing commons as outlined in Ostrom (1990) are clearly defined boundaries, congruence between local appropriation and provision rules and local conditions, collective-choice arrangements, monitoring, graduated sanctions, conflict-resolution mechanisms, minimal recognition of rights to organize, and nested enterprises. These rules have also been expanded and analyzed elsewhere (Stern, 2011; Wilson *et al.*, 2013). For instance, Wilson *et al.* (2013) generalized these principles with evolutionary concepts. See also Dietz *et al.* (2003).

we expect that innovation commons will behave differently and have different rules.

It would be easy to assume that an innovation commons emerges from some altruistic characteristics of its users. But innovation commons do not depend on a form of social provision or altruistic behavior of contribution to the commons. Innovation commons are an institutional solution to economize on the transaction costs to enable proto-entrepreneurs to reap the mutual gains from trade of proto-entrepreneurial information and facilitate the process of entrepreneurial discovery, i.e., they don't necessarily exist for the "social production" of innovation or as some form of political commitment existing "alongside property-based and market-based production."[42] They are a coordinating institution to solve an economic problem of discovering actionable market opportunities and to exit the commons and continue in other phases of the innovation process, such as acting to exploit opportunities in firms across markets.[43]

The core functional role of an innovation commons is to process uncertainty surrounding a potential future opportunity. This contrasts with a natural resource commons, where the ebbs and flows of nature may create a continuing level of uncertainty, and a common property regime may emerge as a perpetually more effective institution than their market and state alternatives. In contrast, the innovation commons exist to coordinate this information and process uncertainty through the coordination of information.

An innovation commons processes uncertainty, and once the uncertainty passes, so too does the efficiency case for this particular governance structure. Innovation commons exist to facilitate non-price coordination to discover "emergent orders of worth."[44] In an innovation commons, proto-entrepreneurs can draw on the subjective perceptions about potential market opportunities of others to define potentially actionable future

---

[42]Benkler (2006, p. 3).

[43]The exit from the commons does not necessarily result in subsequent adoption into a market-capitalist trajectory. The decision of which governance structure to act upon an opportunity once it is discovered lies with the subjective preferences of the proto-entrepreneur. The benefit of a methodologically individualist approach is that we can remain agnostic about the normative intent of the individuals of where to later institutionalize their discovered opportunity and focus on the governance structures, through which they seek to solve the problem of reducing uncertainty about a market opportunity.

[44]See Kuchař and Dekker (2017).

market opportunities. An innovation commons, in this view, coordinates the non-price subjective perceptions over future new combinations of heterogeneous capital in order to discover the potential worth of a market opportunity,[45] i.e., the innovation commons exist to process uncertainty through coordination and discover a *novel* order of worth.

The function of an innovation commons suggests that they are temporary. At the analytical level of the market opportunity or innovation trajectory, an innovation commons is likely to be a transient institutional phenomenon economizing on the microstructure of transaction costs associated with the proto-entrepreneurial problem. When uncertainty dissipates, the basic rationale for the commons substantially weakens. More specifically, the success of an innovation commons in defining market opportunities provides the conditions for other innovation institutions, such as the start-up firm, to outcompete it.

Alternative institutions, such as firms, rely on the reduced uncertainty and stable expectations to make plans and investments. While the innovation commons are born of fundamental uncertainty about innovation opportunities, addressing this problem successfully will collapse their functional rationale. Uncertainty is what engenders the creation of an innovation commons, and the resolution of the same uncertainty instigates their collapse. Unless some other forces hold it together or prolong it, e.g., a legal tool which holds an idea within the commons, the innovation commons will tend to collapse at a point when its functional rationale, the discovery of a market opportunity and an entrepreneurial fundamental transformation, is achieved.

From these perspectives, we can locate the innovation commons in the Schumpeterian innovation trajectory, where an innovation trajectory has three phases: (1) entrepreneurial origination; (2) adoption and diffusion; (3) retention and institutional embedding.[46] An innovation commons theoretically precedes the origination phase. If an innovation commons is successful, it leads to entrepreneurial origination, propelling an innovation trajectory. We can therefore see that innovation commons are complementary to later institutions of firms, markets and states. Innovation commons are not just substitute institutions, but act as

---

[45]The non-price coordination in an innovation commons involves mutual agreement or approval between different individuals to discover the perceived complementarity between bits of heterogeneous capital, and the perceptions of the value of those combinations.
[46]See Dopfer and Potts (2007) and Dosi (1982).

institutional complements to firms, markets and states at later stages of an innovation trajectory.

An innovation commons could be similarly conceived as an "institutional placeholder" for discovering later governance structures within which one can exploit market opportunities.[47] This is consistent with some Austrian theories of the firm where the emergence of the firm is not due to an inefficiency in the market process, but as a product of the market process,[48] or, in the view presented here, a firm may be the product of a commons process.

The recent growth of the literature on peer production, open innovation and open science are often explained using TCE—falling transaction costs render information cheap and ubiquitous, enabling more decentralized organization through civil society. This does not explain whether or not these innovation processes are performing the same role as alternative institutions. We need to ask what economic problem the agents operating in these organizations are trying to solve. These models implicitly assume that these forms of economic organization are substitutes for firms, markets, and governments, whereas an innovation commons may facilitate a complementary process to other institutions.

One example of a function of the innovation commons as a complementary governance structure to later phases in the innovation process is institutional matching. One of the distinct uncertainties around new technologies and opportunities is the best institution in which it can be developed. New ideas and technologies have a variety of characteristics that make them differentially suited to develop in different institutional forms. For instance, some ideas may be better developed in public research institutions. Others are better in private technology start-ups or in large firms.

If each idea had an optimal institution, and if we assumed a world of perfect knowledge and of zero transaction costs, then there would still be

---

[47] Alvarez (2007, p. 437) proposes the entrepreneurial firm in a similar way of acting as a solution to entrepreneurial uncertainty: "One possible solution to this problem is to think of an entrepreneurial firm as an institutional placeholder through which the identity of the most appropriate holders of residual rights of control can be identified over time."

[48] See Ioannides (1999, p. 87): "Unlike the contractarian theories of the firm, the perspective we have derived from Kirzner's theory of entrepreneurship does not have to rely on some sort of inefficiency of the market mechanism but stems, instead, from the very principle that keeps this mechanism in constant motion: entrepreneurial behaviour."

no institutional matching problem: each idea would be seamlessly matched with its governance structure. But we do have transaction costs, and ideas need to be matched. Innovation commons might coordinate the information to match potential opportunities and technologies to their optimal institutions for development and subsequent adoption. The existence of an innovation commons does not predict or even suggest the optimal institutional structure of innovation after an opportunity is discovered. This opportunity may be developed within a firm, a government, or a market. But by coordinating information, an innovation commons might help coordinate information to facilitate this matching.

An innovation commons is likely to emerge in different locations throughout economies, i.e., they are not an economy-wide substitute for other innovation institutions. An innovation commons will exist at many locations in an economy at once, with those locations continually and perhaps frequently shifting. An innovation commons will not exist across an entire economy, sector, or region because its location is emergent with respect to the social organization of the development of a technology. It deals well with a particular, temporary, microstructure of transaction costs. Related to this, we expect that an innovation commons is not a general space—indeed, some of their value will come from their sorting ability around particular technologies. They are likely to be tailored to particular technologies or industries on many different scales.

An innovation commons is predicted to emerge along an innovation trajectory where uncertainty is the highest about the pathways through which a new idea or technology can be developed. It also follows that an innovation commons governance structure is most likely to emerge where the gains from trade of coordinating non-price entrepreneurial information are the highest. This suggests their emergence at the beginning of new highly disruptive technologies, i.e., in situations where proto-entrepreneurs have the incentive to develop governance structures to reveal plentiful market opportunities and their value.

We can look back through history to see some other situations of potential structural uncertainty and see other examples of pooling of information. For instance, throughout the seventeenth and eighteenth centuries, the Societies for Useful Knowledge included groups of pioneers sharing information and contextual knowledge not about commercial opportunities but about how to overcome the institutional problems of agriculture and politics in the New World.[49] Craft guilds in preindustrial Europe also

---

[49]For a recent analysis, see Lyons (2013).

provide a possible example of the pooling of information in order to facilitate innovation.[50] While the innovation commons examined in this book are focused on those around a novel and new technology, the opportunity need not relate to a technology. Rather, the information simply relates to something new.

An innovation commons may act as a defense against enclosure into alternative institutional forms. This function is revealed by taking the perspective of the success of an entire industry, rather than an entrepreneur or their opportunity. An innovation commons could defend against the risk that the technology will not find a viable market niche or that it is locked on a particular technological path. Technologies and markets exhibit path dependency.[51] Innovation commons provide a mechanism to experiment with different paths simultaneously. This mechanism can be observed in the efforts of those committed to open source software to maintain an innovation commons less as a service to potential entrepreneurs, but rather to prevent alternative institutions (e.g., private property rights) enclosing the technology and locking it into one particular path of development.[52] We also know that the very beginning of an industry, market, or product faces the prospect of political resistance by those who would see it as competition.[53] An innovation commons may also act as a bulwark against resistance from incumbent technologies and other entrenched interests with rents to protect.

While from the perspective of an opportunity an innovation commons might be temporary, the optimal period for innovation commons may be relatively long to best discover or shake out hidden costs.[54] Once private property institutions have attached to a technology, or once the technology is fully in the public domain, unintended costs can be particularly costly because of the destruction of investment or the tendency to constrain a technology. Therefore, an innovation commons could serve as a space of what Adam Thierer calls "permissionless innovation."[55] An innovation commons may be able to comparatively quickly and at relatively low cost discover unintended consequences by facilitating small-scale experimental adoption, understood by pooling distributed information.

---

[50] See Epstein (1998).
[51] See Liebowitz and Margolis (1995).
[52] See, e.g., von Krogh *et al.* (2012).
[53] See Juma (2016).
[54] See Klepper (1996, 1997).
[55] See Thierer (2014). Permissionless innovation is discussed further in Chapter 6.

3.5 Conclusion

In modern economics, the institutions that facilitate the process of the development of new technologies are generally constrained to firms, markets, and governments.[56] But, in this chapter, we have seen that solutions to the proto-entrepreneurial problem is not necessarily through vertical integration within a hierarchical firm or trading information across a competitive market.[57] Rather, hybrid governance structures such as innovation commons—with features of both firms and markets—might better coordinate the non-price contextual information necessary to reveal market opportunities.

An innovation commons is a potential transaction cost economizing governance mechanism to deal with the hazards of opportunism and the need for autonomous adaptation to coordinate with others. These polycentric structures precede the emergence of competitive firms and markets by revealing the information necessary to act on an entrepreneurial opportunity. Most importantly, this suggests where we can look to find them, namely, as temporary privately governed structures emerging at the very beginning of new industries and technologies (we turn to examining real innovation commons in the upcoming chapters).

The contributions of this chapter go in two directions. The first direction is to introduce privately developed hybrid governance into the suite of institutional solutions to the innovation problem. In the choice-theoretic conception of the innovation problem, there is little room for privately governed institutional solutions. These governance structures represent the discovery of a new class of commons at the locus of what economic theory informs us is a fundamental driver of the wealth and prosperity of nations, the growth of new technologies. The second direction is to introduce entrepreneurial theory to the commons literature. This adds a third wave of common pool resource governance (to the existing first wave of natural resources and the second wave of cultural and knowledge commons). We have simultaneously extended and enriched commons theory and the economics of the innovation problem.

---

[56]Technologies and their applications emerge in governments and firms and are later adopted and diffused through markets.

[57]In the standard models of innovation economics, there are hierarchically organized innovating firms, contracts for research, and markets for ideas (Aghion & Tirole, 1994; Gans & Stern, 2010; Katz & Shapiro, 1985).

There are no panaceas when it comes to the institutions of innovation. But just as Elinor Ostrom claimed, privatization and government-control solutions are "too sweeping in their claims," so may be the case in the governance of innovation.[58] Just as the "tragedy of the commons" was a misdiagnosis for natural resources, innovation policy may have been mis-diagnosed as a problem of investment rather than a problem of governance. The contemporary status of innovation economics (and, with it, innovation policy) looks strikingly like the state of commons research prior to Elinor Ostrom's systematic rebuttal of Garrett Hardin's pessimism about the "tragedy of the commons." While the specific problem differs (from underproduced innovation resources to overexploited natural resources), the underlying diagnosis and treatment is the same. Both stories began with a supposed market failure that was resolved along a dichotomy of solutions that amounted to privatization on one hand or state regulation and ownership on the other.

In this chapter, the earliest stages of the innovation problem have now been reframed through the contract-theoretic mainline of economic thought, making it a governance problem, with governance solutions. We have predicted where innovation commons might emerge and how they might behave. Now, we can turn to some examples.

---

[58] See Ostrom (1990, p. 14).

PART II

Private Governance Solutions

Chapter 4

The Private Governance of Hackerspaces

4.1 Introduction

Hackers are entrepreneurial because they seek to discover valuable uses for new technologies. The entrepreneurial outputs of hackers are clear from their central contribution to the early 3D printing and personal computing industries.[1] They coordinate this process in privately and collectively governed hybrids called *hackerspaces*.[2] Hackerspaces are often viewed as collections of physical resources—of tools such as 3D printers and laser cutters—or as a collection of norms and values of the hacking and making phenomenon.[3] But hackerspaces are also collections of rules and institutions. They are collectively developed rule systems where hackers attempt to overcome uncertainty around new technologies.

By looking at existing hackerspace evidence, we can see that they have developed mechanisms—from social ostracism to collective action rule formation—to overcome issues of opportunism and to encourage contributions of knowledge. This chapter draws on existing case studies

---

[1]For 3D printing innovations, see Fordyce *et al.* (2015) and Moilanen *et al.* (2014), e.g., the hackerspace *NYC Resistor* was home to the early collaborations of MakerBot Industries, one of the world's largest 3D printing companies. For personal computing, see Freiberger and Swaine (1999).

[2]For a brief introduction to the differences between hackerspaces and their variants (e.g., makerspaces), see Cavalcanti (2013).

[3]Williams and Hall (2015) focus on how technology is used to secure the physical "space" within hackerspace in the context of three of Ostrom's design rules. For the underlying norms and values, see Davies (2017) and Manion and Goodrum (2000).

and analyses of hackerspaces (as well as websites and forums) to lay out some of the mechanisms that have been developed within hackerspaces to solve governance problems.[4] My approach is not to examine any one hackerspace, but draw together a broad understanding of hackerspace governance within the context of entrepreneurial discovery far from the reaches of innovation policy.[5] These mechanisms include the following:

(1) graduated social ostracism and exclusion;
(2) costly signaling as a form of non-price coordination;
(3) processes of collective action rule formation;
(4) nested hierarchies of rules.

At first, the choice of hackerspaces—and hackers—to study the governance of innovation seems obscure and odd. Beginning my analysis far from the conventional institutions of innovation, however, is by design. We want to study private self-governance of entrepreneurship. But studying private governance is analytically difficult. One reason is the complex and entangled nature of innovation with state-led innovation policy. This section outlines some of the analytical difficulties of studying innovation commons within a political economy context and motivates the study of hackerspaces as an extreme form of "entrepreneurial anarchy."

Conventional "additive political economy" assumes that economics and politics can be separately analyzed. Separating economics and politics brings simplicity, but it limits our ability to understand real social phenomena.[6] In contrast, Richard Wagner's "entangled political economy"

---

[4]Kostakis *et al.* (2014), Lindtner and Li (2012), Schlesinger *et al.* (2010), and Williams and Hall (2015). I frame this as an analytic narrative. On analytic narratives, see Boettke et al. (2005, 2013a).

[5]My methodological approach is a trade-off between internal and external validity. The data from a single hackerspace will be more empirically robust and may reveal more fringe and unique governance mechanisms, which only exist in a few hackerspaces. A meta-analysis of hackerspaces, which is adopted here, yields more generalizable comparative institutional implications for hackerspace governance, takes advantage of existing case study methodologies and results, enables a current review of the state of research in the area, and enables more general claims about the class of organizations, including the political economy implications about other competing organizational forms.

[6]Wagner (2014, p. 20) describes an additive political economy as "a scheme of thought where economic equilibrium is conceptualized prior to political activity, with political activity then modifying that equilibrium." See also Pagenelli (2014).

theory argues that the political and economic spheres of activity are closely and inevitably entangled.[7] The implication of an "entangled political economy" is that politics and economics should realistically be examined as operating together, through time, and on the same institutional landscape.[8] They co-evolve together. Governments do not simply diagnose problems, such as market failures, and then intervene. There is complex and ongoing feedback between the various spheres of decision-making. Because economics and politics is entangled, analyzing purely economic or purely political processes is conceptually difficult.

Any claims of pure private governance—including those governing entrepreneurial processes—face the problem of governments lurking behind ready to enforce agreements.[9] This is incredibly difficult in innovation because today the scope of innovation policy subsumes government, university, and industry.[10] It extends into almost all decisions, shaping the behavior of entrepreneurial activity. The entangled nature of political economy is one of the core motivations for analyzing hackerspace governance as an example of the private governance of entrepreneurial activities. How can we analyze the ability of proto-entrepreneurs to come together and create private governance structures to facilitate entrepreneurial discovery?

My approach is to follow the "positive political economy" (or "positive political anarchy") literature, which has sought out extreme

---

[7]As Wagner (2014, p. 25) notes: "Just as market theory is sometimes presented through images of an invisible hand, political activity would be presented in the same fashion." See Wagner (2006, 2016a, 2016b).

[8]See Koppl (2014, p. 2): "The nature of a private or public actor is not given independently of the overall political-economy environment. And that means that they are shaping each other. They co-evolve."

[9]For private governance and the "shadow of the law," see Leeson (2010) and Mnookin and Kornhauser (1979). The private processes of self-governance of entrepreneurship are best described as economic processes, while the interventions of innovation policy are best described as political processes. The question then is what constitutes a private economic solution to the innovation problem, with the focus in this chapter on polycentric hybrid governance in hackerspaces.

[10]See Godin (2009). This nature of entanglement is also important for the political economy analysis in Chapter 6. Policies such as state-based intellectual property or research and development tax credits imply that the political process is interconnected with many of the institutions of innovation. The private choices of entrepreneurs interconnect and co-evolve as innovation policies seek to shift these incentives.

forms of private governance where people are privately engaged in creating and enforcing rules beyond state-based courts and legal systems.[11] Empirical examples of private governance have included prison gangs, private police, stock exchanges, stateless Somalia, and pirate ship constitutions.[12] This literature has pushed back on the conventional understanding that mutually beneficial trade rests on exogenous top-down institutional mechanisms (i.e., coercive states) to create and enforce the institutions necessary (e.g., property rights) to maintain civility.[13] Even where cooperation was assumed to be unattainable, the "positive political anarchy" literature has demonstrated that groups have collectively devised rules to exchange.[14]

This points to the approach of this chapter in examining the private polycentric governance of proto-entrepreneurship in hackerspaces. We know that pirates can run floating corporations on the ocean. We also know that stateless societies and prison gangs can develop complex rules to facilitate order. Why preclude proto-entrepreneurs from creating their own purely private systems of governance to solve the innovation problem outside the scope of innovation policy?[15]

Hackerspaces operate obscurely on the edges of the conventional organizations of firms, markets, and states. Examining hackerspaces, then, as a form of private governance, extends the "positive political anarchy" literature into the study of the governance of entrepreneurial discovery. It enables a greater understanding of the collective action development of rules to overcome the transaction costs of coordinating

---

[11] For this literature, see, among others, Benson (1999), Dixit (2007), Ellickson (2009), and Leeson (2009, 2014). Anarchy in this sense is not the absence of rules, but rather the absence of government rules.

[12] See also Leeson and Skarbek (2010) for the functions of constitutions within criminal organizations. See Bislev (2004) for private police. Others cited above.

[13] See Boettke (2005). The conventional assumption in economics is that where anarchy exists, state-based institutions will fill these vacuums with centralized organization. Moreover, this change is assumed to increase efficiency. Long-held assumptions of the efficiency of states and the failure of markets, however, do not make for a neutral point of departure for institutional analysis. Indeed, the prospect of efficient entrepreneurial anarchy should be examined empirically and not willfully assumed away. This chapter contributes to the examination of the anarchic organization of entrepreneurial discovery within hackerspaces.

[14] See Leeson (2007b).

[15] See Leeson (2007a, 2009).

non-price proto-entrepreneurial information. In this chapter, we first introduce hackers and then look at the rules that they have created in hackerspaces.

4.2 Hackers as Proto-entrepreneurs

In the 1960s and 1970s, a sub-culture of young college students was to play practical jokes, or *hacks*, on one another.[16] Over time, these hacks evolved into more elaborate applications of technologies to meet human needs.[17] This hacking process has variously been described as "transcending boundaries," producing "solutions to complex problems," "playing" and "critical making."[18] Hackers have also been connected through the common values of openness, sharing, creativity, experimentation, free speech, meritocracy, and the power of the individual.[19] Hackers, we will see here, are fundamentally entrepreneurial. They push novelty and newness into the economic, social, and political system. Hackers in hackerspaces are a prime analytical example of the private governance of proto-entrepreneurial discovery.

It is worth noting that the claim hackers are proto-entrepreneurs does not say how an entrepreneurial opportunity is later institutionally developed. Opportunities developed by hackers could be diffused through firms, markets, states, or through other institutional systems, such as the creation of open source software or hardware. Indeed, hackerspaces often exhibit strong open source values (i.e., explicitly keeping some innovation open and in the public domain) rather than seeking profits.

---

[16]A "hack" has been widely misinterpreted as criminals hacking networks, stealing money, and engaging in illegal activities (see Kostakis *et al.*, 2014).

[17]A hack is "an incredibly good, and perhaps time-consuming piece of work that produces exactly what is needed." See https://www.computer-dictionary-online.org/definitions-h/hack.html.

[18]For "transcending boundaries," see Wykretowicz (2013); for "producing solutions to complex problems," see Schlesinger *et al.* (2010); for "playing," see Guthrie (2014), Hatch (2013), and for "critical making," see Ratto (2011).

[19]The hacking sub-culture itself is also closely associated with political ideals, with the connection to freedom constituting a moral discourse for hackers—part of what has become known as the hacker or maker ethic or culture (see Coleman & Golub, 2008; Lindtner, 2012). See also Kostakis *et al.* (2014) and Taylor (2005).

Hacking is not necessarily, or even usually, a solo endeavor. It often takes place in groups within physical *hackerspaces*.[20] At the beginning of 2016, there were "1233 active hackerspaces around the world, and more than 500 in development."[21] The history of hackerspaces traces back to the mid-twentieth century with the founding of the Tech Model Railroad Club at MIT.[22] The Homebrew Computer Club also hosted many of the world's most influential hackers and entrepreneurs in the personal computing industry throughout the 1970s.[23]

Defining hackerspaces is difficult. In part, this is because they are "… constantly on the move; evolving, mixing, forking, hibernating and dying."[24] They are complex rule systems that shift to meet needs and will take different forms in different places. Nevertheless, there are several definitions and perspectives on the hackerspace phenomenon.[25] The potential scope of these innovative spaces further complicate organizational definition.[26] Indeed, other organizations are like hackerspaces but have been differentiated from them (e.g., makerspaces, hacklabs, fab labs, and co-working spaces).

We can think about hackerspaces from the perspective of the patterns, trends, and theories as hackerspaces evolve.[27] This is despite the fact the indeterminate processes of hackerspaces vary. Mitch Altman, founder of the prominent hackerspace Noisebridge, notes:

All [hackerspaces] are unique because they were founded by unique individuals and different groups based on their own sensibilities.

---

[20] See Guthrie (2014) and van Holm (2015a).

[21] Davies (2017, p. 11).

[22] See Farr (2009), Levy (2001), and Schlesinger *et al.* (2010).

[23] See Freiberger and Swaine (1999) and Lash (2007). Other famous spaces include the Chaos Computer Club (founded in 1981 in Germany), and *c-base* (Berlin) and *C4* (Cologne), which were both founded in the 1990s (Tweney, 2009).

[24] Moilanen (2012, p. 1).

[25] Hackerspaces have been variously described as enabling platforms (Seravalli, 2011), shared social studios (Lindtner *et al.*, 2014), collectively governed experimentation (Kera, 2012), third places between the home and the workplace (Moilanen, 2012), location-based user-led innovation networks (Robertson, 2010), intermediaries between scientific knowledge and everyday problems (Kera, 2012), a form of commons-based peer production (Kostakis *et al.*, 2014), and a common pool resource (Williams & Hall, 2015).

[26] See Maxigas (2014) and van Holm (2015b, p. 3). See Capdevila (2014) for a typology of different spaces according to their "creative approach" and "mode of governance."

[27] See Farr (2009).

Of course, they draw on the examples of other hackerspaces. They see what works well and what doesn't work well for the other spaces so they can decide for themselves what they want to try.[28]

The most comprehensive definition of hackerspaces, by Jarkko Moilanen, includes the following characteristics: owned and run by members in the spirit of equality; not-for-profit and semi (regularly) open to the public; share ideas, tools, and equipment; place strong emphasis on technology and invention; shared spaces at the center of a community; and expressing a "spirit of invention and science, based on trial, error, and freely sharing information."[29] They are generally a small social formation of hackers in physical space, such as warehouses and garages, where they can meet and work on their projects and share software, hardware, ideas, and knowledge.[30]

The underlying resource of a hackerspace is not just physical resources but also "group knowledge."[31] It is this access to knowledge for hackers as proto-entrepreneurs that is important given the distributed nature of non-price information they require. Indeed, hackerspaces have been described as intermediaries for the "translation between scientific knowledge produced in the labs ... and the everyday interests, practices and problems of ordinary people in diverse local contexts around the globe."[32] The information within hackerspaces has also been referred to as folk knowledge, "developed by a given community as opposed to knowledge generated through universities, government research centers, and private industry."[33]

From an institutional perspective, hackerspaces are governance structures for people to exchange, share, and coordinate information.[34] We now turn to the question of how this knowledge is privately and collectively

---

[28] Quoted in Han (2015).

[29] Moilanen (2012).

[30] See Lindtner (2012).

[31] Robertson (2010, p. 5).

[32] See Lindtner (2012, p. 1). See also Robertson (2010, p. 5), who argues hackerspaces are "place-based innovation networks act[ing] as a bridge between the local economic development planner and user-led innovation."

[33] See Kera (2012, p. 2).

[34] For instance, hackerspaces have been characterized as a problem-solving network with "free exchange of knowledge in order to create *an optimized final product*" (Seckinger *et al.*, 2012, p. 3).

governed and coordinated by focusing on the institutional mechanisms that overcome the transaction costs of the proto-entrepreneurial problem we saw previously.

4.3 Private Governance Mechanisms in Hackerspaces

This section proposes four main private governance mechanisms in the hackerspace phenomenon, which are interpreted in the context of institutional theory, common pool resource design rules, and the propositions over the characteristics of an innovation commons. These institutional mechanisms are examined as private governance efforts to economize on the transaction costs of the proto-entrepreneurial problem, including the unique challenge of both needing spontaneous coordination and the threat of opportunism and free riding. We examine the transaction hazards and costs hackers face and the emergent private institutional solutions to those costs including the following: (1) graduated social ostracism and exclusion; (2) costly signaling as a form of non-price coordination; (3) processes of collective action rule formation; (4) nested hierarchies of rules.

4.3.1 *Social ostracism and exclusion*

Hackers need to create mechanisms that shift incentives and prevent people from acting poorly. These poor acts include stealing ideas and failing to contribute and share knowledge. When potentially valuable opportunities are revealed, there is a threat that another person will appropriate it, such as by exploiting an opportunity in other organizations (and perhaps utilizing the tools of intellectual property). Hackers may also lack incentives to share ideas and resources with others. The notion of a failure to contribute to the commons has been discussed in the common pool resource management literature relating to knowledge commons.[35] This raises questions of who has access to the resources within a hackerspace and to whom the products of exchange belong to.[36]

---

[35] See Frischmann *et al.* (2014), Madison *et al.* (2010), and Ostrom and Hess (2007).

[36] This is similar to the problem of team production and monitoring of contributions as outlined by Alchian and Demsetz (1972). Given the extreme structural uncertainty as

Given the potential gains from coordination, hackers may be incentivized to develop private governance structures to overcome these hazards. One mechanism to deal with this is *ostracism*, i.e., to exclude people. Ostracism is well known to be an effective mechanism to both induce future cooperative behavior and punish defective behavior.[37] For instance, brokers in the early London Stock Exchange, with no recognition and thus recourse to state law due to the prohibited status of their exchange, would mark on boards those individuals who had cheated others in past dealings.[38] This meant defection was a significant cost to the potential defector as there were few other markets they could go to, and this governance mechanism helped maintain cooperative behaviors. Similar mechanisms exist across many private governance forms: in prison gangs, ostracism could be deadly because it removes the protection the gang provides.[39] For traders across Africa, ostracism excludes defectors from potentially lifesaving food markets.[40]

In hackerspaces, ostracism requires some form of defined resource boundary because this enables defecting individuals to be excluded from the space.[41] This governance problem was captured in the first commons design rule: "defining the boundaries of the CPR and specifying those authorized to use it can be thought of as the first step in organizing for collective action."[42] Defining resource boundaries is the institutional difference between a commons-like club and an open-access resource. The process of excluding defectors from a hackerspace is difficult because of the nature of the underlying distributed, uncertain and non-price proto-entrepreneurial resources. While a formal legal boundary exists between

---

outlined in Chapter 2, however, the economic problem facing the "proto-entrepreneur" makes it difficult to undertake monitoring within a hierarchical firm, and the emphasis within an innovation commons such as a hackerspace is how this process can be undertaken within a polycentric hybrid structure.

[37] Both Section 4.3.1, focusing on ostracism, and Section 4.3.2, on costly signaling, operate largely through the mechanism of reputation. Such mechanisms are generally believed to only work in small groups (note Leeson, 2004 as an exception), which is precisely what hackerspaces provide.

[38] See Stringham (2015).

[39] See Skarbek (2011, 2012, 2014).

[40] See Leeson (2014).

[41] Other transaction cost economizing institutions, such as reputation mechanisms, are discussed in the following sections.

[42] See Ostrom (1990, p. 91).

hackerspace governance and the outside world, a mentality of "openness" and "everyone is welcome" remains.[43] Hackers face a trade-off between openness (that provides more distributed knowledge which is potentially complementary) and the exclusion of potential defectors (to maintain and incentivize cooperation and coordination of information in the hackerspace).

There are several ways in which hackers physically exclude non-members. Physical access to hackerspaces and its resources are restricted through different opening times for members and non-members. Members might have 24-hour access while non-members are only free to come at other times. Exclusive mailing lists or meetings can only be accessed by some people, normally to those who have contributed most to the space. New technologies, such as radio frequency identification keys, can help maintain the physical security of the hackerspace as a common pool resource.[44] Some hackerspaces also impose a formal apprenticeship for new members.

But exclusion of outsiders occurs not just in a formal physical sense. Hackers also choose who they coordinate and share knowledge with. Therefore, we can differentiate between ostracism that is hierarchical and formal and ostracism that is bottom-up and informal. While almost anyone is let into the space initially, individual hackers determine who they coordinate with based on their own discretion. Hackers pay close attention to new members to form an expectation of their reputation.

Given that bottom-up social ostracism is a social barrier, it is more "graduated" rather than "strict." Indeed, hackerspaces rest on very little command and control through hierarchies and "critiques must take the form of a review of respected peers, rather than commands from a supervisor."[45] This type of graduated social ostracism can be seen as a governance mechanism to overcome the transaction costs of the proto-entrepreneurial problem more effectively than through a hierarchical mode of monitoring.

One of the benefits of graduated social ostracism through bottom-up individual action is that individuals in a hackerspace can utilize their local

---

[43] While hackerspaces are generally registered corporations with "an exclusive right of entry and access" (Seckinger *et al.*, 2012, p. 6), this is merely a formal legal requirement and is not enforced in practice.

[44] Williams and Hall (2015).

[45] Seckinger *et al.* (2012, p. 15).

contextual knowledge to perceive a reputation of others. Establishing a top-down mechanism of monitoring and ostracism may be ineffective because defection over the underlying knowledge resources is difficult to determine by third parties and because such top-down coercion may be too hierarchical in relation to the hacker norms and ethic.

Graduated social ostracism within hackerspaces is similar to two commons design rules: (1) the development of a rule system to monitor others' behaviors; (2) the development of a mechanism of graduated sanctions for violators.[46] Bottom-up monitoring, however, also implies a limit on the size of a hackerspace because, as the size of hackerspaces grow, the capacity for individuals to continually develop and update the reputation of other agents diminishes.[47] This graduated bottom-up ostracism is closely linked with a reputation mechanism based on costly signaling in that agents seek to signal their cooperative traits to induce cooperation with others.

4.3.2 Costly signals as non-price coordination

A fundamental problem proto-entrepreneurs, and hackers, face is that they are unclear whether the information held by others will help ameliorate their proto-entrepreneurial problem of revealing opportunities. The value of non-price information—information that helps crystallize a market opportunity—is latent and obscure until combined with other complementary information. The latter uncertainty is a form of the classic "information paradox," where hackers do not know if other information is complementary until it has been disclosed and combined.[48]

A governance mechanism to solve this non-price coordination problem would need to coordinate information on whether another person is likely to cooperate or defect, as well as have an indication whether the exchange of information will help crystallize a market opportunity.

---

[46]Ostrom (1990, p. 94) outlines these two rules as follows: "Monitors, who actively audit CPR conditions and appropriator behavior, are accountable to the appropriators or are the appropriators"; "Appropriators who violate operational rules are likely to be assessed graduated sanctions … by other appropriators, by officials accountable to those appropriators."

[47]See Moilanen (2012) for a description of hackerspace summary statistics, including their size. Hackerspaces are generally small organizations.

[48]See Arrow (1962b).

One potential solution to this economic problem of uncertainty over value, and the problem of defecting agents, is through signaling. While hackers face uncertainty on many fronts, costly signals (e.g., teaching classes, learning the language) can help ameliorate some of this uncertainty and aid coordination.

Costly signaling is understood within the institutional and sociobiology literature to facilitate cooperative trade and behavior in the face of *ex ante* information asymmetries.[49] There are several reasons why signaling mechanisms may be necessary to maintain the efficacy of the hackerspace governance. One function is to filter cooperative entrants coming into the hackerspace. On a lower level, they facilitate individuals making choices about whom to coordinate with. In this way, costly signaling is tightly related to the previous section on social ostracism and exclusion. Signaling is an input into reputation, where reputation is a spontaneously ordered mechanism of contract enforcement.[50]

Perhaps, more deeply, costly signals play a coordinating role. They are inputs into the non-price coordination process of matching hackers. Costly signaling of non-price information may replace the signals of prices within markets to order agents through spontaneous non-price coordination. Signals are a kind of ordering mechanism for matching hackers based on their skills, experiences, and interests.

There are many ways in which hackerspace costly signaling manifests. Voluntary teaching of classes (on topics such as soldering, 3D printing, and laser cutting) involves a signal of cooperative behavior and reveals the skills and interests of others. Learning the "hacker language" and culture can also be conceived as a costly signal or as a kind of "credible commitment."[51] Learning a language is an irreversible, specific

---

[49] See Spence (1973). Signaling is also an important concept within the literature on selection within socio-biology and eusociality, such as the "image-scoring game" (Nowak & Sigmund, 1998). Further parallels can be found in the conception of hackerspaces as innovation commons with the literature on indirect reciprocity (Gintis *et al.*, 2001; Nowak & Sigmund, 2005) and in particular the idea that "the money that fuels indirect reciprocity is reputation" (Nowak, 2006, p. 1561).

[50] Leeson (2010).

[51] For hackerspaces, investing in costly signals can be conceived as a credible commitment in the sense of "reciprocal acts designed to safeguard a relationship" that are "undertaken in support of alliances and to promote exchange" (Williamson, 1983, p. 519).

investment used to encourage cooperative trade and signal the intention for future cooperative exchange and collaboration.

Signaling helps order knowledge coordination. As individuals signal their skills, talents, and interests, this facilitates ordering between hackers. Running regular hack-a-thons, for instance, enables individuals to contribute and coordinate knowledge with others.[52] Non-price costly signaling is necessary, in part, because price signals from markets are insufficient.[53] These costly signals can also act indirectly as other hackers within the space view exchanges of information, i.e., collaborations and coordination in a joint space can act as a multilateral signal to many hackers simultaneously.

The effect of costly signaling within hackerspaces can also be viewed as a "contribution good."[54] Because appropriating the research and products of scientific activity first requires learning the language of science, to reap the benefits of science, scientists must contribute to the body of science itself—therefore, science is a "contribution good."[55] In hackerspaces, costly signaling, such as teaching a class or the growth of the hacker culture and language, also contributes to the resources in the space. Such costly signals may therefore be important in maintaining the underlying common pool of information and preventing hackerspaces from collapsing.

4.3.3 Collective action endogenous rule formation

Hackerspaces are "… set up by hackers for hackers with the principle mission of supporting hacking."[56] The operating governance structure of hackerspaces is a flat hierarchy, generally with some form of horizontally managed democratic collective action process.[57] The process of rule

---

[52]See IFP (2013). See Chapter 5 for a further discussion of the hack-a-thon phenomenon.

[53]See Kuchař and Dekker (2017) for non-price coordination.

[54]Kealey and Ricketts (2014) develop a model of science incorporating both exclusion and openness, where the prisoners' dilemma game is transformed from a public goods problem to a coordination problem.

[55]Specifically, a "pure contribution good is non-rival over contributors but is not accessible by non-contributors" (Kealey & Ricketts, 2014, p. 1015).

[56]Maxigas (2014, p. 4).

[57]See, e.g., Seckinger *et al.* (2012).

formation within hackerspaces are often facilitated through collective action and group decisions. Hackerspaces are often member-owned corporations registered as not-for-profit corporations. They sometimes have formal boards or members (in part, this depends on their jurisdiction). While formal rules prescribe roles to board members, underlying this is a flat and fluid process of collective decision-making.

There are few clearly defined rules within hackerspace governance. The rules that do come to be prescribed, however, are endogenously created through collective group decision-making. Operational voting rights are regularly tied to membership, with members gaining participatory rights in the voting process while outsiders do not.[58] This decision-making is based on participants' perceptions of the contributions and reputations of others. This collective action bottom-up process also means that rules are endogenously created within each space and evolve over time.

There are many descriptions for the different forms of collective action processes within hackerspaces, including "meritocracy," "do-ocracy," and "act-ocracy." As these terms suggest, the commonality across different forms of hackerspace decision-making is that a hackers' position within the organization is closely tied to their contributions to the space in the past. This also relates to the contribution goods literature, with the added dynamic that the more an individual contributes, the more implicit power they gain within the governance structure.

One benefit of embracing bottom-up governance rather than strict hierarchies is the utilization of local contextual knowledge. Collective action rule-making enables a lower level of spontaneous rule-making to occur, which can be developed by the hackers themselves. Endogenous collective action rule-making is a more decentralized form of power than a hierarchical organization. Defections are policed from the bottom-up. The notion of collective action is tightly connected to Elinor Ostrom's third commons design rule, where the individuals who are affected by the rules can modify these rules.

These collective action rules in hackerspaces, however, also filter upwards and are distributed as best-practice rules for other hackerspaces.[59] In this way, hackerspaces use distinct nested hierarchies of rules which enable a form of laboratory federalism that tests and trials effective rules through competition and learning.

---

[58] The process of collective decision-making is explored later in this chapter.

[59] See, e.g., www.hackerspaces.org website on "how to set up a hackerspace."

4.3.4 *Rules are nested in a hierarchy*

Mechanisms of governance often require different systems of rules because each level has a different role in solving different economic problems and institutional challenges. Therefore, to understand the complexity of institutional systems, it is useful to separate rules into sub-levels.[60] Elinor Ostrom's eighth design rule for commons is that "appropriation, provision, monitoring, enforcement, conflict resolution, and governance activities are organized in multiple layers of nested enterprises."[61] We can see three main levels of rules that constitute the private governance of hackerspaces:

- a *meta-constitutional* global network of spaces sharing best-practice rules;
- a *constitutional boundary* of each hackerspace, including the rules that broadly determine the rules of the game;
- a *sub-group* level of polycentric projects where hackers collaborate and collectively determine their own rules.

4.3.4.1 *Meta-constitutional level: A global hackerspace community*

While survey results suggest that 91% of hackers were part of only one hackerspace or makerspace community, there is a strong culture of mutual visiting rights between hackerspaces.[62] Hackerspace passports were created by one prominent hackerspace, Noisebridge, in an attempt to promote visiting rights to other hackerspaces, increase collaboration and cross-pollination, and encourage mutual support between hackerspaces.[63] This broad global community of hackerspaces shares information about governance best practice through "an international network of exhibition fairs, publications, member's clubs, and funding structures."[64] We can call this overarching global hackerspace community as the highest level of self-contained hackerspace rules (the *meta-constitutional* level).

---

[60] See Ostrom (2005, p. 11).
[61] See Ostrom (1990, p. 101).
[62] See Moilanen (2012).
[63] See hackerspaces.org (2011).
[64] See Seckinger *et al.* (2012, p. 5).

The meta-constitutional rules are transferred through a "global and informal network" and relate to their shared "technologies, procedures and values."[65] This provides overarching governance to hackerspaces themselves yet has no direct authority over them. This meta-constitutional level is limited to providing information of the existence of other hacker-spaces and promoting diffusion of best-practice rules. Best-practice design rules are often referred to as Design Patterns—a term that emerged in 2007 from a speech at the 24th Chaos Communication Congress in the discussions of creating and running a hackerspace.[66] An explicit online thread is dedicated to design patterns on the main hackerspaces website.[67] Underlying this broad global network of best-practice rules and sharing of information are the broad rules of each individual hackerspace, which are outlined in Section 4.3.4.2.

4.3.4.2   *Constitutional rules: Broad rules of*
the hackerspace game

The shared community of hackerspaces at the meta-constitutional level described above is made up of self-contained communities of hacker-spaces.[68] Each of these hackerspaces creates their own rules—these are *constitutional*-level rules. These rules "provide a community-oriented space, sustainably funded by members, that supports creation and exploration."[69] These rules delineate activities within an outside the hack-erspace, particularly in differentiating the institutional system from out-side influences.

The constitutional-level rules of hackerspaces align with Elinor Ostrom's commons design rule of a defined resource boundary.[70] Constitutional rules do not direct the goals of hackers as they solve their proto-entrepreneurial problem, but rather enable hackers to coordinate non-price information with others to discover opportunities. Indeed, this constitutional level of rules serves to maintain "arms-length support

---

[65] See Kera (2012, p. 1).

[66] Ohlig and Weiler (2007).

[67] See hackerspaces.org (2016).

[68] See Moilanen (2012).

[69] See Williams *et al.* (2012, p. 18).

[70] To be clear, the hackerspace is not impermeable because such rigid definition would impose artificial boundaries (see Moilanen, 2012).

enabling autonomous creative behaviors" which in turn will "provide the breeding ground for new creative industries to blossom."[71]

Perhaps confusingly, the constitutional rules of a hackerspace—including the collective action voting processes discussed above as well as the informal norms within hackerspaces relating to the sharing of information—are a form of *pre*-constitutional rule-making. They are *pre*-constitutional because they outline the rules by which hackers coordinate to solve their economic problem in the following *post*-constitutional level.[72]

Having broad and fluid *pre*-constitutional rules within which hackers coordinate information may be a mechanism to economize on the unique transaction costs of the proto-entrepreneurial innovation problem, i.e., given the non-price coordination problem proto-entrepreneurs face over potential complementary trading partners, it may be transaction cost economizing for the rules of the game at the level of the hackerspace to remain broad, and then later be made more specific and heterogeneous, which is what occurs at the *sub-group* level, i.e., the *pre*-constitutional rules here exist to enable autonomous spontaneous coordination at lower levels.

4.3.4.3 *Sub-group rules: Forming team rules*

The dynamic processes of developing technologies within hackerspaces tend to be coordinated from the bottom-up. The distributions, duties and goals of hackers are determined collectively by those within each group as they voluntarily enter into informal agreements. Hackers collaborate on projects and develop rules to govern those collaborations—these are the *sub-group* level rules.

At the sub-group level of rules, "various groups and stakeholders (can) negotiate their interests directly."[73] There is a kind of spontaneous proto-entrepreneurial anarchy at this level, where people take on their own positions of leadership. Smaller groups create their own rules to solve problems or to work on projects. These groups may dissipate if a

---

[71] See Seckinger *et al.* (2012, p. 9).

[72] See Buchanan and Tullock (1962) for a distinction between "pre-constitutional" and "post-constitutional" analysis, where the former focuses on the rules of the game and the latter focuses on the play of the game.

[73] See Kera (2012, p. 2).

project fails or may transition the idea into some other form (e.g., a start-up firm, following an "entrepreneurial fundamental transformation").

Sub-group level rules are more specific and heterogeneous than preceding constitutional-level rules. They are also more fluid and dynamic. Indeed, "the autonomous micro communities are constantly on the move; evolving, mixing, forking, hibernating and dying."[74] This level of rules is where hackerspaces gain the impression of lacking specifically designed or defined goals and that they rest on indeterminate and dynamic processes.[75] The creative process, due to its necessary failures and revisions, "does not deal with administration well."[76]

Sub-group levels of rules are similar to the concept of "entrepreneurial teams."[77] The sub-groups or teams that form within a hackerspace give hackerspaces an accurate description as a polycentric ordering, i.e., many centers of decision-making (each sub-group), but these centers sit within a larger framework of central mechanisms to resolve conflicts (constitutional-level rules).[78] The sub-group level of rules is a polycentric ordering within the constitutional level of rules described above. In this way, the grouping of entrepreneurial sub-groups within a hackerspace—based on the combination of complementary information between proto-entrepreneurs—enables the polycentric decision-making to occur at a potentially more efficient scale of decision-making.[79]

These polycentric rule systems may economize the transaction costs associated with fundamental structural uncertainty over trading partners and the costs of trial and error with different trading partners.

---

[74] See Moilanen (2012, p. 94).

[75] Seravalli (2011).

[76] See Seckinger *et al.* (2012, p. 15).

[77] The sub-groups of hackers in hackerspaces are "entrepreneurial teams" in the sense that Harper (2008, p. 614) defines "an entrepreneurial team as a group of entrepreneurs with a common goal that can only be achieved by appropriate combinations of individual entrepreneurial actions." As Harper notes, this definition of an entrepreneurial team is extremely broad. In the context of a hackerspace, there may be multiple overlapping polycentric entrepreneurial teams because the entrepreneurial team itself must be first discovered. See also Cooney (2005) for a review of entrepreneurial teams.

[78] Polycentrism in the sense of Ostrom *et al.* (1961). For polycentric governance, see also Aligica *et al.* (2014), Aligica and Tarko (2012), McGinnis and Ostrom (2012), and Ostrom (2010).

[79] See Tarko (2015a, 2016).

The benefits of such a polycentric approach, however, may decline as groups of proto-entrepreneurs begin to crystallize market opportunities. At the two levels of rules in hackerspaces discussed above (meta-constitutional and constitutional), hackerspaces appear as a perpetual institutional solution to the innovation problem. From the perspective of the choosing proto-entrepreneur attempting to solve their economic problem, however, the polycentric sub-group rules within a hackerspace may only be a temporary institutional solution. Therefore, this sub-group level is where the "entrepreneurial fundamental transformation" takes place. As hackers begin to work on a project collaboratively, they may develop increasingly asset-specific investments with the others in the group. The asset specificity here is not necessary in the form of physical investments, but rather human capital understanding of a market opportunity that has quasi-rents as a project opportunity is identified and developed. These quasi-rents exist because (potential) economic value would be sacrificed if the trading relationship were to be terminated. Once hackers discover what they perceive to be an actionable market opportunity, they may decide to integrate within a centralized firm due to the increase in the potential for opportunism.

Only at the level of polycentric sub-group rules can the constitutional rules of hackerspaces described above be outlined as *pre*-constitutional rules, enabling the spontaneous ordering and formation at lower levels. The constitutional rules in a hackerspace create a playing field within which hackers can devise and test their own rules, including, e.g., the ownership of the project through bargaining. For instance, it's been noted that "creatives are constantly coming and going, trading projects and resources the way most others trade currency."[80]

The question then becomes why hackers create a constitutional level of rules to undertake polycentric coordination outside the traditional institutions of the innovation system, including firms and markets. In Section 4.4, we observe that hackerspaces themselves can be viewed as a form of entrepreneurial secession—from the entangled institutions of innovation policy to private governance.

---

[80] See Seckinger *et al.* (2012, p. 17).

4.4 Hackerspaces as Entrepreneurial Institutional Secession

Why do hackers choose to secede from the institutions of innovation policy (e.g., intellectual property) in favor of governance in hackerspaces? This institutional choice of private governance is examined through the analytical framework of "positive political anarchy" (or "efficient anarchy").[81] From this perspective, hackerspaces represent secession from the institutional controls of innovation policy analogous to economic shatter zones that are "found wherever the expansion of states, empires, slave-trading, and wars, as well as natural disasters, have driven large numbers of people to seek refuge in out-of-the-way places."[82]

Examining hackerspaces as a form of institutional secession raises many questions within comparative political economy. For instance, are hackers explicitly seceding because innovation policy distorts the costs of other institutional solutions? What are the transaction cost conditions under which this choice to secede may be made?[83] Economist Peter Leeson lays out a useful analytical model for thinking about when private governance (i.e., anarchy) may be an efficient institutional choice for rational self-maximizing people.[84] Assume that each person receives some gains from trade when there is a government and some payoffs when the government is absent. Assume that there is also a higher level of trade (and payoffs) when the government is present. For a society to prefer anarchy—private governance—the cost of government must be lower than the social benefit it brings.[85]

We can apply this simple model to think about the choices of proto-entrepreneurs. Private governance in hackerspaces may be efficient because the relative cost of governing the entrepreneurial process else-where—within the entanglement of innovation policy—may be comparatively expensive. Given that the costs of government are subjectively perceived, to demonstrate the cost of government intervention in this

---

[81] See Leeson (2007b).

[82] See Scott (2014, p. 8).

[83] For a further discussion of how institutional choice is a trade-off between the subjective costs of dictatorship and disorder, see Chapter 6.

[84] See Leeson (2007b).

[85] This assumes a social contract theory of government where the presence or absence of government is in efficiency terms.

process, we can look at the perceptions of hackers themselves: do hackers perceive innovation policy as an effective institutional solution to the economic problem they face? Hackers' focus on maintaining governance autonomy is evidence they are seceding from both governments and hierarchical firms. Hackers delineate what practices are acceptable within their constitutional rules and what is only acceptable outside the ordering. This manifests in eschewing of intellectual property rights, subsidies, credits, and public funding. Hackers tend to shun both hierarchical firms (i.e., corporations) and governments (e.g., defense departments). Hackerspaces maintain their autonomy from these other institutions in several ways.

The main source of funding in hackerspaces varies, but the financial independence and autonomy constitute an important principle.[86] Funding is often sourced from monthly fees or dues and subscriptions, as well as "donations, sponsorships and grants."[87] Furthermore, "company donations (money) are less disagreeable than governmental support, but only slightly" while membership fees "seem to be the most approved source of funding."[88] These donations preferably come "without strings" attached.[89]

The extent of governance autonomy within a hackerspace may also change as the microstructure of transaction costs shifts throughout an innovation trajectory. A proto-entrepreneurial hacker may move from a hackerspace to a fab lab, to an incubator, and then on to a start-up firm. This includes gradations of autonomy from a fully privately governed hackerspace to other institutions that may be embedded more tightly with a national innovation system.

Shifting between governance structures to solve different entrepreneurial problems creates tension with underlying hacker norms. There is a sentiment in hackerspaces that the creative process may not "function in the traditional business model, where income generation is the primary measure of success."[90] Indeed, at first, it seems that hackers are entrepreneurs because of the revealed sentiment of opposing commercialization because "commercialization undermines the spirit that drives the space's

---

[86] See Guthrie (2014).
[87] Seckinger *et al.* (2012, p. 6).
[88] See Moilanen (2012).
[89] See Kostakis *et al.* (2014, p. 566).
[90] Seckinger *et al.* (2012, p. 9).

innovative engine."[91] There exist some evidence that hackers eschew commercialization within the space, but not outside it: "We dislike intellectual property and I don't think we would keep people from using the knowledge they gained on the 'outside' world. In fact, one of our goals is to enable people to go outside and apply what they learned at the hackerspace."[92] It is clear that one of the dominant themes of the maker movement is "open-source, non-proprietary intellectual property," partially because the traditional form of intellectual property protection runs counter to their desires.[93] This reveals a clear tension between the open-source principles within hackerspaces and the commercialization and diffusion of opportunities discovered in the space.

While on the surface it appears that hackers dislike commercialization, this might only be a temporary norm. Many hackers eschew the commercialization of ideas (pushing back on the institutions of firms, markets, and governments) while simultaneously understanding that ideas may later enter these institutions. Put another way, hackers first begin coordinating and cooperating within hackerspaces, but, if successful in discovering some perceived actionable economic value outside the space, and as agreed by other members involved in the project, the discovery of a market opportunity may be commercialized elsewhere. What begins with cooperation in hackerspaces between many autonomous agents may end in commercialization within the hierarchical firm of only a few people.

The comparative efficiency of hackerspaces in solving the proto-entrepreneurial problem may have also improved over time through institutional learning. Sharing may be prevalent not only because it is the right thing to do but also because it is an efficient and superior development model for making software (in contrast to intellectual property models).[94] Effective private collective action mechanisms make the benefits of engaging with the institutions that are entangled with innovation policy comparatively ineffective. More effective private orderings imply a smaller benefit from engagement in the state-based system.

From this perspective, hackers have discovered unique and contextual sets of rules to overcome the problems they face. Some of these

---

[91] See Robertson (2010, p. 6).
[92] See interviews in Kostakis *et al.* (2014).
[93] See Seckinger *et al.* (2012, p. 16).
[94] See Raymond (1999).

governance institutions become more effective through the application of technology. For instance, social media has enabled different hackers to come together and sort themselves into relevant hackerspaces.[95] Cheaper and more easily accessible security measures, such as cameras and SSID cards, have aided the maintenance and governance of the physical resources of hackerspaces,[96] i.e., hackerspaces not only help develop technologies but also leverage technologies to solve governance problems and economize on transaction costs. New institution-creating technologies such as blockchains may further decrease the costs of private orderings to coordinate the discovery of value. Indeed, the private development of institutional solutions to the proto-entrepreneurial problem may improve over time as proto-entrepreneurs learn—pushing us further toward entrepreneurial anarchy and private governance as solutions to knowledge coordination problems.

4.5 Conclusion

In this chapter, we have analyzed hackerspaces as an example of a polycentric private collective action solution to the proto-entrepreneurial problem. In hackerspaces, hackers coordinate non-price entrepreneurial information within collectively developed rules to discover opportunities. The barrier to proto-entrepreneurial coordination in hackerspaces is not just physical or formal, but rather the individual decision to collaborate with others. The benefit of this—through graduated social ostracism—is that it draws on the local contextual reputation of other hackers, helping to suppress opportunism. Hackers also use various forms of costly signaling (e.g., voluntary teaching of classes) to signal future cooperative behavior and facilitate ordering of tacit skills, talents, and interests. Many of the rules of hackerspaces are made through collective action processes—rather than through hierarchy and control—that create a kind of laboratory federalism.

Hackerspaces are best understood as having distinct hierarchies of rules at three main levels. First, *meta-constitutional rules* coordinate best-practice rules across the thousands of hackerspaces globally. Second, *constitutional rules* govern each individual hackerspace, including their

---

[95]See Seckinger *et al*. (2012, p. 5).
[96]See Williams and Hall (2015).

constitutions and formal rules as well as operational rules such as voting, and that act to set the playing field for the creation of further rules at the lower level. Third, *sub-group rules* are created at the level of project or team. They make hackerspaces polycentric. These rules spontaneously emerge from the typically flat hierarchical structure of hackerspaces. It is at this lower-level of rulemaking—at the level of proto-entrepreneurial teams—where the temporary nature of hackerspaces along an innovation trajectory becomes clear. This level of rules is also where the dynamics of the "entrepreneurial fundamental transformation" manifest.

More broadly, hackerspaces may emerge as a form of secession from other institutions of innovation, including innovation policy. Coordinating the proto-entrepreneurial process within the institutions of innovation policy may be comparatively costly. The autonomy of hackerspace governance outside of the reach of innovation policy was evidenced by hackers' explicit eschewing of the efficacy of state-based innovation policy and the hierarchical firm. One further reason for the secession to the private governance structures of hackerspaces may be that the continual development and refinement of private hybrid governance solutions may make them comparatively effective in solving the proto-entrepreneurial problem.

The contributions of this chapter have expanded our understanding of the mechanisms hackers develop to solve the proto-entrepreneurial problem. The implication of this is to reveal some of the feasible bounds of the institutional possibility set of proto-entrepreneurial coordination. Enquiring into the private governance of proto-entrepreneurial discovery can also be examined from the perspective of a single technology, i.e., rather than directing analysis around a class of institutional governance—hackerspaces—we can alternatively look at an early-stage technology. This is the task of Chapter 5, which focuses on blockchain.

Chapter 5

Developing the Blockchain Cryptoeconomy

5.1 Introduction

Blockchain and other distributed ledger technologies are decentralized institutional technologies for governing trusted information and creating new types of economic, social, and political organizations.[1] Blockchains have clear complementarities to other technologies (e.g., artificial intelligence) that rely on value being transferred across secure digital infrastructure. Given this scope, blockchains are predicted to be widely applied across many industries—from supply chains to healthcare data—and compete with alternative forms of governance (e.g., firms and governments) in providing digital trust. This chapter looks at blockchain technology and the governance processes of entrepreneurial discovery seeking to develop it.

My analysis is organized into two intertwined parts. The first part examines the private governance of blockchain proto-entrepreneurship. The focus is on hybrid organizations such as conferences, workshops, and online forums as ways to facilitate knowledge coordination, and the diversity of mechanisms these governance structures use. The second part explores more deeply the challenges of institutional entrepreneurship,

---

[1] Some of the ideas in this chapter have been outlined in various other places, including Allen (2019, 2020) and MacDonald *et al.* (2016). This work contributes to the field of "institutional cryptoeconomics." See, e.g., Allen *et al.* (2018, 2019a, 2019b, 2019c, 2020a), Berg *et al.* (2019, 2020), and Davidson *et al.* (2018).

underscoring the importance of entrepreneurial coordination for block-chain technology. The central argument is that developing the crypto-economy is analogous to the problem of economic development, but this process is coordinated through hybrid private governance.

Blockchain technology was invented in 2008 as the infrastructure for the digital cryptocurrency bitcoin.[2] The core innovation is to combine cryptography with economic incentives to create publicly accessible ledgers, stored in a decentralized way, that provide tamper-resistant infor-mation. Blockchain protocols employ consensus mechanisms to facilitate a distributed network of computers to come to agreement over shared data. These consensus mechanisms convert resources (e.g., energy) into economically valuable trust.[3] Blockchain infrastructure is therefore an alternative mechanism to provide the trusted inputs into economic exchange (e.g., property rights). Coupled with other technologies— such as self-executing smart contracts that can be executed across block-chain infrastructure—blockchains are next-generation digital economic infrastructure.

As we can see, blockchain is a potentially highly disruptive technol-ogy for decentralized governance. But the technology remains nascent because the entire scope of applications is yet to be entrepreneurially tested and discovered. Indeed, the process of entrepreneurial discovery around technologies with general application is well known to involve a lengthy period of trial-and-error experimentation.[4] Steam power, for instance, took over a century and half to move from the steam-powered pump to textiles.[5] Discovering the applications of blockchain technology will be a long entrepreneurial process of institutional disruption. The way that entrepreneurial process happens will be framed by the institutional environment within which entrepreneurs coordinate information and act.[6]

The blockchain industry was selected as an effective place to look for examples of private governance of proto-entrepreneurship for several reasons. Throughout this book, we have emphasized the temporary and transient nature of innovation commons at the very beginning of inno-vation trajectories. This suggests the emergence of private polycentric

---

[2] See Nakamoto (2008). For an early history of bitcoin, see Popper (2015).
[3] See Berg *et al.* (2019, 2020).
[4] For GPTs, see, e.g., Griliches (1957).
[5] For steam power, see Landes (1969).
[6] See Allen (2020).

governance structures around nascent technologies, such as blockchain. The temporary nature of these private governance structures implies they are harder to observe later in innovation trajectories and industries (e.g., because of information loss about their existence). Furthermore, because blockchains have a wide scope of potential opportunities, this suggests that the costs of developing private governance mechanisms to coordinate them can be recovered. Large gains from trade to be made from entrepreneurial coordination incentivize the creation of private orderings to realize these benefits.

5.2 Entrepreneurial Coordination Around Blockchain Technology

Collaboration within the cryptography community spans back beyond the invention of blockchain.[7] Attempts to create a digital currency, for instance, trace back to the early 1980s.[8] Communication between cypherpunks included mailing lists, one of which had almost every major cryptography figure pass through, including the elusive creator of Bitcoin, Satoshi Nakamoto.[9] Blockchain technology emerged from this long-term effort to develop new decentralized governance mechanisms. While early players in the blockchain and cryptography ecosystem focused almost solely on overcoming *technical* problems, the present economic problem surrounding blockchain technology is primarily an *entrepreneurial* problem.[10]

The entrepreneurial discovery problem continues in a collaborative range of hybrid governance structures today. The aim here is not to provide a comprehensive mapping of these governance structures (partly because the space of private governance solutions shifts constantly and rapidly) but to demonstrate that these spaces do exist and that they are

---

[7]Collins (2009) proposes that this collaboration between actors in the blockchain ecosystem may prove vital for its success.

[8]See, e.g., Bargar (2016) and Chaum (1983).

[9]For the mailing list, see Cypherpunks (2016). The mailing list grew to 700 subscribers in 1994 and over 2,000 by 1997 (Manne, 2015).

[10]This is not to downplay existing technical issues around scalability, privacy, and security of blockchain infrastructure. But it is reasonable to say that there are more entrepreneurial efforts today—in applying the technology for human needs—than there was in the earlier cypherpunk movement.

diverse. We can see three broad classes of private governance efforts to coordinate proto-entrepreneurial discovery around blockchain: (1) physical and short-lived blockchain coordination (e.g., conferences and hack-a-thons); (2) physical but ongoing governance (e.g., hackerspaces as above); (3) digital coordination (e.g., messaging forums). Some of these are covered.

There are many different types of blockchain conferences (and their variants such as workshops and hack-a-thons) that act as places to share entrepreneurial information. These temporary coordinating structures occur in physical space, but only for short-lived periods. Following are some examples:

- Blockchain *conferences* regularly occur for less than a week and repeat annually. There are often hundreds of presentations and collaborations between developers, thought leaders, and academics. The emphasis of these conferences is not only on technological development (and seeking investors for start-ups) but also on broader industry issues, such as regulation and coordination of standards. At the time of writing, major blockchain conferences include Consensus, DevCon, Cryptoeconomic Systems and the Crypto Valley Conference. Conferences range widely in terms of their size (up to tens of thousands of attendees) and focus (e.g., cryptocurrency or blockchain).
- Blockchain *hack-a-thons* are gatherings of people to collaborate intensively over a short period of time (a day to a week).[11] They are variously known as codefests, hack fests, or hack days and are regularly held or sponsored by software companies.[12] Some hack-a-thons will have a specifically defined goal, while others will be more aligned to a technology or a programming language.[13] Hack-a-thons generally begin with presentations before participants form teams, and from here, the "hacking" begins. This hacking can continue for

---

[11] See Briscoe and Mulligan (2014). Hack-a-thons are distinct from hackerspaces outlined in Chapter 4 because they are a temporary event that occurs over a short period of time.
[12] Nandi and Mandernach (2016).
[13] Some more specifically designed focuses for hack-a-thons include software application type (e.g., mobile apps), a specific programming language (e.g., Ruby), within a company (e.g., Google), a specific cause (e.g., health applications), or a single application (e.g., blockchain).

several hours, days, or even up to a week. Teams often present their work in front of a panel of judges selecting a winning team for prizes. Hack-a-thons are often created as side events to major blockchain conferences and are regularly run out of universities.

We can understand these as examples of blockchain innovation commons, i.e., hybrid polycentric collectively governed spaces, where participants are proto-entrepreneurs seeking to coordinate information over the potential applications for blockchain technology. These hybrid entrepreneurial organizations facilitate the coordination of information between dispersed individuals who may have not otherwise met, thereby helping to overcome uncertainty about opportunities. In hack-a-thons, for instance, there is an emphasis on meeting people: "where people who are not normally collocated converge for a few days."[14] They may be used as a mechanism to discover real usable applications of blockchain rather than abstract theories.[15] Conferences and hack-a-thons can also take a more industry-wide coordinating role. For instance, the founder of Blockchain Labs, Bo Shen, says "the focus is on blockchain as a whole" and participants will "achieve a better understanding on the potential of Blockchain applications."[16]

Hack-a-thons can act as a coordination mechanism prior to the "entrepreneurial fundamental transformation" in an innovation trajectory. Indeed, the collaboration, links, and networks generated through hack-a-thons (and conferences) often extend farther than the short temporary focus of the event, leading to business collaborations.[17] When some potentially actionable value is discovered, the economizing structure may shift from the hybrid fluid structure of a hack-a-thon toward integration within a start-up firm. This process of group formation, i.e., of group formation of complementary bits of proto-entrepreneurial information, has recently received academic attention.[18]

---

[14]See Trainer *et al.* (2016).

[15]Reutzel (2016).

[16]This concept of focusing on "blockchain as a whole" is further developed here in relation to economic development.

[17]See Briscoe and Mulligan (2014).

[18]See, e.g., Lederman (2015, p. 80): "Some of the groups showed a tendency to break into sub-groups at different stages of the Hackathons."

Forming groups in hack-a-thons has some similarity to hacker-spaces, except with a further emphasis on speed and shorter time frame. Hack-a-thon teams are, like those in hackerspaces, polycentric forms of governance. The Chainsmith blockchain hack-a-thon in Dublin, for instance, states that "the whole point is to network and learn; [people are] encouraged to mingle and spread in different teams." This collaborative process, however, comes with transaction costs (as outlined in Chapter 2). One novel mechanism to overcome the hazards of the transaction costs of the collaborative process is Hackonomy, which uses blockchain technology itself to create a currency facilitating the collaborative process.[19]

We can also identify more long-lived governance structures coalescing around blockchain technology, such as the following:

- Bitcoin Embassies were particularly popular early in the development of the cryptocurrency industry. They were a global network of membership-based physical locations that aimed to bring together "fellow like-minded cryptocurrency enthusiasts to learn about Bitcoin and cryptocurrencies." While fulfilling this basic role, each embassy maintained a high degree of autonomy in its projects and rules. Many of these spaces self-identified as providing a place coordinating information for entrepreneurs and enthusiasts as well as regulatory compliance issues and interaction with state institutions.

- Bitcoin and Blockchain Centers are more closely described as incubators and consulting services and are (comparatively) less focused on socializing. They are targeted more specifically at start-ups or people seeking to develop an opportunity (i.e., proto-entrepreneurs). They are therefore more representative of innovation "markets" in the sense that more standardized innovation services are provided. One of the largest Bitcoin Centers in the world, in New York, "aims to be a place where developers can really take their software developments to town." There is also a greater focus on the physical resources in the space and on learning resources to incubate start-ups.

Some hybrid governance structures around the blockchain industry are digital. For instance, online forums and mailing lists are mechanisms to pool information and coordinate around the discovery of opportunities.

---

[19] See Aitken (2016) and hack.ether.camp (2017).

Cypherpunks have coordinated online through forums and mailing lists since at least the 1980s. While their original mailing list has closed down, there are several current lists which can be traced directly back.[20] The original list "spawned not just commerce but an entire philosophy."[21]

Today, many distributed communities of developers—often relating to a specific blockchain protocol—utilize open and closed online coordination tools, such as Telegram, Slack and Keybase channels. We can understand these as digital mechanisms to coordinate and match entrepreneurial talent and to overcome issues of uncertainty in developing a blockchain-based digital protocols.

The range of innovation commons coalescing around blockchain technology are remarkably diverse. They all provide a place where people can come to coordinate information and learn about opportunities for blockchain technology, but they also differ along a range of key margins, including hierarchy, control, and the autonomy of agents to create their own exchange relations with others.

Blockchain innovation commons tend to have flat but emergent hierarchical rules. We know that in markets there are few hierarchies, while firms are generally hierarchical organizations that are planned from top-down, with interactions based on authority relations between its agents. Blockchain innovation commons sit somewhere in between. Where hierarchical control does exist in blockchain innovation commons, these rules tend to emerge through reputation and thus participant discretion. For instance, in hackerspaces and blockchain centers, individuals who are more prominent within the space generally have a higher position in the hierarchy (even informally). Through hack-a-thons, there are fewer hierarchies in part because there is less time for a hierarchy to emerge. For online forums, the degree of hierarchy depends on the openness of the group and also on whether there is a reputation system, which may increase the extent to which some comments are more influential (indeed, sometimes this is leveraged effectively to filter content).

Blockchain innovation commons also differ in how free individuals are to coordinate with others (i.e., individual autonomy) and collaborate. We know that in markets autonomous coordination is high, while in firms autonomy tends to be low due to the extent of administrative control and

---

[20]For example, the cryptography list (gryptography@matzdowd.com) and financial cryptography list (fc-announce@ifca.ai).
[21]Rodger (2001).

monitoring. Generally, blockchain innovation commons have high degrees of autonomy. For instance, hack-a-thon participants are encouraged to form teams with participants to work on projects based on their own interests and skills in proposed projects. There may be less autonomy, however, within incubators and centers. Autonomy matters because it might ameliorate some of the transaction costs of coordinating proto-entrepreneurial information under uncertainty (i.e., high levels of autonomous interaction may facilitate the process of non-price coordination and discovery).

Blockchain innovation commons set goals in different ways. Within a firm, goal orientation tends to be explicitly top-down controlled and directed, while markets rely on bottom-up individual goals. While blockchain innovation commons are, once again, somewhere in between, goal setting tends to be emergent from individual entrepreneurs and the groups within which they interact. Goals tend to be first generated through an emergent process of interaction and then potentially later enforced through the creation of a hierarchy around that goal (i.e., through the formation of teams). In hackerspaces and centers, for instance, project groups may create their own goals—to work on a project together—from which some form of hierarchy may emerge within this group to overcome the hazards in organizing this group.[22] Similarly, hack-a-thons may begin with a set of projects, which are then voted upon, and then the losing participants merge into the projects of the winning groups.

Blockchain innovation commons also have different safeguards—and therefore potential—for opportunistic behavior. The capacity for opportunism varies greatly based on how different events and spaces are governed and the extent to which the governance structure itself exists to detect, punish, and deter opportunism. Smaller blockchain innovation commons, such as hackerspaces and centers, have few participants, have multiple interactions with other participants, and exist in a physical place. These environments are perhaps more conducive to monitoring and thus guarding against opportunism—both because agents are more likely to know the reputation of other members (and thus change their exchange behavior based on those reputations) and because punishments for opportunism may more effectively be monitored. Larger conferences, in

---

[22] See also Chapter 4 for the private governance in hackerspaces.

contrast, lack tight reputation-based safeguards (and interactions are often once-off). This reveals a trade-off in innovation commons: a larger group not only increases the potential for complementary and valuable knowledge coordination through a larger pool of knowledge resources but also opens the scope for opportunism by diluting monitoring through reputation.

We can also see varying scope of participant interaction, i.e., in how many people interact simultaneously. Much of the coordination in an innovation commons is multilateral, with the sharing and exchanging of information occurring between many participants at once. More people coordinating at once may help overcome uncertainty in knowledge coordination. We can think of this as the "lateralness" of exchange. In hackerspaces, there are fewer people working in small teams on projects, while at conferences, there are larger groups with information being broadcast. The degree of "lateralness" also changes depending on the level of rules: hackerspaces often have classes where many people are involved, and online forums and communication systems vary by the number of agents within each group, forum, Slack group, and so on. We can also consider "lateralness" relating to whether coordination is between two individuals or more indirect between multiple individuals at the same time. This relates to the concept in evolutionary biology of direct versus indirect reciprocity.[23] A proto-entrepreneur could either expect to reap their entire benefits from one exchange, or they may be exchanging with this individual to gain from someone else in the group. Such an indirect system of reciprocity may be effective for overcoming the structural uncertainty of coordinating proto-entrepreneurial information.

What we have seen here is that blockchain innovation commons exist and that they are diverse governance structures to ameliorate some of the costs of proto-entrepreneurial coordination—both in terms of opportunism and in terms of spontaneous collaboration to deal with the uncertainties of coordinating information. Section 5.3 turns to a deeper explanation for the prevalence of blockchain innovation commons, given the unique entrepreneurial challenge that blockchains present. Drawing on "new development economics," we explain these governance structures—hackerspaces, conferences, hack-a-thons, and messaging groups—as a form of private economic development of the cryptoeconomy.

---

[23] See Nowak and Sigmund (1998, 2005).

5.3 Institutional Blockchain Entrepreneurship

In the first half of this chapter, we implicitly assumed that the institutional environment in which blockchain entrepreneurs were applying the technology was given. We now step away from this assumption and analyze more fundamental applications of blockchains as a tool for institutional secession—cryptosecession. Applications of blockchain by entrepreneurs are not constrained to integration within the existing institutions of a territorial economy. Blockchain is also a technology for exit—away from existing territorial political systems such as the law and courts—to create the new decentralized institutions of the *cryptoeconomy*.

The entire suite of blockchain applications, each of which operate on their own rule systems or protocols, can together be described as forming a new decentralized economy called the cryptoeconomy. The cryptoeconomy does not have a geographic location, or a centralized political structure, or a legal system. Rather, the cryptoeconomy is defined as using "cryptographic techniques to constrain behavior (in place of using trusted third parties)."[24] At first glance, the cryptoeconomy appears similar to other techno-economic paradigms, such as "peer-to-peer" or "sharing economy."[25] The cryptoeconomy is unique, however, because it involves non-territorial political exit away from the institutions of the state, such as the law and courts.[26] This process is known as *cryptosecession*.[27]

The process of creating the cryptoeconomy is an entrepreneurial process,[28] i.e., for entrepreneurs to use blockchain technology to exit from existing institutions they need to discover where blockchain institutions can outperform other institutional alternatives. In this way, the economic problem of cryptosecession and developing the cryptoeconomy remains a proto-entrepreneurial problem of coordinating dispersed information.

---

[24]Babbitt and Dietz (2014, p. 1).

[25]See Benkler (2006) and Allen and Berg (2014).

[26]Just as the organization of industry is "dense network of co-operation and affiliation by which firms are inter-related" (Richardson, 1972, p. 883), the cryptoeconomy is an order of networks and complementarities between individuals exchanging across different blockchains. The spontaneous ordering of cryptoeconomy exchange is generated by the complex and competing interactions of individuals and organizations operating within the constraints of blockchain technology. This draws heavily from the "catallaxy" definition by Hayek (1973).

[27]See MacDonald (2019).

[28]See Allen (2019, 2020).

Analyses of entrepreneurial discovery generally take the territorial institutional environment as given.[29] From this perspective, entrepreneurs discover profitable market opportunities within the existing territorial institutions, such as the law. But entrepreneurs can also discover new "protective-tier" institutional technologies aimed at changing the "rules of the game."[30] For instance, entrepreneurs can develop technologies to secure property rights for exchange and provide private legal systems.

Institutional entrepreneurs face a higher-order economic problem than entrepreneurs operating within existing institutions.[31] Here, we take some of the insights from institutional entrepreneurship within development economics—where in developing countries entrepreneurs create institutional technologies that "restrict predation in the absence of a well-functioning government"—and apply those insights to the discovery and development of the cryptoeconomy.[32] Unlike territorial developing nations, the lack of a centralized government within the cryptoeconomy implies that the discovery and development of the cryptoeconomy must be privately governed. From this perspective, the diversity of blockchain innovation commons outlined above is a type of private economic development.

We can roughly distinguish between two broad types of blockchain applications. On the one hand, blockchains can be integrated within the existing institutions and organizations of territorial economies (e.g., firms) while maintaining *public* protective-tier technologies (e.g., courts). This type of entrepreneurship is conventional. Entrepreneurs integrate their opportunities within the existing institutional architecture of the territorial state. The steam engine, for instance, did not seek to provide new enforcement or institutional structures; it was gradually integrated into the

---

[29]See, e.g., Baumol (1990). As Leeson and Boettke (2009, p. 252) note: "Conventional discussions of entrepreneurship focus on entrepreneurship at a 'lower tier' of economic activity—entrepreneurial activity within a given institutional framework." Indeed, this was the case here.

[30]See, e.g., Leca *et al.* (2008). Also, as outlined in Leeson and Boettke (2009, p. 253): "Productive-tier entrepreneurship is 'concerned with investments that improve productivity (innovation) and better service consumer needs (arbitrage)' while protective-tier entrepreneurship is 'concerned with the creation of protective technologies that secure citizens' private property rights vis-à-vis one another (governance).'"

[31]Kuchař (2016).

[32]Leeson and Boettke (2009).

existing institutions of trade, such as the courts, price mechanisms, and private property. On the other hand, blockchain entrepreneurs can cryptosecede to create *private* protective-tier technologies. Blockchains are a technology of trust that can be used to cryptosecede from political institutions. If the latter path is taken by the entrepreneur, they must discover blockchain cryptographic code as an institutional enforcement mechanism that does not maintain recourse to the institutions of territorial states. While the core focus here is on the entrepreneurial problem of seceding, i.e., of creating the new frontier cryptoeconomy, it is useful to begin by briefly outlining the political economy choice by the entrepreneur to secede or to integrate.

Entrepreneurs can use blockchain technology while maintaining resource to state-based public protective institutions. Blockchains can be applied within existing organizations and institutions in the shadow of existing state-based institutions of enforcement.[33] Application of blockchain within the organization of the financial industry, for instance, mainly achieves efficiency gains within the existing financial organizations of banking (e.g., clearing houses). Costs are reduced while maintaining the underlying public infrastructure of territorial states. Here, the benefits of decentralization might remain within the centralized organizational structure. Indeed, blockchains can be applied by governments themselves (e.g., to create property registries and other applications to the machinery of government).

Alternatively, entrepreneurs could cryptosecede and develop self-enforcing institutions facilitated by cryptographic technology.[34] Entrepreneurs may apply blockchain to push economic exchange away from centralized organizations toward decentralized economic systems. Here, blockchains are not integrated into the public protective institutions, they compete with them. Where blockchains are comparatively effective in solving economic problems, i.e., where they more effectively economize on transaction costs, individuals engaging in economic exchange will exit from existing institutions and move toward decentralized private blockchain-based institutions.[35] This form of political rupture

---

[33] Mattila (2016).

[34] MacDonald (2019).

[35] The costs of integration within the existing political and regulatory process are subjective costs and the political context in which blockchains emerged suggest that the costs of integration were perceived to be high.

occurs because blockchain lowers the costs of exit by providing decentralized trust.[36] Blockchains maintain their institutional segregation or sovereignty in several ways, including as autonomous agents or decentralized autonomous organizations. As these applications are completely autonomous and self-executing, they cannot easily be stopped by centralized entities.

Why would an entrepreneur decide to integrate or secede? Integrating or seceding is an economic choice, with costs in both directions. One of the central costs of integrating blockchain can be understood from the motivations of discovering the technology itself. Blockchain was developed as a tool to decentralize hierarchical firms and states to overcome the centralization of power.[37] The initial intention of blockchain was as a technology to create new self-contained and self-executing institutions to replace centralized firms and states. The original intention of smart contracts and decentralized autonomous organizations was to eschew all reliance on legal contracts.[38] Integration of blockchains within existing institutions and organizations does not satisfy the underlying motivations of much of the blockchain industry. Indeed, there was no mention in the original blockchain white paper of integration within existing institutions such as firms or governments.[39]

The motivation to cryptosecede can be understood through the Institutional Possibility Frontier (IPF).[40] The IPF proposes that institutions trade-off the dual costs of disorder (private expropriation) and dictatorship (public expropriation). Blockchains help ameliorate both the costs of dictatorship and disorder. In particular, the cypherpunks who developed blockchain sought to lower the social losses from disorder by developing decentralized yet trusted ledgers that reduced the need to trust and rely on intermediaries. Integration of blockchain within existing political economy structures does not necessarily alter the centralization of power and may even make the processes of coercion and control more efficient.

Blockchain proto-entrepreneurs also face regulatory barriers. Regulatory uncertainty and hostility are challenges for any new

---

[36] See MacDonald (2019). One of the defining aspects of smart contracts on the blockchain is that they theoretically eliminate contractual opportunism.

[37] See Popper (2015).

[38] See, e.g., DuPont (2017).

[39] Mougayar (2016) notes this.

[40] See Djankov *et al.* (2003). The IPF is further extended and applied in Chapter 6.

technology.[41] Incumbents can lobby to defend their territory and draw blockchain technology within existing regulations. This notion of regulatory resistance with new technologies is well known in other technologies, including when regulators are captured by incumbents with entrenched interests who suffer future losses.[42] Combining this understanding of political resistance with a broader "precautionary principle" adopted by governments suggests blockchain integration might not be the optimum strategy.[43]

Cryptosecession lowers the costs of dictatorship—by relying on code rather than the discretionary power of governments—and can reduce some of these political economy costs of entrenched interests. The decentralized nature of cryptosecession may substantially increase the transaction costs of rent-seeking. One of the benefits of non-territorial cryptosecession, in this view, is the development of a "permissionless innovation" environment where entrepreneurs can elaborate and improve applications through trial and error with few constraints. While "permissionless innovation" is where agents are free to innovate without first having to ask for permission from the state, the unique aspect of blockchain permission is that it doesn't stem from changing the culture of government regulation, but rather by first developing a new jurisdiction with no coercive sovereign state.[44] Choosing to cryptosecede, therefore, can be seen as a new form of "technological civil disobedience" or even "spontaneous private deregulation" necessitated by the regulatory pressures on blockchain (and on governance more broadly).[45]

---

[41] As Harwick (2016, p. 579) notes: "In addition to the intrinsic network hurdles, regulatory uncertainty and hostility also constitute an extrinsic hurdle for intermediation in a way that they do not for the protocols themselves."

[42] See Juma (2016).

[43] The precautionary principle, according to Thierer (2014, p. 1), "refers to the belief that new innovations should be curtailed or disallowed until their developers can prove that they will not cause any harm to individuals, groups, specific entities, cultural norms, or various existing laws, norms, or traditions."

[44] One drawback from this, however, is when these experimental rules created within the cryptoeconomy prove ineffective (for instance, a failed smart contract), and agents attempt to fulfill these agreements using the conventional institutions (i.e., courts) of the formal economy. This remains an ongoing legal issue.

[45] Following Thierer (2016), civil disobedience "represents the refusal of innovators (individuals, groups, or even corporations) or consumers to obey technology-specific laws or regulations because they find them offensive, confusing, time-consuming, expensive, or

But cryptosecession comes with its own set of costs—*entrepreneurial costs*. The institutions of the cryptoeconomy, if they do not rely on state enforcement, must be discovered and developed. These institutions must outcompete state-based and other centralized institutions in economizing on the transaction costs of exchange. Therefore, on the one hand, cryptosecession partially overcomes the resistance within the reigning regulatory environment, and on the other hand, the additional cost is an entrepreneurial challenge of discovering the cryptoeconomy.

The core challenges of cryptosecession can be seen through the development of new blockchain-based digital platforms to facilitate trade. For instance, OpenBazaar is a peer-to-peer decentralized marketplace based on blockchain technology.[46] It has been described as an "anarchist eBay."[47] To create a decentralized marketplace, OpenBazaar had to form trusted institutions that verify and secure pseudonymous trades without recourse either to state-based institutions (e.g., courts) or indeed any other centralized organization (e.g., a tech firm). This required the discovery of new governance mechanisms for reputation and enforcement of rules. Another prominent blockchain platform, Ethereum, facilitates the creation and decentralized execution of peer-to-peer smart contracts. It was one of the first major extensions beyond the bitcoin protocol and sought to bring more development flexibility through its own Turing-complete programming language. We can understand Ethereum as a platform on which entrepreneurs can create their own systems of cryptosecession, including the secure creation of online markets, programmable transactions, and many other functioning applications.

The entrepreneurial examples of OpenBazaar and Ethereum are just two of thousands of blockchain-based platforms seeking to service the cryptoeconomy. They use technologies to create institutions to order human exchange. Furthermore, these examples show the entrepreneurial challenge of discovering trusted decentralized private protective-tier institutions of the cryptoeconomy. What we can see here is that the process

---

perhaps just annoying and irrelevant." Of course, only time will tell whether territorially based states will, or indeed can, halt or slow the development of blockchain technology by constraining it through regulation.

[46]There were already over 12,000 listings one month after its launch (BazaarBay, 2016). Further, the company has received several rounds of substantive venture capitalist funding, including prominent Andreessen Horowitz and Union Square Ventures (Allison, 2015).

[47]Fox-Brewster (2016).

of cryptosecession requires the discovery of self-enforcing and self-executing institutional mechanisms to outcompete territorial institutions. Cryptosecession is a type of institutional "protective-tier" entrepreneurship to economize on the costs of disorder using cryptography and economic incentives. In Section 5.4, these examples are interpreted within the context of the "new development economics" literature, which sheds light on the broader proto-entrepreneurial problem that is the core focus of this book.

5.4　Private Economic Development of the Cryptoeconomy

Here, we connect two seemingly disparate fields of research: *development economics*, or the study of how poorer economies grow, and *institutional cryptoeconomics*, or the analysis of blockchain as an institutional technology.[48] Development economics enables us to better understand the economic problem of discovering and developing the decentralized cryptoeconomy. The economic problem facing blockchain proto-entrepreneurs is analogous to the understanding of developing the institutional structures of developing economies. But rather than this process occurring hierarchically through government planners, the cryptoeconomy is being developed privately through blockchain entrepreneurship and coordinated through private governance in blockchain innovation commons. In this way, we have a deeper explanation of the polycentric private orderings as a type of *private economic development.*

Before we turn to the cryptoeconomy, we must first understand the contributions of development economics and, in particular, "new development economics." The arc of thought in the economics of development ranges from the mainstream approaches of the mid-twentieth century "old development economics" to the mainline approaches of "new development economics."[49]

The resurgence of the mainline tradition of economics brought new perspectives to the forefront of development economics. Some of the

---

[48] Some of the ideas in this section were extended into a separate working paper with Chris Berg and Jason Potts: Allen *et al.* (2020b). See also Allen (2019).

[49] For the "old development economics," see, e.g., Chenery and Strout (1966), Domar (1946), and Harrod (1939).

drivers of economic growth came to include the complexity, stickiness, and path dependence of both formal and informal institutions, the epistemological limits of allocating investment through centralized governments, and the importance of bottom-up entrepreneurial discovery for overcoming uncertainty.[50]

Given that development comes through economic growth, theories of economic growth are also theories of economic development.[51] When development economics emerged as a sub-discipline in the 1950s, the sources of economic growth centered on the allocation, investment, and accumulation of capital.[52] As the story went, given that developing nations had a savings–investment gap, the key to economic development was through increasing savings,[53] i.e., the source of economic growth for developing countries was seen to come through increased foreign aid.[54] The relevant question for a developing country was, first, whether they saved enough to invest, and second, how that gap could be ameliorated through aid or intervention.

One example of the analytical approach of this "old development economics" is the need for a "big push" of state-led investment.[55] While the big push theory also attributed underdevelopment to insufficient investment, its unique addition was that economic development requires several coordinated investments in different sectors of the economy because the marginal product of investments was higher when made simultaneously (i.e., investments exhibit complementarity).[56] As it was theoretically irrational for individual agents to privately coordinate

---

[50]See, e.g., Bauer (1976) and Boettke *et al.* (2008).

[51]See, e.g., High (2009) on Holcombe (1998).

[52]See Engel (2010). For examples of contributions in "old development economics," see Domar (1946), Harrod (1939), Rostow (1990), and Swan (1956).

[53]See Chenery and Strout (1966).

[54]As Chenery and Strout (1966, p. 268) note in the first paragraph: "For most underdeveloped countries, foreign assistance is already a critical source of development finance and one of the main hopes for accelerated growth in the future."

[55]For the "big push," see Murphy *et al.* (1989), Rosenstein-Rodan (1943, 1961), and Sachs (2005).

[56]Complementary investments are investments which raise any potential profits (or, generally, success) from the use of a new technology (i.e., an increase of investment A leads to an increase in the productivity of investment B). As Murphy *et al.* (1989, p. 1004) note: "Spillovers give rise to the possibility that coordination of investments across sectors— which the government can promote—is essential for industrialization."

investment, countries would become stuck in the second-best poverty trap. A big push required not only foreign aid to meet the minimum level of investment but also some centralized government planning of these investments.[57]

The "new development economics" sought to remedy many shortcomings of this capital-centered and planning-centered approach to economic development. Economist William Easterly referred to the concept of the big push as a "legend."[58] Focusing solely on investment and capital accumulation ignores the reality that information is imperfect and economies are complex. How will investments, including through aid, be coordinated and allocated to their most efficient use? As such, many criticisms of "old development economics" revolve around the idea that while a minimum quantity of investment may be a necessary condition for development, it is not a sufficient one:

> *The allocation of investment, however, unlike the allocation of given stocks of consumer goods (equilibrium of consumption), or of producer's goods (equilibrium of production) is necessarily an imperfect market, i.e., a market on which prices do not signal all the information required for an optimum solution. Additional signalling devices apart from market prices are required.[59]*

As seen throughout this book, throughout the 1980s, there was a resurgence of fields of mainline of economic thought and a range of historical failures of centralized planning. Combining these advancements with the falling of the neoclassical consensus led to the realization that investment and centralized planning was not the standalone key to development.[60] It became increasingly clear that the study of economic development needed to incorporate institutions and entrepreneurship. A greater focus on knowledge coordination and entrepreneurial discovery was the starting point for what has become known as the "new development economics," which "builds directly on the voluminous body of research that examines the emergence, operation, and effectiveness of spontaneously ordered institutional arrangements."[61]

---

[57] See Jomo and Reinert (2005).
[58] See Easterly (2006).
[59] See Rosenstein-Rodan (1961, p. 2).
[60] See Coyne and Boettke (2006).
[61] See Boettke *et al.* (2008, p. 333).

"New development economics" emerged on a different set of analytical principles and intellectual traditions, including from advancements in entrepreneurial theory, new institutional economics, and Austrian economics.[62] Institutional analysis, governance, and knowledge coordination were brought to the foreground of the economics of development and growth.[63] This new understanding of economic development sat in tension with the old growth economics, returning development economics back to the mainline of economic thought, which itself has always been concerned with growth, and thus development. The implication of the "new development economics" was that economic development was no longer driven solely by investment, allocation, and central planning, but emphasized how distributed and dispersed contextual information can be coordinated through institutions and put to use to meet human needs.[64]

Persistent critiques of the role of government in economic development slowly severed the connection between central planning and development. Effective state-led investment requires both an omnipresent state (to overcome the complementarity and allocation of investment problem) and an omniscient state (to know those sectors or investments which are necessary for success). Governments are made of individuals, who are neither omnipresent nor omniscient. Widespread intervention can destabilize existing institutions and investments.

One prominent critic of this centralized approach to development was Peter Bauer.[65] For Bauer, the central problem with foreign aid was a knowledge problem: how could a planner ever hold the necessary information for aid to be successful and effective? Rather, development was better understood as a discovery problem, and the determinants of development had been "underrated, or even ignored, in most of the development literature ... These determinants are not among the familiar variables of economic analysis; they are not readily quantifiable; and they cannot easily be manipulated by official policy."[66] Bauer's development economics analysis incorporates many of the core methodological understandings of mainline and Austrian economics, including radical uncertainty,

---

[62] See Boettke *et al.* (2008), Coyne and Boettke (2006), Fine (2006), and Rodrik (2008). For entrepreneurial theory, see Kirzner (1978a, 1982, 1997). For new institutional economics, see North (1990) and Williamson (1975, 1985a, 2005).

[63] See Acemoglu and Robinson (2010, 2012) and Nabli and Nugent (1989).

[64] See Glaeser *et al.* (2004).

[65] See Bauer (1976).

[66] *Ibid.*, p. 80.

knowledge coordination, and heterogeneous capital combinations.[67] The work of Austrian economists—particularly relating to the market mechanism and the role of entrepreneurship—reintroduced the idea of privately ordered spontaneous institutions into the economics of development. The entrepreneur became the driving force of the economic system—a premise which is now widely accepted within the development literature.[68]

It is largely through the Austrian conception of development economics where the analogies with the economic problem of the cryptoeconomy surface. Here, development comes from entrepreneurial discovery of the complementarity of various combinations of heterogeneous capital.[69] Particularly because blockchain technology is extremely fast-moving, entrepreneurial discovery of the institutions of the cryptoeconomy occur under fundamental and radical uncertainty. Blockchain entrepreneurs require information about future changes in the state of the world, business models, financing, timing, and consumer demand, competitors, failed ventures, and so on. The development of the blockchain cryptoeconomy, like all entrepreneurship, is a knowledge coordination problem and is analogous to the economic problem facing territorial developing economies, as examined in the "new development economics" literature.

In the same way that entrepreneurship manifests itself in many ways in the formal economy—from starting a new corner store, developing a new smart phone application, or arbitraging foreign exchange markets—blockchain entrepreneurship manifests itself in many different ways.[70] The notion that a new industry, and the entrepreneurs within it, face a different set of challenges than a completely formed industry is not a novel concept.[71] Blockchain proto-entrepreneurs, in the earliest stages of the new industry, can be seen to be navigating "an institutional vacuum of indifferent munificence."[72] On deeper inspection, however, there are multiple economic problems facing the blockchain proto-entrepreneur.

---

[67] For some of the major contributions, see Böhm-Bawerk (1891), Hayek (1945), Menger (1871), and Mises (1949).

[68] See Kasper and Streit (1998). This is in contrast to the earlier old development economics, where Leff (1979, p. 47) explains how "since approximately the 1970's, the topic of entrepreneurship has virtually disappeared, suggesting that in some sense the problem has been 'solved.'"

[69] See Manish and Powell (2015).

[70] Arthur (2009) and Ziman (2000).

[71] See, e.g., Aldrich and Fiol (1994).

[72] See Aldrich and Fiol (1994, p. 645).

When blockchain proto-entrepreneurs *integrate*, they must look to the institutions of the formal economy for information over price points, products, opportunities, complementary investments, and so on, which, when arranged in the right order, will define market opportunities for blockchain integration. But when blockchain entrepreneurs *cryptosecede* to the cryptoeconomy, they face a different higher-order entrepreneurial challenge.

Discovery, creation, and testing of novel institutional structures and mechanisms are required to build this new frontier cryptoeconomy. As we saw above, cryptosecession requires the discovery of self-contained and self-executing mechanisms of blockchain governance that are not embedded in the existing institutional environment. Blockchain proto-entrepreneurs lack precedent over the institutional structure in which they operate and are seeking to change. The proto-entrepreneurial process of cryptosecession is best viewed not just through the lens of a *new industry*, but rather from the perspective of a developing protective tier of a *new economy*.

There are two tiers of entrepreneurial activity necessary for economic development: (1) productive-tier entrepreneurship and the discovery of productive technologies necessary to better support human needs; (2) protective-tier entrepreneurship and the discovery of protective technologies that are institutional mechanisms to secure property rights and trade.[73] Development of the cryptoeconomy requires both. While the former occurs within a given institutional environment, the latter does not take the institutional environment as given: the institutional environment itself must be discovered by entrepreneurs. When blockchain proto-entrepreneurs integrate into existing institutions, they are closer to productive-tier entrepreneurship. But when they cryptosecede to create the cryptoeconomy, this is protective-tier entrepreneurship.

Proto-entrepreneurs must develop a protective-tier of institutional solutions that outcompete existing state-based institutions. Indeed, the development of the cryptoeconomy is perhaps the most explicit form of protective-tier entrepreneurship yet, or at least amenable to analysis, given that there are no existing protective institutions, and that these institutions must be publicly secure and verifiable as well as trusted. As the cases of cryptosecession revealed, cryptosecession requires the discovery of institutions necessary to enforce exchanges of information on

---

[73] See Leeson and Boettke (2009).

distributed and secure public ledgers. These institutions include property rights, contracting, and dispute resolution.[74]

The economic problem of blockchain cryptosecession faces higher structural uncertainty than integration because proto-entrepreneurs must discover an entirely new set of institutions which is detached from the formal economy. This aligns with Oliver Williamson's hierarchy of institutions and entrepreneurship.[75] At deeper levels of institutional entrepreneurship—of shaping public affairs and institutions—entrepreneurs face more structural uncertainty. Indeed, cryptosecession and development of the cryptoeconomy require its own knowledge structures, enforcement, and incentive mechanisms built in. The institutional environment cannot be taken as given; it must be created. To develop the cryptoeconomy, entrepreneurs have to discover not only institutional enforcement mechanisms but also the most basic institutional structures that connect these applications together.

Cryptosecession requires the discovery of complex complementarities. Blockchains exhibit complementarity both with existing technologies (e.g., the internet of things) and institutions (e.g., firms and government) and also with other heterogeneous blockchains within the cryptoeconomy. Capital goods are heterogeneous and exhibit complementarities in the sense that they satisfy different plans for human actors. They also have "multiple specificity" in the sense that capital can be used in different plans.[76] The range of blockchains within the cryptoeconomy similarly exhibit heterogeneity and multiple specificity. Blockchain technology can be applied to multiple problems and can also be combined and used in multiple plans.

The entrepreneurial development task, then, is to ask how these bits of capital will be structured to form the cryptoeconomy. This is an entrepreneurial problem requiring discovery of how each potential blockchain-based institution will fulfill a need yet also discover how the other blockchains within the cryptoeconomy will interact with the new institution. Blockchains also exhibit complementarity with other blockchains within the cryptoeconomy because the technology multiplier applies on inter-blockchain interactions (an investment in one application of

---

[74]For dispute resolution and blockchains, see Allen *et al.* (2020c).

[75]Bylund and McCaffrey (2017).

[76]As Lachmann (1956, p. 114) outlines, multiple specificity implies that "their mode of use changes as circumstances change."

blockchain will alter the return of a different blockchain). Multiple decentralized processes of blockchains in the cryptoeconomy can interact, which lowers the cost of additional blockchain applications (i.e., a multiplier effect).

The entrepreneurial problem facing blockchain proto-entrepreneurs involves simultaneously satisfying the discovery of both the protective-tier and the protective-tier. As we saw previously, the decentralized marketplace OpenBazaar is a complementary application to other cryptocurrencies. The success of a remittances business not only relies on transferring value between different individuals but also requires exchanges in each jurisdiction. The complementarities between these protective-tier technologies, however, are yet to be fully discovered.

Discovering the structure of the cryptoeconomy is a proto-entrepreneurial economic problem that is similar to the entrepreneurial problem of developing a territorial nation state. There are, however, two critical differences between the economic development of a territorial economy and the economic development of the non-territorial crypto-economy. First, the cryptoeconomy has few existing institutional systems. While development economics tends to recognize that the existing indigenous institutions matter—including for instance skills, culture, and conventions—the blockchain ecosystem has few existing institutions.[77] Cryptosecession could be understood as a private effort to "shock" and overcome the path dependence of existing sovereign institutions.

Second, there is no central planning authority to guide the discovery of institutions. While, as discussed above, the economics of development shifted from a focus on capital and investment toward institutions and change, the question of precisely how these institutions change given issues such as stickiness and path dependence remains unanswered. Recent efforts include the use of private cities and charter cities, both of which are attempts to push significant shifts in institutional mechanisms through the development of special economic zones.[78] However, such territorial special economic zones require state-based political change. Cryptosecession, on the other hand, requires no sovereign permission to

---

[77] See Coyne and Boettke (2006) for a discussion of the importance of indigenous institutions.

[78] For private cities, charter cities, and special economic zones, see Allen and Lane (2020), Bell (2017), Fuller and Romer (2012), Lutter (2016), Moberg (2015), and Rajagopalan and Tabarrok (2014).

change institutions—it is a privately driven entrepreneurial process—but can still be viewed through the same lens of changing existing institutions.

The entrepreneurial process of discovering the institutions of the cryptoeconomy does not occur within an institutional vacuum. Blockchain entrepreneurship, like all early-stage proto-entrepreneurship, requires non-price coordination of distributed information about market opportunities. Indeed:

> *Economic development is an eternal process of innovation, in which economies make progress as they discover a better combination of activities, or a better system of coordination. The discovery of any new system, by its nature, cannot be designed or even anticipated; all we can do is to design a better search mechanism or discovery procedure.*[79]

When William Easterly criticized the "old development economics" paradigm, he shifted attention away from "planners" toward "searchers" in directing this development process. Searchers are entrepreneurs and are necessary because of the inherent epistemological challenges in economic development. The blockchain cryptoeconomy does not have a central planner—it is governed by the consensus of the nodes maintaining each of the various blockchain protocols. Indeed, developing blockchain governance is a complex task.[80] Although attempts have been made to create quasi-state bodies—such as foundations—to coordinate some aspects and facilitate debates, the cryptoeconomy itself has no sovereign. This is despite the fact that regular debates within the blockchain community concern the most effective mechanisms to maintain the robustness and efficiency of the cryptoeconomy.

As there is no centralized sovereign state within the cryptoeconomy, the entrepreneurial development process must be *privately governed* by "searchers" rather than *publicly governed* by "planners." The development of the cryptoeconomy must entirely be a bottom-up process of search. While the "new development economics" literature has previously examined how the private governance of development may be optimal (i.e., development under anarchy), as compared to poorly performing

---

[79] Matsuyama (1997, p. 149).
[80] See Allen and Berg (2020).

states, the discovery and development of the blockchain cryptoeconomy is unique because by definition it must be privately governed.[81] Entrepreneurial coordination within the blockchain ecosystem requires commingled discovery of protective-tier technologies. Blockchain entrepreneurs are concerned not only with their own market opportunity but also with how other agents are acting on their opportunities. How do blockchain entrepreneurs solve this problem? Privately governed hybrids such as innovation commons. They are collaborating and coordinating in private governance mechanisms. These blockchain innovation commons involve entrepreneurs pooling and coordinating non-price information about discovering and developing the cryptoeconomy under collective action rules. Through the findings of this chapter, the collaborative nature of the blockchain ecosystem can be viewed as a robust system of private institutional controls in order to develop the cryptoeconomy.

There are therefore two levels of protective-tier technologies within the development of the cryptoeconomy. The first level is the collectively developed rules within blockchain innovation commons where blockchain entrepreneurs govern non-price information necessary to apply blockchain technology. This level includes the reputation mechanisms, signaling, and nested hierarchies of rules that constitute conferences, hack-a-thons, and online forums. Each of these involve protective-tier entrepreneurship in the sense that proto-entrepreneurs must overcome the hazards of coordinating non-price information, which the state is comparatively ineffective at protecting. These institutions support a higher-level protective tier—the new decentralized cryptoeconomy, where individuals use new mechanisms to create and exchange property rights far from the reach of the territorial nation state.

5.5 Conclusion

Blockchain is a nascent and widely applicable institutional technology, incentivizing the creation of private governance structures to facilitate entrepreneurial discovery. Several different types of privately self-governed innovation commons coalesce around blockchain technology, including hack-a-thons, conferences, and online forums. These governance structures differ widely (e.g., how goals are generated and the level

---

[81] See Leeson and Williamson (2009).

of autonomy). The diversity of blockchain innovation commons can be interpreted as a form of institutional diversity to overcome the uncertainty of which precise governance structure will ameliorate the proto-entrepreneurial problem, i.e., diversity as a way to overcome the uncertainty of designing and choosing institutions to coordinate information.

My argument in this chapter has been that these governance structures emerge to coordinate the non-price information necessary to discover entrepreneurial opportunities—to discover the cryptoeconomy. Blockchains and other distributed ledger technologies are institutional technologies that enable cryptosecession, i.e., exit from existing institutions. Blockchains can be applied specifically to change the rules of the game. In doing so, blockchain proto-entrepreneurs are forming a new non-territorial decentralized economy: the cryptoeconomy. This is an entrepreneurial problem, but one that can be understood through the lens of economic development.

Developing the cryptoeconomy is analogous to an economic development problem. The institutional mechanisms of the cryptoeconomy—those that protect digital property rights and facilitate exchange—must be discovered through entrepreneurial coordination of dispersed non-price information. Cryptosecession is a hard entrepreneurial problem, requiring dispersed knowledge about complementarities with other institutions. This knowledge coordination process requires governance. But, unlike in a territorial nation, there is no overarching sovereign state to coordinate and direct investment within a decentralized cryptoeconomy. Development of the cryptoeconomy must be *privately governed* by entrepreneurs rather than governments. This understanding provides a higher-order explanation for blockchain innovation commons.

PART III

Implications for Innovation Policy

Chapter 6

Rethinking Innovation Policy

6.1 Introduction

Economic thought on the governance of common-pool resources can be divided into two stages.[1] The first stage was outlined in the parable of an open access pasture as the "tragedy of the commons."[2] This view assumes that individuals will fail to pull themselves out of social dilemmas (e.g., over depleting a fishery) because the costs of developing self-governance solutions is prohibitively high. This led to recommendations for shifting incentives along two dimensions: privatization to internalize the costs of individual actions and lead groups away from tragedy, or government regulation to prevent overappropriation through coercion and control. These market-based or state-based interventions were seen to minimize the social losses from the commons as the institutional solutions to social dilemmas.[3]

Nearly 50 years on, since the recent expansion of the economics of common-pool resources, the political economy thinking about the social dilemmas of common property has decisively shifted. This second stage of thinking, which took off largely in the 1990s through the work of Vincent Ostrom and Elinor Ostrom within the Bloomington School,

---

[1] The core theoretical framework developed in this chapter—the "subjective political economy" framework—is outlined in further detail in Allen and Berg (2017).
[2] This was built on Gordon (1954) and Scott (1955) and was outlined in Hardin (1968).
[3] See Ostrom (1990, p. 2) for an outline of the influential models in this line of thinking, including the tragedy of the commons, the prisoners' dilemma, and the logic of collective action.

developed a new—more optimistic—understanding of the potential for private self-governed commons.[4] The implication of this research was to expand the potential suite of governance solutions to social dilemmas. We moved beyond markets and states through empirical research into fisheries, forests, and irrigation systems, as well as game-theoretic analyses of how individuals cooperate.[5] While ameliorating social dilemmas through polycentric private orderings and collective action was no panacea, it could be comparatively optimal.[6] Over time, these findings translated into policy prescriptions.

This dramatic shift in thinking about commons governance did not come from new and more effective types of self-governing institutions. Commons governance did not necessarily get better, but our understanding about them did. Many of the commons that have been studied were old and historical. Much of the empirical work in Ostrom's landmark *Governing the Commons*—from the mountain-grazing villages in Japan to the Alicante *huerta* irrigation systems—focused on historical "long-enduring, self-organizing, and self-governed" common-pool resources. The objective costs of commons did not change, but our subjective perceptions of them did.[7]

While it was previously assumed that the transaction costs of developing self-governance solutions to social dilemmas were too high, the new commons research program revealed that the social losses to common property—at least to the individuals within the game itself—may be lower than privatization or regulation. Through robust empirical and theoretical analysis, the Bloomington School convinced and persuaded others of the potential for polycentric commons-based solutions. Together with greater appreciation for institutional diversity, this research program stretched beyond natural resource commons, shedding light on broader questions of comparative institutional choice and political economy. We now extend this further to the choice of proto-entrepreneurs to develop and coordinate within private self-governance institutions.

Before we synthesize our findings into a political economy context, it is first useful to summarize what these findings are. A contract-theoretic institutional perspective of the innovation problem suggests that from the

---

[4] See Aligica and Boettke (2009), Boettke and Coyne (2005), and Boettke *et al.* (2013b).
[5] See Mitchell (1988), Ostrom (1990, 2005, 2010), and Tarko (2016).
[6] See Cole (2014), Feeny *et al.* (1990), and Hess (2008).
[7] Ostrom (1990, p. 58).

perspective of the proto-entrepreneur, the innovation problem is a governance problem. Polycentric collective action governance in the innovation commons is one potential transaction cost-economizing solution to this early-stage governance problem. We then examined some of these governance mechanisms in practice, including the hackerspace phenomenon and the blockchain industry.

But examining such private collective action structures is not to say that they are the optimal solutions to the innovation problem in any objective sense. Rather, these spaces reveal institutional choices of proto-entrepreneurs. Hackerspaces and other forms of private governance emerge from the decisions by entrepreneurs to try and solve their governance problem. The central task of this chapter is to place this decision into a broader political economy context of innovation policy. My intention is not to draw specific policy implications. Such policy claims would go beyond the logical remit of my findings. Rather, my aim is to examine how private governance of entrepreneurial discovery is squared with the interventions of innovation policy. To do so, we modify the IPF to incorporate subjective costs and apply this new framework to the private governance of entrepreneurship.

6.2 New Comparative Economics

The Institutional Possibility Frontier (IPF) is a theoretical framework representing institutional choice over the social losses of various forms of governance.[8] It has a basic premise: institutions are imperfect and face a trade-off between the costs of dictatorship (from state actors) and from the costs of disorder (from private actors). The IPF framework has proved to be insightful in a range of policy areas, including innovation.[9]

The IPF demonstrates that societies implement institutions to control the dual costs of dictatorship and the costs of disorder. While institutions lower the disorder costs of the supposedly "nasty, brutish and short" life

---

[8] See Djankov *et al.* (2003) and then Shleifer (2005).

[9] For instance, the IPF has been applied to innovation policy (Davidson & Potts, 2016a) as well as a range of more specific policy questions, including media regulation (Berg & Davidson, 2015), productivity reform (Davidson, 2013), tobacco control (Davidson, 2016) and free speech (Berg & Davidson, 2016), connected to total factor productivity (Lokshin, 2015), democratic structures (Allen *et al.*, 2018, 2019), and dispute resolution services (Allen *et al.*, 2020a).

of statelessness, institutions also increase the costs of dictatorship from state coercion.[10] That all institutions imperfectly minimize social losses is the analytic core of the IPF framework as one of comparative institutional choice.

There are two types of costs in the IPF framework.

When governments intervene into the polity, there are social losses relating to the *costs of dictatorship*, such as the "risk to individuals and their property of expropriation by the state and its agents in such forms as murder, taxation, or violation of property."[11] While some dictatorship costs are clear, such as a communist regime, others are subtler, such as individuals using the power and enforcement mechanisms of the state to control others through regulatory capture.[12]

When private individuals impose costs on each other through private expropriation, there are social losses from the *costs of disorder*, i.e., there is a "risk to individuals and their property in such forms as banditry, murder, theft, violation of agreements, torts, or monopoly pricing."[13] These costs come from the development of private orderings, often stemming from asymmetric information or unequal power or bargaining between private agents.

Given that no institution is perfect, a space of institutional possibilities can be traced through the points at which a given institution trades-off the costs of dictatorship and disorder, thereby forming the IPF (Figure 6.1). While the costs of institutional controls within a political economic system can never be completely mitigated, the convexity of the IPF implies a cost-minimizing point where the costs of dictatorship and disorder are minimized. The convexity assumption is based on the comparative properties of different institutions and enables an interior efficient solution to a constellation of dictatorship and disorder threats.

The distance of the 45-degree line from the origin could represent a function of the "civic capital" within a given society (see Figure 6.2).[14] Such an amorphous interpretation of the relationship to the origin,

---

[10]See Hobbes (2006 [1651]) for statelessness.

[11]Djankov *et al.* (2003, p. 7).

[12]See, e.g., Dal Bó (2006), Laffont and Tirole (1991), Peltzman (1976), and Stigler (1971).

[13]Djankov *et al.* (2003, p. 6).

[14]See Djankov *et al.* (2003). However, the 45-degree line within the IPF framework should not be confused as being representative of some objective institutional possibilities. Rather, it is an analytical tool for an individual to solve the point closest to the origin.

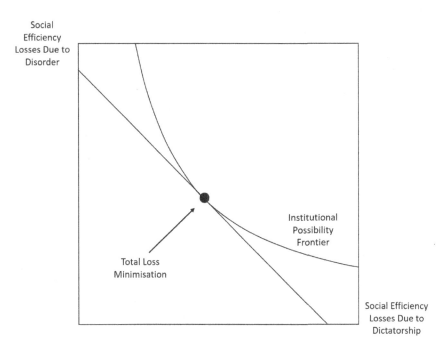

Figure 6.1:   An Institutional Possibility Frontier (IPF).

however, has rightly been criticized as "poorly defined, if not downright flimsy."[15] Nevertheless, despite the ambiguity of the distance from the origin, it remains that different societies begin with different available institutional possibilities within the IPF space, and even further, because the institutional space is unstable, the availability of these points will change through time.

The nature of the IPF will alter depending on the time horizon. In the shorter term, institutional possibilities remain fixed. In the longer term, however, several factors change the shape, the slope, and the position of the curve. Shifts in the IPF are a result of multiple complex factors, many of which are out of our control.[16] Societies also begin with different institutional possibilities. For instance, in Figure 6.2, the society represented by IPF$_1$ has a potentially more efficient suite of institutional possibilities than the societies represented by IPF$_2$ and IPF$_3$, respectively.

[15]Rosser and Rosser (2008, p. 95).

[16]See Boettke *et al.* (2005).

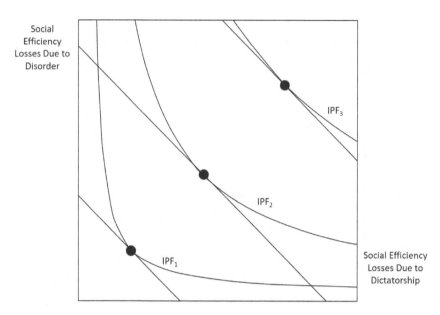

Figure 6.2:   IPF distance to origin.

The differences in the cost-minimizing solution, and the available space of institutional change, may be a result of different social fabrics or civic capital.

The IPF is an ordering of institutional possibilities, not an absolute representation of the social losses they seek to mitigate. Moving from "private orderings" (e.g., firms) on the top left, down and across to "public orderings" (e.g., socialism) on the bottom right, we can see rising costs of state intervention and declining powers of the individual, i.e., while moving from top left to bottom right, social losses stemming from disorder fall while the social losses from dictatorship rise. A society may implement an institution at some point on either side of the cost-minimizing tangency, thereby utilizing a set of institutions that are "inefficient." For instance, Figure 6.3, which represents the regulation of business, implies that independent judges and the regulatory state are both inefficient solutions.[17] This is an example of implementing a representative set of institutional

---

[17]Adapted from Djankov *et al.* (2003).

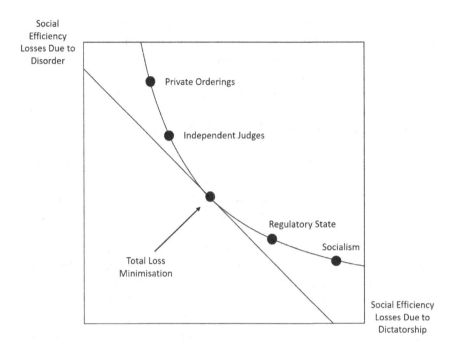

Figure 6.3:   The institutional possibilities of business regulation.

systems at a society-wide level, where, for instance, socialism produces inefficiencies due to the costs of dictatorship, while purely private orderings produce costs relating to disorder and private appropriation.

From here, we can examine some of the shortcomings of the IPF framework. These shortcomings relate to the dynamics of institutional change, which are described below in two ways: the *transition* between institutional points and the *discovery* of these points.[18] First, how does a group, such as a territorial nation state, transition toward the theoretically efficient loss-minimizing tangency point? Put another way: is it true

---

[18]Several criticisms of the IPF framework have been outlined in the literature. For instance, the IPF provides "no endogenous reason or mechanism leading to institutional inefficiency" and the new comparative economics more broadly "really overlooks the qualitative aspects of the issues ... we must account also for consistent (systemic) qualitative differences in the nature of the state and the actors operating within it" (Dallago, 2004, p. 65).

that, through time, a society will move towards the efficient point through an evolutionary process? There are at least four possibilities: spontaneous evolution, the activity of interest groups favoring efficiency, Coasean bargaining, and democratic voting.[19]

Institutional evolution and selection, however, is well known to be slow and perhaps inefficient due to transaction costs.[20] The convexity of the IPF in societies that hold different aversions toward dictatorship versus disorder may lead countries to become "trapped" at certain points.[21] There may also be forms of institutional stickiness or path dependence in institutions,[22] or problems of multiple equilibria by a "failure of convexity,"[23] or public choice suggestions that politicians will make choices to keep themselves in power rather than seeking the efficient point.[24]

Even assuming that the institutional transition process is efficient still leaves a deeper epistemological question: how does a society determine the location of institutional possibilities within the IPF space? Given the dispersed and contextual information necessary in order to help discover the point of tangency, the IPF is representative of the knowledge problem of the nation state.[25] There is uncertainty over institutional optimality. The institutional controls of a regulatory state or a legal system—and their cost-minimizing capacity—must themselves be discovered. This discovery could come through a form of political entrepreneurship to overcome the instability of the institutional space.[26] The following section extends the IPF framework to incorporate subjective costs, which both helps mitigate some of the shortcomings outlined here, and enables the new subjective political economy framework to be applied to the innovation problem.

---

[19] See Dallago (2004, p. 68) for these possibilities.

[20] See Nelson (1995).

[21] See Rosser and Rosser (2008).

[22] See Boettke *et al.* (2008), Glaeser and Shleifer (2002), and La Porta *et al.* (2008).

[23] See Djankov *et al.* (2003) and Rosser and Rosser (2008).

[24] See Berg (2008) and Buchanan and Tullock (1962).

[25] See Hayek (1989).

[26] See Koppl *et al.* (2015). This understanding, of uncertainty relating to the efficient set and the possible set of institutions, is clear in new development economics, and in particular, the Austrian conception of development economics as it was explored in Chapter 5 (Bauer, 1976; Boettke *et al.*, 2008; Leeson & Boettke, 2009; Matsuyama, 1997).

6.3 Subjective Innovation Institutions

We tend to think of innovation policies regarding their benefits, i.e., of the positive spillovers and the societal gains from economic growth that spread throughout society due to innovative discoveries.[27] From the perspective of an institutional approach to the innovation problem, however, institutions also impose costs. In the context of the IPF, innovation policies can be conceived in terms of social losses. In this light, Sinclair Davidson and Jason Potts arrayed innovation policies as institutions along an IPF curve (see Figure 6.4).[28] The main benefit of this new institutional approach to innovation policy is not just to recognize that innovation policies impose costs but also to understand that these costs are not equivalent. The innovation IPF is a depiction of the institutions applied to ameliorate the innovation problem.

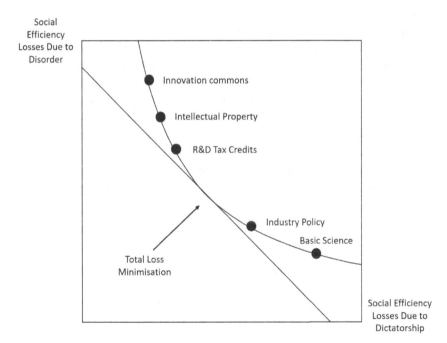

Figure 6.4: An innovation IPF.

---

[27]For spillovers, see Griliches (1991), and for the connection to growth, see Lucas (2009) and Romer (1990).

[28]Davidson and Potts (2016a, 2016b).

Figure 6.4 outlines some of the institutions of innovation. In the upper left portion of the IPF, the costs of private orderings relate largely to the costs of private appropriation from a lack of state-based control.[29] The social losses here are a form of disorganization and entail whether this disorganization leads to underinvestment, or overlapping of investment, or predatory opportunistic behavior in the sharing of ideas.

Moving down the curve, we find intellectual property, which has theoretically fewer costs of disorder, as compared to private orderings, but also has dictatorship costs. Intellectual property rights, such as patents and copyright, are a form of intellectual privilege monopoly rights.[30] They create a trade-off between static and dynamic efficiency.[31] This trade-off includes the emergence of the anti-commons and patent thickets, and is traded off against increased appropriability for innovators.[32] There are also disorder costs relating to the use of intellectual property for patent trolling.[33]

Moving further down the innovation IPF, we find innovation policies administered through the tax system. Research & Development (R&D) tax credits, for instance, act as a subsidy to fund innovative activity. As with all innovation polices, it is an empirical question whether these R&D tax policies are effective.[34] Even further is industry policy, which targets innovation funding toward particular industries. The social losses from industry policy are largely in the form of dictatorship costs, such as regulatory capture.[35]

While the innovation IPF is useful to outline and discuss the various institutions of the innovation problem, it fails to explain how the curve

---

[29] Davidson and Potts (2016b).

[30] Bell (2007, 2014).

[31] For static and dynamic efficiency, see Wu (2006), and for the cumulative growth of knowledge over time, see Scotchmer (1991).

[32] See Boldrin and Levine (2008), Heller (1998), and Shapiro (2001).

[33] See, e.g., Bessen *et al.* (2011) and Dourado and Tabarrok (2015).

[34] Bloom *et al.* (2002).

[35] See Stigler (1971) for regulatory capture. Other examples include rent-seeking (Krueger, 1974), identification of externalities (Davidson & Spong, 2010), and agency problems (Holmstrom, 1989). Indeed, a public choice approach to innovation economics has long been understood (Link, 1977) where, for instance, increases in government research and development have been shown to significantly increase the wages of scientists, suggesting that government funding directly crowds out private behavior (Goolsbee, 1998).

shifts through time or how the institutional solutions to the innovation problem come about. This also raises a problem of placing the findings of this book within the innovation IPF framework.

How can proto-entrepreneurs seceding from the conventional institutions of innovation policy be understood as a point within the IPF space? How can the "entrepreneurial fundamental transformation" and the range of different economic problems of an innovation trajectory be placed on a static society-wide innovation IPF?

Rather than discarding the IPF, we can extend it by incorporating the notion of subjective costs. By maintaining the underlying valuable concept of a trade-off between dictatorship and disorder, but extending the framework to incorporate subjectivist underpinnings, the simplicity and clarity of the IPF can be maintained, but its flexibility, nuance and explanatory power can be expanded.

The IPF represents the potential institutional solutions to an economic problem. To develop a representation of the proto-entrepreneurial problem, we must recognize that there is not one IPF for the entire suite of the institutions of innovation. This idea that IPF curves are heterogeneous is outlined briefly in the original analysis: "[t]he shape and the location of the IPF—and hence the efficient choice—various across activities within a society, as well as across societies."[36] Dallago noted that "the portion of the IPF that is relevant for particular societies would be different."[37]

Because the IPF is generally drawn as a continuous function, this implies one economic problem, with one optimal solution to these problems at the cost-minimizing tangency point. While representing the IPF as a continuous function is useful to demonstrate, there are indeed different institutions within the innovation system and they occupy different locations within the IPF space, this conception is not reconcilable at the more granulated level of each of the different economic problems within the innovation problem.

The innovation problem consists of multiple economic coordination problems—there is no one cost-minimizing tangency point for the innovation system. The threats of dictatorship and disorder are of a different

---

[36] Djankov *et al.* (2003, p. 9).
[37] Dallago (2004, p. 71). Furthermore, in relation to economic development, which is at its heart the comparative institutional economics of growth, Leeson and Boettke (2009, p. 256) note that "the efficient 'mix' of more or less reliance on private vs. public protection technologies will consequently depend upon the specific case."

structure for a multinational company with a large R&D lab, for instance, compared to the hacker in a hackerspace or the proto-entrepreneur seeking valuable uses for blockchain technology.[38]

That the institutions of innovation are interrelated throughout the innovation process has been a key to the innovation systems literature.[39] The innovation systems approach suggests that different institutions deal with different problems in different ways and that there are different sets of institutions for each economic problem throughout the innovation process.[40]

For the institutions of innovation, different types of innovations, e.g., the development of nuclear weapons compared to the development of new business models, face different costs of disorder and dictatorship.[41] Furthermore, the transaction costs of economic problems change throughout an innovation trajectory, suggesting different cost-minimizing institutional solutions. Each of the different economic problems that constitute the process of innovation face different constellations of economic costs.

The innovation IPF should be represented differently for each coordination problem because each of these are different economic activities with different cost structures. This involves a disaggregation of the IPF down from the level of the entire innovation system (which incorporates all IPFs within one single institutional space) to the level of the economic problem. Therefore, the innovation IPF would represent a class of economic problem, where a range of institutional controls could be implemented (ranging from private to public) in order to minimize the social losses of this problem.

While disaggregating the innovation IPF enables us to examine the specific economic problem associated with proto-entrepreneurship, it fails to explain the nature of the costs of institutions themselves. How do proto-entrepreneurs discover the costs of various institutional solutions to their economic problem? The nature of the costs underpinning the IPF is critical because the framework is fundamentally a representation of individual institutional choice. This examination reveals a further extension of the innovation IPF—the costs of dictatorship and disorder for each economic problem are *subjective*.

---

[38] See, e.g., Kealey and Nelson (1996) and Kealey and Ricketts (2014).
[39] See, e.g., Freeman (1995) and Lundvall (1992).
[40] See Chapter 1 for an introduction to innovation systems theory.
[41] Davidson and Potts (2016b).

The shape or position of an IPF can never be represented objectively. This is not only because of the complexity and uncertainty relating to the choice of institutions but also because all perceptions of costs are based on opportunity costs, which are fundamentally subjective.[42] Indeed, the costs of disorder and dictatorship are subjective both to the actors which impose them and the societies which endure them.

Building on early theories of subjective value, the concept of subjective costs has sat at the center of the Austrian school of economics.[43] A subjectivist view focuses on the mental states and subjective determinations of each of the members within a society rather than some objectively verifiable measure of society.[44] Most generally, costs are subjective accounts of the preferences of individuals.[45] Subjectivism, therefore, has extended beyond the idea of value to knowledge more broadly.[46] Some of the deepest questions in economics stem from subjectivism and the level to which an individual economist is willing to extend their commitment to it.[47]

Costs are subjective because they rely on opportunity costs of institutional implementation that are perceived in the minds of the individual agent. Indeed, as James M. Buchanan argues: "(1) Cost is subjective; it exists in the mind of the decision maker and no-where else. (2) Cost is based on anticipations; it is necessarily a forward looking or ex ante concept."[48] Similarly, it is true that individual perceived costs of society's social losses to any given institutional arrangement are deeply and necessarily intertwined with their subjective preferences. Subjectivism can not only be applied to a good or service, but more broadly to the perception of the costs of institutional choice.

The costs of dictatorship and the costs of disorder represented in the IPF space are subjective costs in the mind of the individual agent perceiving them and can never be objectively known. This implies that the particular location of a given institution within the innovation IPF space

---

[42] See Buchanan (1979a).
[43] See Menger (1871) on the subjective value in economics. See also Buchanan and Wagner (1977) and Yeager (1987).
[44] See Lachmann (1990).
[45] See Stringham (2010).
[46] See Horwitz (1994).
[47] See Horwitz (1994), Shackle (1992), and Stringham (2010).
[48] See Buchanan (1979c, p. 43).

is based on the decision makers' anticipations over the constellations of available institutional setups and that these subjective costs are the inputs into institutional choice.[49] This subjectivity is apparent because the costs of any given institution are highly distributed and intangible, and are highly framed by the ideological assumptions of the individual.

Introducing a subjectivist understanding into the institutional costs of the IPF helps overcome some of the persistent shortcomings of the IPF, including its bluntness, clumsiness, and lack of general theoretical applicability. For instance, the IPF, even disaggregated to each individual economic problem, would strain to understand the various 'traps' between South Korea and North Korea.[50] While subjectivity of costs is also alluded to by Rosser and Rosser, it is only mentioned once elsewhere across the new comparative economics literature.[51]

> *even if it is very fuzzy and imperfect, if we observe reasonably functioning democracies, and we observe them consistently over long periods of time choosing to have very different balances between their public and private sectors, we would not be too unreasonable in asserting that these political outcomes may to some degree indicate differences in preferences among at least broad sectors of the populations in the respective countries.*[52]

Other comments clearly demonstrate the implicit nature of subjective costs, such as "the Chicago School's confidence in private orderings and in courts is excessive."[53] While the claim that institutional costs are subjective is a simple observation, it has major implications for the understanding of the institutions of innovation and for the usefulness of the new comparative economics approach more generally.

Given that costs are subjective, societies do not make institutional choices, while individuals do. The dynamics of individual disagreement and bargaining over institutional costs become the analytical heart of comparative institutional analysis. Introducing subjectivity brings the idea of discovery of these institutional costs to the forefront of analysis.

---

[49] See Pasour Jr. (1978).

[50] Rosser and Rosser (2008, p. 86).

[51] See Whitford and Lee (2012).

[52] Rosser and Rosser (2008, p. 87).

[53] Shleifer (2005, p. 3).

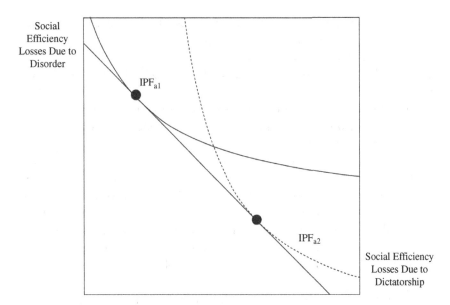

Figure 6.5:   Subjective perceptions of the institutions of innovation.

The economic problem is then one where a political economic process, such as a democracy, or a catalytic processes, such as a market, coordinates the contextual information of subjective perceptions (see Figure 6.5).[54]

This process of coordinating information about institutional costs plays out within a political economic system. While in aggregate the IPF may appear to be a single, societywide IPF, it is better understood as the outcome of a process of inter-agent bargaining and coordination between people and the groups, networks, and factions within which they engage. As there are no objective dictatorship and disorder costs—institutional costs are mental states rather than objective facts—any observed institution emerges as a function of both a diverse range of ideas about the costs of these institutions and a social bargaining process. Institutional costs are a function of both the institutional environment in which they emerge and the economic coordination problem that is being solved, and also the perception of these agents making the choices within a complex and entangled political economy.[55] Because the costs of disorder or dictatorship are

---

[54] See Hayek (1937, 1945, 1948, 1989).
[55] See Wagner (2006, 2016a, 2016b).

complex, uncertain and subjective, their perception is strongly influenced by the ideology of those analyzing the policies.[56]

If any given institutional possibility on an IPF is subjectively and dynamically determined by people, the IPF should be disaggregated down not only to each economic coordination problem within the innovation process but also to incorporate the perceptions of each person. Each person holds their own distinct perception of the shape of the IPF based on their subjectively determined costs of dictatorship and disorder.

Our focus on individual perceptions, however, does not imply that analysis should end at the individual. We begin from individual but then move upward into the meso and macro levels in order to understand the implementation of innovation policies.[57] Without beginning with the individual, the discussion of the IPF remains as one of objective costs, of which there are none. Therefore, each economic agent will have a different curve relating to the same economic problem (see Figure 6.6) with different perceived cost-minimizing points.

If everyone perceives their own costs of a given institution, then there will indeed be a different shape and slope for every individual. One source of these perceptions might be individual ideology.[58] We can see how these views change over time. For instance, literature suggesting that the market failure in the discovery of basic scientific knowledge is not as clear as once thought. There has been a case built, for instance, against public science that suggests the perception of this curve has indeed been influenced, for instance, by rent-seeking and regulatory capture.[59] This literature would suggest that the curve may be flatter than previously suggested and indeed that the costs of dictatorship and disorder may be minimized using some other institutional set up.

---

[56] Almudi *et al.* (2017), for instance, describes civilization as the result of a contest between competing utopian visions.

[57] This concept of methodological individualism was at the heart of the Bloomington school (Boettke & Coyne, 2005; McGinnis, 2005).

[58] Ideology has been part of positive political economy at least since Downs (1957). Ideas—"shared mental models" of norms and custom—have been a part of institutional economics since its conception (Denzau & North, 1994; North, 1993). Further, Tarko (2015b) recently outlined that the direction in which institutions change depends on the ideas, beliefs, and values of those who change them.

[59] See Greenberg (2001) and Kealey and Nelson (1996).

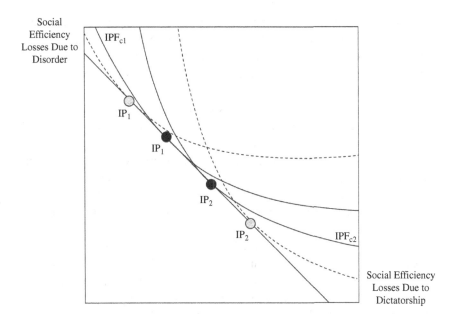

Figure 6.6:   A subjective innovation IPF.

Figure 6.6 shows a disaggregated representation of two agents possessing subjective perceptions over two different economic problems (c1 and c2) within the innovation system. The result is four different perceptions of cost-minimizing institutional solutions to separate dilemmas within the innovation system. This shows how the subjective political economy framework enables the analysis of the political economy process of the implementation of innovation policy. By incorporating subjective costs within the IPF framework, it becomes clear that the transition process between different IPF points is a political economy *process*. In a modern liberal democracy, the processes of bargaining between the different agents through some political process, where agents with different subjective costs over the relative costs of dictatorship and disorder bargain between their two cost-minimizing tangency points. Even when these bargaining processes occur between coalitions—including, for instance, political parties—the underlying premise remains the same: each individual has their own perceptions on the various costs of dictatorship and of disorder, of which a given set of institutions will impose on society to solve a given problem.

The economy-wide IPF as represented is the result of a political economy process where institutional interventions are applied.[60] It also follows, however, that the structure of the individual subjectively determined cost curves underpinning the IPF will result in a different implementation of policies.

An aggregated society-wide innovation IPF representing the selected institutions of innovation policy is to individual subjective costs what prices are to preferences—it ignores the process of getting to these institutions. An economy comprising people more sympathetic to government intervention, for instance, will see a policy outcome different from a more government suspicious society.[61] While observing and moving an IPF—in the same way as prices—may provide some indication of the underlying dynamics of the actors, the real detail of the analysis only emerges when the IPF is disaggregated to a lower level. Indeed, aggregate measures (and indeed any aggregate representations) ignore the fundamental underlying economic problem because the detail of individual movements is lost.

The future of new comparative economics may similarly involve disaggregating the IPF down to the level of the individuals who make up the polity. The movement of the IPF, or more accurately the perceived movement in the IPF, can then be split into two main categories: (1) a movement of the underlying subjective costs of individuals; (2) some exogenous force which changes underlying transaction costs (i.e., civic capital).

6.4 Private Governance and Innovation Policy

Several chapters in this book have demonstrated that private ordering solutions to the hazards of coordinating the non-price information

---

[60]See Davidson and Potts (2016b).

[61]One further consequence of viewing institutional costs as an agreement between different individuals in a society is the notion of ignorance and certainty. In Djankov *et al.* (2003), the IPF is convex toward the origin, reflecting society's knowledge about the costs of the institutions on the curve. However, it has been observed that agents are not always well informed about policy alternatives (Caplan, 2011; Somin, 2013). While in a subjective political economy, all agents are equally ignorant of "true" or "objective" costs, not all agents may feel they are able to produce a well-formed, well-ordered, and complete ranking of institutional alternatives in the subjective IPF space relative to other agents. This is a question of the intensity of perceptions of institutional costs, where the convexity is a function of the relative certainty of costs.

necessary to act entrepreneurially may minimize the dual costs of dictatorship and disorder. In the context of the IPF framework, collective action polycentric governance may minimize, on the one hand, the costs of dictatorship, which would hinder entrepreneurial discovery through hierarchies and path dependence, and, on the other hand, the costs of disorder, in which opportunism, for instance, may reduce the sharing and exchange of information. This section examines three main implications of this finding of the potential efficacy of private governance solutions to the innovation problem:

1. The choice-theoretic market failure perspective on the innovation problem may have systematically overweighted the disorder costs of private governance solutions to the innovation problem of proto-entrepreneurial discovery.
2. The institutional solutions to the innovation problem face a "knowledge problem" of discovering and coordinating the constellations of subjective perceptions of institutional controls.[62]
3. Examples of secession from the innovation system to private governance (e.g., hackerspaces) imply the need to understand the entanglement of public and private solutions to the innovation problem as well as the institutional objective of robustness.[63]

That groups of entrepreneurs have collectively developed private governance solutions to the innovation problem sits in stark contrast to the reigning conception of innovation as facing a market failure of suboptimal investment, thereby requiring public intervention through innovation policy. Conventional perceptions of innovation policy place private ordering solutions to the innovation problem in the background of economic analysis. These two contrasting conceptions are partially reconciled through the development of subjective political economy framework for innovation policy.

The perceived costs of dictatorship for innovation may have been underweighted in the design of innovation policy, i.e., policymakers may have underweighted the costs of intervention within the innovation system.[64] In contrast, we have seen throughout this book that the costs of

---

[62] See Hayek (1989).
[63] For robustness, see Pennington (2011).
[64] See Davidson and Potts (2016b).

disorder for proto-entrepreneurial discovery may have been overweighted in the application of innovation policy. The position of subjective innovation IPF, from the perspective of entrepreneurs making the institutional choice to engage in innovation commons, and for the specific coordination problem in the early proto-entrepreneurial stages of new technology, is flatter than that assumed within innovation policy.

That the potential for groups of proto-entrepreneurs to privately come together and develop institutional solutions to the costs of dictatorship and disorder have been assumed infeasible, or at least inefficient, however, is not clear through the conventional lens of market and systems failure of the innovation problem. Put another way, the costs of disorder may have been systematically overweighted in the analysis of entrepreneurial discovery. This discrepancy can perhaps be attributed to the reigning market failure view of innovation, which, since the early 1950s, has consistently suggested that private agents are unable to overcome social dilemmas in the innovation system through private orderings.

What this also demonstrates is that, because the costs associated with institutional choice are subjective, they are highly influenced by academic discourse. Ideas, rhetoric, and culture all play an important role in framing subjective perceptions.[65] When policymakers, for instance, begin their search of the institutions of innovation policy, with, for example, a starting perspective of market failure, this is tantamount to assuming that the costs of disorder are higher than those of dictatorship and indeed will implement policies in other portions of the curve.

While the benefits of innovation policies are considered to be extremely high, and the costs of innovation policy (e.g., rent seeking and distortions) are rarely discussed, the subjective political economy framework suggests that the costs of the institutions of innovation are subjective, unstable, and entangled. The points within the IPF space are shrouded in fundamental uncertainty. The microstructure of costs underpinning each institutional solution is unknown and is subjectively held within the mind of each individual.

Implementing an efficient innovation system would involve discovering each of the institutions constituting the cost-minimizing point for each economic problem throughout an innovation trajectory. This process would include each of the complementarities and substitutes between

---

[65]For ideas, see López and Leighton (2012), for rhetoric, see McCloskey (2010, 2016), and for culture, see Mokyr (2016).

each of the curves, and take into account that this space is not stable and moving through time. It also follows that the relevant curve for the entrepreneur would change throughout an innovation trajectory, i.e., the cost-minimizing interior solution to the economic problem changes as the microstructure of transaction costs change along an innovation trajectory.

Disaggregating the innovation IPF by each coordination problem brings into clear view the enormous intellectual knowledge coordination task that would have to be surmounted for achieving such a feat. The question for a society is no longer to find the efficient institutional set up which is located at the tangency between the IPF and the cost-minimizing line. The policy question is one of coordinating all the distributed bits of information over the perceptions of the location and efficiencies of the institutional possibilities. This discovery process is not necessarily effectively solved through top-down planning.

We can now see that innovation policy is itself an evolving *discovery process* over the cost-minimizing structure of each IPF. This suggests a common thread between many comparative institutional questions: because the social costs of dictatorship and disorder are shrouded in fundamental uncertainty, and thus have subjective costs, the institutions implemented to mitigate these dual concerns must themselves be discovered and will change through time as the actors perceiving them change their view.

Because the eventual structure of implemented innovation policy is influenced largely by ideas of their subjective costs, academic enquiry into the private governance of entrepreneurial discovery acts to slowly shift the perceptions of the IPF. This dynamic process will not occur directly, but through bargaining processes as subjective perceptions of the polity are aggregated through the political process, and as various coalitions of the polity, including organized coalitions of rent-seekers, attempt to influence the subjective perceptions of the institutions of innovation for other agents within the economy. It will emerge from a bargaining process of individual perceptions, but these perceptions are influenced by the reigning academic view of the costs. The search frame of institutional solutions to the innovation problem is highly influenced by academia, which thus far has been characterized by choice-theoretic market failures, thereby providing a further theoretical explanation for why the innovation commons have thus far played little role in innovation economics.

The current views of the scope and structure of innovation policy, largely through market failure and systems failure, should therefore be viewed within their historical context. Innovation policy traces back the mercantilist efforts of mid-nineteenth century Germany to catch up with the Industrial leader Britain. Germany built the first modern research universities and engaged in what we now call industrial policy. In 1945, Vannevar Bush, Head of the US Office of Scientific R&D, advocated a vast expansion of government support for science.[66] The aim was to replicate the success of government sponsorship of science during WWII (e.g., the Manhattan project) toward civilian ends. Basic science was funded by government that would then be developed by large private corporations into new consumer goods.

Modern innovation policy is built around the idea of a relationship between government and corporations as well as the idea of many different institutions, which together constitute an innovation system, solving the innovation problem, stimulating innovation and propelling economic growth.[67] Governments lead the invention of new fundamental science and technologies. These technologies and insights will then be developed for civilian consumer use by large corporations, who will release these technologies to market.

Governments have long sought to discover the interventions necessary to propel economic growth and development by solving the innovation problem. There is also evidence that governments have not quite got those settings right yet, with mounting critiques of some of the major institutions of innovation policy.[68] It is similarly clear that the perception of the innovation problem, and the proposed public institutional solutions to those innovation problems, have changed through time. Governments have been attempting to discover the cost structure of each economic problem and its corresponding solution within the innovation system.[69]

The knowledge problem of overcoming the subjectivity of the innovation system can be viewed within the context of both entangled political

---

[66] See Bush (1945).

[67] See Chapter 1 on these perspectives on the innovation problem society faces.

[68] For some recent critiques, see Boldrin and Levine (2005, 2008, 2013) and Box (2009).

[69] There are various caveats with this claim, the largest of which is assuming that governments are indeed seeking the cost-minimizing tangency point. This, however, is politics with romance.

economy and robust political economy.[70] The first perspective suggests that the polity and the economy co-dependently exist. The institutions of innovation, for instance, face complementarities in their implementation.[71] The idea of complementarity of different IPFs which is clear in the findings in Chapter 4 relating to hackerspace secession, i.e., hackers are seceding from the conventional institutions of the innovation system because they *perceive* the costs to be high, is an example of how a suite of innovation policies can shift the subjective perceptions of agents and thereby influence behavior. It similarly holds, however, that the perceptions in these costs will change as individuals move throughout an innovation trajectory.

One key upshot from this interaction between the public and private spheres is that when scholars and policymakers are conceptualizing the interdependencies of the innovation policy mix, they should both (1) incorporate an understanding that not only the costs they perceive are different for the people making the institutional choice but also that (2) intervening within the process can have unintended consequences as agents shift their behaviors,[72] i.e., implemented points in the IPF space interact and change the incentives of other perceived points within the space.

Given the subjective nature of the institutions of innovation, this suggests that one objective of innovation policy should be *robustness*.[73] The robust political economy framework relaxes the assumptions that humans are all-knowing and benevolent. The principle behind robust political economy is that institutions should be analyzed to the extent they deal with these human imperfections. Robust institutions are those which deal with the dual weaknesses of human behavior—both in government and outside government. Robust institutional systems "generate prosperity in the face of less than ideal conditions."[74] This suggests an important

---

[70]For entangled political economy, see Smith *et al.* (2011) and Wagner (2014, 2016a, 2016b), and for robust political economy, see Leeson and Subrick (2006) and Pennington (2010, 2011).

[71]See Mohnen and Röller (2005). Indeed, as Dourado and Tabarrok (2015, p. 149) note in the context of intellectual property, "it is important to consider the ways in which nonmarket decision—both political and institutional—interact with intellectual property."

[72]Flanagan *et al.* (2011).

[73]Pennington (2010, 2011).

[74]Leeson and Subrick (2006, p. 107).

connection between a robust system and a disentangled system. Indeed, in relation to entangled political economy:

> *Turbulence and not placidity is the normal state of a system of entangled political economy. A system based on private ordering, however, is generally better able to calm turbulence than a system where public ordering occupies the social foreground.*[75]

This is relevant for understanding the private governance of proto-entrepreneurship, where the production of novelty is a spontaneous ordering of entrepreneurs.[76] Perhaps, the comparative institutional choice of hackers' interactions within private orderings, as compared to public ordering institutions, is because the former institutions are relatively robust rather than fragile.[77] A polycentric system of rules, such as those in hackerspaces, may be a more robust system than centralized state-centered innovation policies because they deal better with the reality of limited human rationality and benevolence, i.e., because entrepreneurs face high transaction costs relating to the discovery of knowledge and the institutions to coordinate this knowledge, having polycentric decision-making, in the spontaneously ordering sub-groups, enables trial and error institutional learning to overcome uncertainty. Such a robust polycentric decentralized system enables institutional exit rather than monopoly rules.[78]

Proto-entrepreneurs, such as hackers, can be understood to be seceding from the conventional institutions of the innovation system. This is an attempt to escape the entanglement of the institutions of innovation policy. Integrating hackerspaces into the innovation system may affect their internal processes and decrease the robustness of the innovation system more broadly. The robustness of a system of rules to facilitate entrepreneurial discovery exists at multiple levels. At the level of the entrepreneur,

---

[75] Wagner (2016a, p. 541).

[76] See Potts (2014).

[77] In the same way as previous studies such as Wagner (2006) and Leeson and Subrick (2006) note that those systems with more polycentric nodes of decision-making in terms of economic organization are more robust.

[78] This idea of robustness is closely tied to the Austrian conceptions of the market economy in terms of time, change, and processes, i.e., Austrian economics itself is the examination of robustness of various institutional systems.

the choice to engage in private polycentric governance through reputation mechanisms may be more robust than founding an entrepreneurial firm (because, for instance, it enables cheaper exit). At the innovation system level, individuals contracting in mechanisms outside the state have the capacity to increase the robustness of the system.

Integrating these independent autonomous innovation institutions and entangling them with the political process may have two effects: (1) to impede the processes of spontaneous order on which hackerspaces are based; (2) to decrease the robustness and adaptability of the innovation system more broadly. State intervention can undermine the ability of individual agents to create polycentric structures or shift their potential benefits. For instance, intellectual property rights artificially raise the return and incentives of entering the state-based system, distorting proto-entrepreneurial activities. Such innovation polices might make the innovation system more fragile. Furthermore, because private polycentric governance structures are dynamic systems conducive to spontaneous ordering of entrepreneurial information and actors, caution should be exercised when attempting to integrate these institutions within the state-led sector. The sovereignty of the private governance of entrepreneurship should be maintained to induce ordering and prevent ideas being pushed toward minimum viable products. Intervening in these spaces—which is a growing phenomenon—may diminish the coordination benefits of the indeterminate, dynamic, spontaneous processes, and make the entire suite of institutions of innovation more fragile.[79]

6.5 Conclusion

In this chapter, we theoretically extended the IPF framework to the proto-entrepreneurial innovation problem. Given that each economic problem has different cost-minimizing institutional solutions, the IPF should not be represented as a societywide function, but rather disaggregated down to the level of the individual economic problem. This understanding enables a focus on the specific proto-entrepreneurial innovation problem outlined in this book. Further, the costs of institutional choice are not objectively known—they are subjectively perceived. Therefore, we must also

---

[79]This is similar to how government intervention distorts the structure of production in Austrian capital theory.

consider an IPF from the perspective of the individual perceiving it. This new "subjective political economy" framework was applied to understand private governance solutions to the proto-entrepreneurial problem.

There are several implications for innovation policy. First, the costs of disorder may have been systematically overweighted because of a disregard for the potential of collective action self-governance solutions. Second, given the uncertainty and instability of a subjective political economy, innovation policy itself must undergo an institutional discovery process. The process of forming innovation policy is framed by the reigning academic orthodoxy. Third, the evidence of secession from the institutions of innovation policy speaks for the entanglement of innovation policies. This raises questions over the complementarity and substitutability of various innovation policies and their impact on the capacity of individuals to develop private polycentric orderings to solve the economic problems they perceive they face.

Chapter 7

Conclusion

7.1 Introduction

In modern economics, the two main perspectives of the innovation problem that society faces are market failure and systems failure. The market failure perspective is that innovation outputs are public goods that will be sub-optimally produced in a competitive market due to lack of investment incentives. In this view, the innovation problem is a problem of allocation of private innovation resources. This view leads to innovation policy, which is an attempt to correct the misaligned microeconomic incentives through intervention. The systems failure perspective views the innovation problem as the complex interplay of different organizations and institutions. However, the solutions to systems failure come primarily through governments directing resources toward different institutional parts of the innovation system.

Both conceptions of the innovation problem society faces are choice-theoretic analyses, emphasizing the investment and the allocation of resources. Further, both choice-theoretic approaches to the innovation problem obscure from the process of entrepreneurial discovery of market opportunities and particularly the governance and institutional mechanisms entrepreneurs use to coordinate the information to discover market opportunities.

This book has developed and applied a mainline contract-theoretic approach to the innovation problem in economics. Factors such as uncertainty, institutions, and entrepreneurship have been in the foreground of analysis. We analyzed the private governance solutions to this contract-theoretic problem and placed these institutional choices within the context of the political economy of the institutions of innovation and innovation policy.

A contract-theoretic institutional perspective of the innovation problem does not place investment or allocation of innovation resources at the forefront of analysis. Rather, it begins from the perspective of the entrepreneur and their economic problem of coordinating dispersed and contextual information through comparatively effective governance structures to discover market opportunities. This perspective emphasizes the institutional mechanisms that people privately and collectively develop to economize on the transaction costs of coordinating information to discover opportunities.

My approach begins from the perspective of the entrepreneur, understands the limits of the human mind owing to bounded rationality and the subjectivity of the future, and acknowledges the potential for private ordering solutions to economic problems. I have variously drawn on entrepreneurial theory, the logic and framework of transaction cost economics, the economics of common pool resource management and the economics of collective action governance more broadly, and the new comparative economics and its focus on choice over institutional governance.

The analysis of hackerspaces and the governance of blockchain innovation demonstrated that early-stage proto-entrepreneurs do indeed develop privately governed polycentric structures to coordinate the information they require and that, at least in their subjective perceptions, these may be transaction cost economizing institutional solutions to the economic problem they perceive they face. This sits in contrast to conventional understandings of the origins of entrepreneurship.

The findings of this book have implications for the political economy of innovation policy. Innovation policy is informed and motivated by choice-theoretic understandings of innovation economics. The contract-theoretic approach developed here turns attention to how the costs of governance solutions to the various stages of the innovation problem are subjectively perceived by entrepreneurs and that government intervention must acknowledge the entanglement of the costs of institutional solutions.

7.2   Contributions

7.2.1   *A new institutional approach to the innovation problem*

Part I of this book developed a mainline institutional contract-theoretic approach to the innovation problem in economics.

In Chapter 2, we focused on the earliest stages of entrepreneurial discovery and proposed that the proto-entrepreneur must coordinate non-price information with others in order to define an actionable market opportunity and that they must do so in comparatively effective governance structures facing non-zero transaction costs.

The characteristics of the knowledge necessary to define market opportunities were proposed as being both distributed and uncertain. This suggests that, given some potential gains from trade of coordinating this proto-entrepreneurial information, the early-stage proto-entrepreneur must escape innovation autarky to engage and coordinate information with others. An institutional definition of the innovation problem, therefore, focuses on the governance choice by the entrepreneur on how they perceive governance structures economize on the transaction costs in their economic problem.

We also introduced the "entrepreneurial fundamental transformation," i.e., as a proto-entrepreneur coordinates non-price information with others about market opportunities, their microstructure of transaction costs changes and so does the potential range of transaction cost economizing governance structures. This suggests that the earliest stages of an innovation trajectory, where proto-entrepreneurs are seeking to discover actionable market opportunities, may have a different transaction cost economizing governance structure to the entrepreneurial process of acting on or exploiting those opportunities. Therefore, the economic problem of entrepreneurial discovery not only occurs with others in an institutional context, but also this governance problem has an intertemporal dimension.

The transaction cost economizing institutional solutions to the innovation problem are no longer constrained to firms or governments to align incentives. Rather, my contract-theoretic approach to the innovation problem is institution-neutral—it is defined by the economic problem that the entrepreneur perceives they face.

In Chapter 3, we introduced hybrid polycentric governance in the innovation commons as a potentially optimum institutional solution to economize on the transaction costs of the proto-entrepreneurial problem. This suggests that the private governance of entrepreneurial discovery, particularly in the earliest stages of the innovation trajectory where structural uncertainty is the highest, may be more important to innovation, and therefore to economic growth, than previously believed.

An innovation commons is a rule-governed space where proto-entrepreneurs coordinate the distributed, contextual, and uncertain non-price information about market opportunities with others. Hybrids might deal well with the transaction costs of non-price coordination and opportunism under uncertainty.

Several unique behavioral characteristics of innovation commons were revealed. An innovation commons might emerge as a mechanism to realize the mutual gains from the trade of coordinating information to reveal opportunities. We expect that an innovation commons is most likely to emerge at the beginning of new technologies and industries where structural uncertainty is the highest and where there are great potential gains from the trade of coordinating proto-entrepreneurial information with others.

The effectiveness of innovation commons is only temporary. They process the uncertainty about the potential of a market opportunity. If an innovation commons is successful at whittling away this uncertainty, then other governance forms will begin to outcompete it. An "entrepreneurial fundamental transformation" at the level of the individual market opportunity will shift the transaction cost economizing governance structure perhaps toward start-up firms or other hierarchical governance. The function of the innovation commons suggests that they are complements to other institutions of innovation, including firms and markets, rather than being direct substitutes to them.

7.2.2   Private governance of entrepreneurial discovery

Part II of the book examined the cases of proto-entrepreneurial private governance.

In Chapter 4, hackerspaces were introduced as a potentially analytically pure example of an innovation commons. Hackers have developed a range of mechanisms that can be interpreted as attempts to economize on the transaction costs they face in discovering opportunities, including the following:

(1) graduated social ostracism and exclusion that draws on the local knowledge of hackers and their reputation;
(2) costly signaling to facilitate non-price coordination and to induce contributions to pooled resources;
(3) processes of collective action decision-making to form rules, enabling laboratory federalism between hackerspaces;
(4) nested hierarchies of rules that facilitate dynamic polycentrism.

In Chapter 5, we turned to examining blockchain technology. The first part of the analysis focused on the self-definitions of a range of governance structures, such as workshops, conferences, hack-a-thons and online forums. This demonstrated the diversity of hybrid institutions coalescing around blockchain technology and facilitating knowledge coordination.

The second part emphasized the fundamental entrepreneurial problem at the heart of a new institutional technology—as a tool for exit or cryptosecession. Blockchains facilitate institutional entrepreneurship to create the new decentralized cryptoeconomy. The economic problem of creating the institutions of the cryptoeconomy is analogous to the economic development problem. The difficultly of this problem provides a higher-order explanation for the existence of privately governed proto-entrepreneurial hybrids around the blockchain industry.

What these examples demonstrate is that private governance of entrepreneurship is possible and may even be optimal (from the perspective of those choosing these institutions). Therefore, the institutional ecosystem within which entrepreneurial discovery occurs—particularly at the beginning of new technologies and industries—may look starkly different from what is conventionally believed. Private governance may be more central to the discovery and development of new technologies than previously assumed perhaps because of the transient and temporary nature of these governance institutions.

7.2.3 Subjective political economy of the innovation commons

Part III of the book outlined some of the political economy implications of the private governance of entrepreneurship within an innovation commons. What form of economic organization a proto-entrepreneur engages in is a question of comparative institutional choice within an entangled political economy ranging from purely private to purely public governance.

In Chapter 6, we turned to the political economy of the private governance of entrepreneurship. The aim of this contribution is not to draw specific policy implications but to examine how successful private governance in the innovation commons can be squared within the political economy of innovation policy. We first extended the IPF framework to incorporate subjective costs.

The IPF is based on a trade-off between the costs of disorder and the costs of dictatorship in institutional choice. However, these costs are subjectively perceived by individuals because they are based on the opportunity costs of institutions. Given that each individual economic activity has a different cost-minimizing institutional solution, the IPF should not be represented at the level of a society, but rather must be disaggregated downward to the level of the individual economic problem.

We then applied this subjective political economy framework to understand how the private governance of proto-entrepreneurship is squared with the institutions of innovation policy. In this view, each of the institutions of innovation, including each of the institutions of innovation policy, can be placed as points within the IPF space. This enabled an examination of the economic problem of proto-entrepreneurial discovery.

Several implications for innovation policy flow from this. The costs of polycentric organization within the innovation commons may have been subjectively and systematically underweighted in the application of innovation policy, i.e., the costs of disorder of developing private solutions to the innovation problem may have been assumed to be prohibitively high. This discrepancy also has implications for the understanding of the design and development of policies to stimulate innovation.

The process of innovation policy is itself a discovery process. Governments must discover the entire constellation of subjective costs of institutions within the IPF space and for each individual economic problem throughout the innovation process. This discovery process is an economic problem, which must be solved within the context of an entangled political economy where there are interdependencies between the social losses of the different innovation policies.

7.3   Some Limitations and Future Directions

This book has sought to tackle a complex topic. It has focused on the specific economic problem facing proto-entrepreneurs as they seek to coordinate information to discover actionable market opportunities. In contrast to the conventional choice-theoretic perspectives, this economic problem was viewed through the contract-theoretic lens of mainline economic thought and then applied and contextualized within the framework of political economy.

My aim has not been to develop a detailed institutional analysis of a single solution to the innovation problem. Rather, my analytical approach entails a broad enquiry into entrepreneurial institutional choice over a wide range of potentially comparatively economizing solutions. Connecting such seemingly disparate bodies of work within the mainline of economics—from transaction cost economics to new development economics—into a single coherent book, and with a constrained length, is a task that has many limitations. Some of these limitations are noted here, while others have been noted throughout the book.

This book has not examined the entire suite of collaborative hybrid governance structures within which entrepreneurs engage or indeed the literatures on hybrid institutions within the innovation process. Rather, this book has developed the foundations of a contract-theoretic institutional approach to the collaboration between entrepreneurs within mainline institutional analysis. This leaves open the question of how the framework and contributions made here can be applied to understand some of the other examples of collaborative entrepreneurship and innovation activities elsewhere.

My study of existing innovation commons was through mixed methods over secondary data of contemporary innovation commons and has not examined the specific motivations of entrepreneurs who are choosing to enter an innovation commons or, in particular, whether those motivations are to later exploit these opportunities within firms and markets. The norms and values of the proto-entrepreneurs who choose to coordinate in innovation commons, such as hackerspaces, will influence the comparative efficacy of different forms of economic governance. Indeed, norms are an input into the subjective perceptions of institutional choice.

In the same way, I have not formally modeled the entrepreneurial choice of the comparative transaction cost economizing properties of the various institutions of innovation. Such an approach would need to consider the subjective perceptions of the proto-entrepreneur and their institutional choices.

Each of these limitations presents opportunity for further examination. These future research opportunities sit variously on the boundary of institutional economics, entrepreneurial theory, and private governance. This new mainline institutional approach to the innovation problem opens up lines of economic enquiry in two directions:

(1) **To the sources of economic growth and prosperity:** This book began with a brief discussion of the drivers of modern economic growth, emphasizing the structure of institutions and the process of entrepreneurial discovery. The theory of the innovation commons raises questions over how the culture or the values preceding this take-off in global prosperity shaped the formation of polycentric groups of proto-entrepreneurs. Can innovation commons be observed further back in history? How did proto-entrepreneurs organize themselves when they embraced a culture of growth following the Enlightenment? Can we find examples of innovation commons failures?

(2) **To the dynamics of political economy:** The subjective political economy framework developed within this book helps expand the domain of new comparative economics. When taken into an intertemporal dimension, the subjective political economy framework helps inform the dynamics of coordination of subjective perceptions over institutional choice. How are institutional costs discovered through bargaining and through politics? Does the intensity of subjective perceptions of institutional costs alter the path of institutional change? How does this process of institutional choice play out as new technologies, such as blockchain, expand the suite of institutional possibilities? What does the potential for political exit and cryptosecession mean for institutional choice?

More generally, this book presents the scope for further case studies into the micro-institutional mechanisms of innovation commons. These studies could be undertaken within a modified version of the Institutional Analysis and Development (IAD) Framework developed by Elinor Ostrom and could be combined into a broader database of innovation commons, as has been the case with the study of natural resource commons. These case studies need not be constrained to modern technology-centered innovation commons, but could include a broader range of innovation commons throughout history, such as craft guilds or scientific societies, shedding light on the intertemporal proposition of an entrepreneurial fundamental transformation.

References

Acemoglu, D. & Robinson, J. A. (2010). The Role of Institutions in Growth and Development. In D. Brady & M. Spence (Eds.), *Leadership and Growth* (pp. 135–164). Washington, DC: The World Bank.

Acemoglu, D. & Robinson, J. A. (2012). *Why Nations Fail: The Origins of Power, Prosperity, and Poverty*: Crown Business.

Aghion, P. & Holden, R. (2011). Incomplete contracts and the theory of the firm: What Have we learned over the past 25 years? *The Journal of Economic Perspectives, 25*(2), 181–197.

Aghion, P. & Howitt, P. (1990). A model of growth through creative destruction. *60*, 323–351.

Aghion, P. & Tirole, J. (1994). The management of innovation. *The Quarterly Journal of Economics, 109*(4), 1185–1209.

Aitken, R. (2016). The Rise Of Blockchain, Hackathons & The Hackonomy. *Forbes*. Retrieved from https://www.forbes.com/sites/rogeraitken/2016/11/03/the-rise-of-blockchain-hackathons-the-hackonomy/#5ff5eef61065.

Alchian, A. A. & Demsetz, H. (1972). Production, information costs, and economic organization. *The American Economic Review, 62*(5), 777–795.

Aldrich, H. E. & Fiol, C. M. (1994). Fools rush in? The institutional context of industry creation. *Academy of Management Review, 19*(4), 645–670.

Aligica, P. D. & Boettke, P. J. (2009). *Challenging Institutional Analysis and Development: The Bloomington School*: Taylor & Francis.

Aligica, P. D., Ostrom, E., Ostrom, V., Tiebout, C. M., Warren, R., Cole, D. H., & McGinnis, M. D. (2014). *Elinor Ostrom and the Bloomington School of Political Economy: Polycentricity in Public Administration and Political Science* (Vol. 1): Lexington Books.

Aligica, P. D. & Tarko, V. (2012). Polycentricity: From Polanyi to Ostrom, and beyond. *Governance, 25*(2), 237–262.

Allen, D. W. (1999). Transaction Costs. In *Encyclopedia of Law and Economics*.

Allen, D. W. (2011). *The Institutional Revolution: Measurement and the Economic Emergence of the Modern World*. Chicago, USA: University of Chicago Press.

Allen, D. W. E. (2019). Entrepreneurial Exit: Developing the Cryptoeconomy. In M. Swan, J. Potts, S. Takagi, F. Witte, & P. Tasco (Eds.), *Blockchain Economics* (pp. 197–214). London, United Kingdom: World Scientific.

Allen, D. W. E. (2020). Governing the entrepreneurial discovery of blockchain applications. *Journal of Entrepreneurship and Public Policy, 9*(2), 194–212.

Allen, D. W. E. & Berg, C. (2014). *The Sharing Economy: How Over-regulation Could Destroy an Economic Revolution*. Retrieved from Melbourne, Australia: https://ipa.org.au/wp-content/uploads/archive/Sharing_Economy_December_2014.pdf.

Allen, D. W. E. & Berg, C. (2017). Subjective Political Economy. *New Perspectives on Political Economy, 13*(1-2), 19–40. Retrieved from https://papers.ssrn.com/sol3/papers.cfm?abstract_id=2799032.

Allen, D. W. E. & Berg, C. (2020). Blockchain governance: What we can learn from the economics of corporate governance. *The Journal of the British Blockchain Association, 3*(1), 1–10.

Allen, D. W. E. & Lane, A. M. (2020). Cryptodemocratic Governance of Special Economic Zones. *The Journal of Special Jurisdictions*. Retrieved from https://papers.ssrn.com/sol3/papers.cfm?abstract_id=3491481.

Allen, D. W. E. & Potts, J. (2016). How the Innovation Commons Contribute to Discovering and Developing New Technologies. *International Journal of the Commons, 10*(2), 1035–1054.

Allen, D. W. E., Berg, C., Lane, A. M., & Potts, J. (2018). Cryptodemocracy and its institutional possibilities. *The Review of Austrian Economics*. DOI: https://doi.org/10.1007/s11138-018-0423-6.

Allen, D. W. E., Berg, C., Davidson, S., Novak, M., & Potts, J. (2019a). International policy coordination for blockchain supply chains. *Asia & the Pacific Policy Studies, 6*(3), 367–380.

Allen, D. W. E., Berg, C., Novak, M., Markey-Towler, B., & Potts, J. (2020a). Blockchain and the evolution of institutional technologies: Implications for innovation policy. *Research Policy, 49*(1), 1–8.

Allen, D. W. E., Berg, C., & Lane, A. M. (2019b). *Cryptodemocracy: How Blockchain Can Radically Expand Democratic Choice*. Lanham, US: Lexington Books.

Allen, D. W. E., Berg, A., & Markey-Towler, B. (2019c). Blockchain and supply chains: V-form organisations, value redistributions, de-commoditisation and quality proxies. *The Journal of the British Blockchain Association, 2*(1), 57–65.

Allen, D. W. E., Berg, C., & Potts, J. (2020b). *Blockchain Technology and the Theory of Economic Development*. Retrieved from https://papers.ssrn.com/sol3/papers.cfm?abstract_id=3333568.

Allen, D. W. E., Lane, A. M., & Poblet, M. (2020c). The governance of blockchain dispute resolution. *Harvard Negotiation Law Review, 25,* 75–101.

Allison, I. (2015). Move over eBay: Countdown to OpenBazaar and the Decentralised Marketplace Revolution. *International Business Times.* Retrieved from http://www.ibtimes.co.uk/move-over-ebay-countdown-openbazaar-decentralised-marketplace-revolution-1529767.

Almudi, I., Fatas-Villafranca, F., Izquierdo, L. R., & Potts, J. (2017). The economics of Utopia: A co-evolutionary model of ideas, citizenship and sociopolitical change. *Journal of Evolutionary Economics, 27*(4), 629–662.

Alvarez, S. A. (2007). Entrepreneurial rents and the theory of the firm. *Journal of Business Venturing, 22*(3), 427–442.

Alvarez, S. A. & Barney, J. B. (2005). How do entrepreneurs organize firms under conditions of uncertainty? *Journal of Management, 31*(5), 776–793.

Andersen, E. S. (2012). Schumpeter's core works revisited. *Journal of Evolutionary Economics, 22*(4), 621–625.

Arrow, K. J. (1962a). The economic implications of learning by doing. *The review of economic studies, 29*(3), 155–173.

Arrow, K. J. (1962b). Economic Welfare and the Allocation of Resources for Invention. In R. R. Nelson (Ed.), *The Rate and Direction of Inventive Activity: Economic and Social Factors* (pp. 609–626): Princeton University Press.

Arthur, W. B. (2009). *The Nature of Technology: What it is and How it Evolves*: Free Press.

Auerswald, P. E. (2008). Entrepreneurship in the theory of the firm. *Small Business Economics, 30*(2), 111–126.

Babbitt, D. & Dietz, J. (2014). *Crypto-Economic Design: A Proposed Agent-Based Modeling Effort.* Paper presented at the University of Notre Dame, Notre Dame, USA.

Bajari, P. & Tadelis, S. (2001). Incentives versus transaction costs: A Theory of procurement contracts. *RAND Journal of Economics, 32*(3), 387–407.

Bargar, D. (2016). *The Economics of the Blockchain: A study of its engineering and transaction services marketplace.* (Master of Arts (Economics)). Clemson University, https://tigerprints.clemson.edu/all_theses/2417/.

Bauer, P. T. (1976). *Dissent on Development.* USA: Harvard University Press.

Baumol, W. J. (1968). Entrepreneurship in economic theory. *The American Economic Review, 58*(2), 64–71.

Baumol, W. J. (1990). Entrepreneurship: Productive, unproductive, and destructive. *The Journal of Political Economy, 98*(5), 893–921.

Baumol, W. J. (1993). Formal entrepreneurship theory in economics: Existence and bounds. *Journal of Business Venturing, 8*(3), 197–210.

BazaarBay. (2016). Stats. Retrieved from http://bazaarbay.org/stats/year.

Bell, T. W. (2007). Copyright as intellectual property privilege. *Syracuse Law Review, 58*, 523–546.

Bell, T. W. (2014). *Intellectual Privilege: Copyright, Common Law, and the Common Good.* USA: Mercatus Center at George Mason University.

Bell, T. W. (2017). *Your Next Government? From the Nation State to Stateless Nations.* Cambridge: Cambridge University Press.

Benkler, Y. (2006). *The Wealth of Networks: How Social Production Transforms Markets and Freedom.* USA: Yale University Press.

Benson, B. L. (1999). An economic theory of the evolution of governance and the emergence of the state. *The Review of Austrian Economics, 12*(2), 131–160.

Berg, C. (2008). *The Growth of Australia's Regulatory State: Ideology, Accountability and the Mega-Regulators.* Melbourne, Australia: Institute of Public Affairs.

Berg, C., & Davidson, S. (2015). Media regulation: A critique of Finkelstein and Tiffen. *Available at SSRN 2669271.*

Berg, C. & Davidson, S. (2016). Section 18C, Human rights, and media reform: An institutional analysis of the 2011–13 australian free speech debate. *Agenda, 23*(1), 5–30.

Berg, C., Davidson, S., & Potts, J. (2019). *Understanding the Blockchain Economy: An Introduction To Institutional Cryptoeconomics*: Edward Elgar Publishing.

Berg, C., Davidson, S., & Potts, J. (2020). Proof of work as a three-sided market. *Frontiers in Blockchain, 3*, 2.

Bessen, J. E., Meurer, M. J., & Ford, J. L. (2011). The Private and Social Costs of Patent Trolls. *Boston University School of Law, Law and Economics Research Paper*(11–45).

Bislev, S. (2004). Privatization of security as governance problem: Gated communities in the San Diego region. *Alternatives: Global, Local, Political, 29*(5), 599–618.

Bleda, M. & Del Rio, P. (2013). The market failure and the systemic failure rationales in technological innovation systems. *Research Policy, 42*(5), 1039–1052.

Bloom, N., Griffith, R., & Van Reenen, J. (2002). Do R&D tax credits work? Evidence from a panel of countries 1979–1997. *Journal of Public Economics, 85*(1), 1–31.

Boettke, P. J. (2005). Anarchism as a progressive research program in political economy. In E. P. Stringham (Ed.), *Anarchy, state and public choice* (pp. 206–219). Cheltenham, UK: Edward Elgdar.

Boettke, P. J. (2007). Liberty vs. power in economic policy in the 20th and 21st centuries. *The Journal of Private Enterprise, 22*(2), 7–36.

Boettke, P. J. (2012). *Living Economics.* Oakland, CA: Independent Institute.

Boettke, P. J. & Coyne, C. J. (2005). Methodological individualism, spontaneous order and the research program of the workshop in political theory and policy analysis. *Journal of Economic Behavior & Organization, 57*(2), 145–158.

Boettke, P. J., Coyne, C. J., & Leeson, P. T. (2008). Institutional stickiness and the new development economics. *American Journal of Economics and Sociology, 67*(2), 331–358.

Boettke, P. J., Coyne, C. J., & Leeson, P. T. (2013a). Comparative historical political economy. *Journal of Institutional Economics, 9*(3), 285–301.

Boettke, P. J., Coyne, C. J., Leeson, P. T., & Sautet, F. (2005). The new comparative political economy. *The Review of Austrian Economics, 18*(3-4), 281–304.

Boettke, P. J., Palagashvili, L., & Lemke, J. (2013b). Riding in cars with boys: Elinor Ostrom's adventures with the police. *Journal of Institutional Economics, 9*(4), 407–425.

Böhm-Bawerk, E. V. (1891). *The Positive Theory of Capital.* London, UK: Macmillan and Co.

Boldrin, M. & Levine, D. K. (2005). *The Economics of Ideas and Intellectual Property.* Paper presented at the Proceedings of the National Academy of Sciences of the United States of America.

Boldrin, M. & Levine, D. K. (2008). *Against Intellectual Monopoly.* Cambridge, MA: Cambridge University Press.

Boldrin, M. & Levine, D. K. (2013). The case against patents. *The Journal of Economic Perspectives, 27*(1), 3–22.

Box, S. (2009). *OECD Work on Innovation — A Stocktaking of Existing Work* (1815–1965).

Boyle, J. (2007). Mertonianism Unbound? Imagining Free, Decentralised Access to Most Cultural and Scientific Material. In C. Hess & E. Ostrom (Eds.), *Understanding Knowledge as a Commons: From Theory to Practice* (pp. 123–143). Cambridge, MA: The MIT Press.

Briscoe, G. & Mulligan, C. (2014). *Digital Innovation: The Hackathon Phenomenon.* CreativeWorks London Working Paper No. 6.

Buchanan, J. M. (1975). A contractarian paradigm for applying economic theory. *The American Economic Review, 65*(2), 225–230.

Buchanan, J. M. (1979a). *Cost and Choice: An Inquiry in Economic Theory*: University of Chicago Press.

Buchanan, J. M. (1979b). General Implications of Subjectivism in Economics. In *What Should Economists Do* (pp. 81–92). US: Liberty Press.

Buchanan, J. M. (1979c). *What Should Economists Do?* Indianapolis, IN, USA: Liberty Fund Inc.

Buchanan, J. M. (1990). The domain of constitutional economics. *Constitutional Political Economy, 1*(1), 1–18.

Buchanan, J. M. (2001). Game theory, mathematics, and economics. *Journal of Economic Methodology, 8*(1), 27–32.

Buchanan, J. M. & Tullock, G. (1962). *The Calculus of Consent* (Vol. 3). Ann Arbor: University of Michigan Press.

Buchanan, J. M. & Vanberg, V. J. (1991). The market as a creative process. *Economics and Philosophy, 7*(2), 167–186.

Buchanan, J. M. & Wagner, R. E. (1977). *Democracy in Deficit*. Indianapolis, IN, USA: Liberty Fund Inc.

Busenitz, L. W. (1996). Research on entrepreneurial alertness. *Journal of Small Business Management, 34*(4), 35–44.

Bush, V. (1945). Science: The endless frontier. *Transactions of the Kansas Academy of Science (1903-), 48*(3), 231–264.

Bylund, P. L. (2015). Explaining firm emergence: specialization, transaction costs, and the integration process. *Managerial and Decision Economics, 36*(4), 221–238.

Bylund, P. L. & McCaffrey, M. (2017). A theory of entrepreneurship and institutional uncertainty. *Journal of Business Venturing, 32*(5), 461–475.

Caloghirou, Y., Ioannides, S., & Vonortas, N. S. (2003). Research joint ventures. *Journal of Economic Surveys, 17*(4), 541–570.

Cantillon, R. (1772). *Essai sur la nature du commerce en général*. London, UK: Frank Cass and Company Ltd.

Capdevila, I. (2014). Different Entrepreneurial Approaches in Localized Spaces of Collaborative Innovation. *Available at SSRN 2533448*.

Caplan, B. (2011). *The Myth of the Rational Voter: Why Democracies Choose Bad Policies*. New Jersey, USA: Princeton University Press.

Casson, M. (1982). *The Entrepreneur: An Economic Theory*. New Jersey, USA: Barnes and Noble.

Casson, M. (2005). Entrepreneurship and the theory of the firm. *Journal of Economic Behavior & Organization, 58*(2), 327–348.

Cavalcanti, G. (2013). Is it a Makerspace, Hackerspace, TechShop or FabLab? *Make*. Retrieved from http://makezine.com/2013/05/22/the-difference-between-hackerspaces-makerspaces-techshops-and-fablabs/.

Chaum, D. (1983). *Blind Signatures for Untraceable Payments*. Paper presented at the Advances in Cryptology.

Chenery, H. B. & Strout, A. M. (1966). Foreign assistance and economic development. *The American Economic Review, 56*(4), 679–733.

Chesbrough, H. W. (2003). *Open Innovation: The New Imperative for Creating and Profiting From Technology*. Boston, USA: Harvard Business Press.

Cheung, N. (1990). *On the New Institutional Economics*. Department of Economics, University of Hong Kong, pp. 66.

Chiles, T. H., Bluedorn, A. C., & Gupta, V. K. (2007). Beyond creative destruction and entrepreneurial discovery: A radical Austrian approach to entrepreneurship. *Organization Studies, 28*(4), 467–493.

Clark, J. B. (1918). *Essentials of Economic Theory: As Applied to Modern Problems of Industry and Public Policy*. New York, USA: Macmillan.

Coase, R. H. (1937). The nature of the firm. *Economica, 4*(16), 386–405.

Coase, R. H. (1960). The problem of social cost. *Journal of Law and Economics, 3*, 1–44.

Coase, R. H. (1998). The new institutional economics. *The American Economic Review, 88*(2), 72–74.

Cole, D. H. (2014). Lessons from Lin: Lessons and Cautions from the Natural Commons for the Knowledge Commons. In B. M. Frischmann, M. J. Madison, & K. J. Strandburg (Eds.), *Governing Knowledge Commons* (pp. 45-68). New York: Oxford University Press.

Coleman, E. G. & Golub, A. (2008). Hacker practice moral genres and the cultural articulation of liberalism. *Anthropological Theory, 8*(3), 255–277.

Collins, R. (2009). *The Sociology of Philosophies*: Harvard University Press.

Commons, J. R. (1931). Institutional economics. *The American Economic Review, 21*, 648–657.

Contreras, J. L. (2014). Constructing the Genome Commons. In B. M. Frischmann, M. J. Madison, & K. J. Strandburg (Eds.), *Governing Knowledge Commons* (pp. 99–136). New York: Oxford University Press.

Cooney, T. M. (2005). What is an entrepreneurial team? *International Small Business Journal, 23*(3), 226–235.

Coyne, C. J. & Boettke, P. J. (2006). The role of the economist in economic development. *Quarterly Journal of Austrian Economics, 9*(2), 47–68.

Cypherpunks. (2016). Cypherpunks Mailing List. Retrieved from http://cypherpunks.to/list/.

Dahlander, L. & Gann, D. M. (2010). How open is innovation? *Research Policy, 39*(6), 699–709.

Dahlman, C. J. (1979). The problem of externality. *Journal of Law and Economics, 22*(1), 141–162.

Dal Bó, E. (2006). Regulatory capture: A review. *Oxford Review of Economic Policy, 22*(2), 203–225.

Dallago, B. (2004). Comparative economic systems and the new comparative economics. *The European Journal of Comparative Economics, 1*(1), 5–86.

Davidson, S. (2013). Productivity Enhancing Regulatory Reform. *Australia Adjusting: Optimising National Prosperity*, Committee for the Economic Development of Australia, pp. 66–71.

Davidson, S. (2016). Submission to Parliamentary Joint Committee on Law Enforcement Inquiry into Illicit Tobacco.

Davidson, S., De Filippi, P., & Potts, J. (2018). Blockchains and the economic institutions of capitalism. *Journal of Institutional Economics, 13*(4), 639–658.

Davidson, S. & Potts, J. (2016a). A new institutional approach to innovation policy. *Australian Economic Review Policy Forum: Research and Innovation, 49*(2), 200–207.

Davidson, S. & Potts, J. (2016b). The social costs of innovation policy. *Economic Affairs, 36*(3), 282–293.

Davidson, S. & Spong, H. (2010). Positive externalities and R&D: Two conflicting traditions in economic theory. *Review of Political Economy, 22*(3), 355–372.

Davies, S. R. (2017). *Hackerspaces: Making the Maker Movement.* Cambridge, UK: Polity Press.

Dekker, E. (2016). *The Viennese Students of Civilization*: Cambridge University Press.

Denzau, A. T. & North, D. C. (1994). Shared mental models: Ideologies and institutions. *Kyklos, 47*(1), 3–31.

Dietz, T., Ostrom, E., & Stern, P. C. (2003). The Struggle to govern the commons. *Science, 302*(5652), 1907–1912.

Dixit, A. K. (2007). *Lawlessness and Economics: Alternative Modes of Governance*: Princeton University Press.

Djankov, S., Glaeser, E., La Porta, R., Lopez-de-Silanes, F., & Shleifer, A. (2003). The new comparative economics. *Journal of comparative economics, 31*(4), 595–619.

Dodgson, M., Hughes, A., Foster, J., & Metcalfe, S. (2011). Systems thinking, market failure, and the development of innovation policy: The case of Australia. *Research Policy, 40*(9), 1145–1156.

Domar, E. D. (1946). Capital expansion, rate of growth, and employment. *Econometrica, 14*(2), 137–147.

Dopfer, K. (2006). The origins of meso economics: Schumpeter's legacy. *0610*, 1–43.

Dopfer, K. & Potts, J. (2007). *The General Theory of Economic Evolution.* London, UK: Routledge.

Dopfer, K. & Potts, J. (2009). On the theory of economic evolution. *Evolutionary and Institutional Economics Review, 6*(1), 23–44.

Dosi, G. (1982). Technological paradigms and technological trajectories: A suggested interpretation of the determinants and directions of technical change. *Research Policy, 11*(3), 147–162.

Douglas, E. J. & Shepherd, D. A. (2000). Entrepreneurship as a utility maximizing response. *Journal of Business Venturing, 15*(3), 231–251.

Dourado, E., & Tabarrok, A. (2015). Public choice perspectives on intellectual property. *Public Choice, 163*(1-2), 129–151.

Downs, A. (1957). An economic theory of political action in a democracy. *The Journal of Political Economy, 65*(2), 135–150.

DuPont, Q. (2017). Experiments in Algorithmic Governance: A History and Ethnography of "The DAO," a Failed Decentralized Autonomous Organization. In *Bitcoin and Beyond: Cryptocurrencies, Blockchains, and Global Governance* (pp. 157–177): Routledge.

Earl, P. E. & Wakeley, T. (2005). *Business Economics*. UK: MaGraw-Hill.

Easterly, W. (2006). *The White Man's Burden: Why the West's Efforts to Aid the Rest Have Done So Much Ill and So Little Good*. London, UK: Penguin.

Ebner, A. (2005). Hayek on Entrepreneurship: Competition, Market Process and Cultural Evolution. In J. G. Backhaus (Ed.), *Entrepreneurship, Money and Coordination: Hayek's Theory of Cultural Evolution* (pp. 131–149). Cheltenham: Edward Elgar Publishing.

Ellickson, R. C. (2009). *Order Without Law: How Neighbors Settle Disputes*. Cambridge, MA: Harvard University Press.

Endres, A. M. & Harper, D. A. (2013). Wresting Meaning from the market: A reassessment of Ludwig Lachmann's Entrepreneur. *Journal of Institutional Economics, 9*(3), 303–328.

Endres, A. M. & Woods, C. R. (2006). Modern theories of entrepreneurial behavior: A comparison and appraisal. *Small Business Economics, 26*(2), 189–202.

Engel, S. N. (2010). Development Economics: From Classical to Critical Analysis. In R. A. Denemark (Ed.), *The International Studies Encyclopedia Volume II* (pp. 874–892). West Sussex: Blackwell Publishing.

Epstein, G., Pérez, I., Schoon, M., & Meek, C. (2014). Governing the invisible commons: Ozone regulation and the montreal protocol. *International Journal of the Commons, 8*(2), 337–360.

Epstein, S. R. (1998). Craft guilds, apprenticeship, and technological change in preindustrial Europe. *Journal of Economic History, 58*(3), 684–713.

Fagerberg, J. (2012). A Guide to Schumpeter. *Confluence: Interdisciplinary Communications*, 20–22.

Fagundes, D. (2014). Labor and/as Love: Roller Derby as Constructed Cultural Commons. In B. M. Frischmann, M. J. Madison, & K. J. Strandburg (Eds.), *Governing Knowledge Commons* (pp. 417–444). New York: Oxford University Press.

Farr, N. (2009). Respect the Past, Examine the Present, Build the Future. In: hackerspaces | flux.

Feeny, D., Berkes, F., McCay, B. J., & Acheson, J. M. (1990). The tragedy of the commons: twenty-two years later. *Human ecology, 18*(1), 1–19.

Fine, B. (2006). The New Development Economics. In K. S. Jomo & B. Fine (Eds.), *The New Development Economics: Post Washington Consensus Neoliberal Thinking* (pp. 1–21). London and New York: Zed Books.

Fischer, S. (1977). Long-term contracting, sticky prices, and monetary policy: A comment. *Journal of Monetary Economics, 3*(3), 317–323.

Flanagan, K., Uyarra, E., & Laranja, M. (2011). Reconceptualising the 'policy mix' for innovation. *Research Policy, 40*(5), 702–713.

Fordyce, R., Heemsbergen, L., Mignone, P., & Nansen, B. (2015). 3D printing and university makerspaces: Surveying countercultural communities in institutional settings. *Digital Culture & Education, 7*(2), 192–205.

Foss, N. J., & Klein, P. G. (2012). *Organizing Entrepreneurial Judgment: A New Approach to the Firm*. Cambridge, UK: Cambridge University Press.

Fox-Brewster, T. (2016). OpenBazaar is Not the Next Silk Road—It's an Anarchist eBay on Acid. *Forbes*. Retrieved from https://www.forbes.com/sites/thomasbrewster/2016/03/16/openbazaar-silk-road-dark-web-drugs-ebay/#2e5990555ab4.

Freeman, C. (1995). The national system of innovation in historical perspective. *Cambridge Journal of Economics, 19*(1), 5–24.

Freeman, C. (2002). Continental, national and sub-national innovation systems—Complementarity and economic growth. *Research Policy, 31*(2), 191–211.

Freiberger, P. & Swaine, M. (1999). *Fire in the Valley: The Making of the Personal Computer*: McGraw-Hill Professional.

Frischmann, B. M., Madison, M. J., & Strandburg, K. J. (2014). *Governing Knowledge Commons*. UK: Oxford University Press.

Fuller, B. & Romer, P. (2012). *Success and the City: How Charter Cities Could Transform the Developing World*: Macdonald-Laurier Institute for Public Policy.

Gaglio, C. M. & Katz, J. A. (2001). The psychological basis of opportunity identification: Entrepreneurial alertness. *Small Business Economics, 16*(2), 95–111.

Gans, J. S. & Stern, S. (2010). Is there a market for ideas? *Industrial and Corporate Change, 19*(3), 805–837.

Gintis, H., Smith, E. A., & Bowles, S. (2001). Costly signaling and cooperation. *Journal of Theoretical Biology, 213*(1), 103–119.

Glaeser, E. L., La Porta, R., Lopez-de-Silanes, F., & Shleifer, A. (2004). Do institutions cause growth? *Journal ofEeconomic Growth, 9*(3), 271–303.

Glaeser, E. L. & Shleifer, A. (2002). Legal origins. *Quarterly Journal of Economics, 117*(4), 1193–1229.

Globerman, S. (1980). Markets, hierarchies, and innovation. *Journal of Economic Issues, 14*(4), 977–998.

Godin, B. (2009). National innovation system: The system approach in historical perspective. *Science, Technology & Human Values, 34*(4), 476–501.

Goolsbee, A. (1998). Does government R&D policy mainly benefit scientists and engineers? *American Economic Review, 88*(2), 298–302.

Gordon, H. S. (1954). The economic theory of a common-property resource: The fishery. *Journal of Political Economy, 62*(2), 124–142.

Greenberg, D. S. (2001). *Science, Money, and Politics: Political Triumph and Ethical Erosion*. US: University of Chicago Press.

Griliches, Z. (1957). Hybrid corn: An exploration in the economics of technological change. *Econometrica, 25*(4), 501–522.

Griliches, Z. (1991). The search for R&D spillovers. *The Scandinavian Journal of Economics, 94*, 29–47.

Grossman, G. M. & Helpman, E. (1991). Trade, knowledge spillovers, and growth. *European Economic Review, 35*(2–3), 517–526.

Grossman, S. J. & Hart, O. D. (1983). An analysis of the principal-agent problem. *Econometrica, 51*(1), 7–45.

Grossman, S. J. & Hart, O. D. (1986). The costs and benefits of ownership: A theory of vertical and lateral integration. *Journal of PoliticalEeconomy, 94*(4), 691–719.

Guthrie, C. (2014, 2–5 April 2014). *Empowering the Hacker in Us: A Comparison of Fab Lab and Hackerspace Ecosystems.* Paper presented at the 5th LAEMOS (Latin American and European Meeting on Organization Studies) Colloquium, Havana Cuba.

hack.ether.camp. (2017). Hacker Gold. Retrieved from https://hack.ether.camp/home.

hackerspaces.org. (2011). Hackerspaces Passport. Retrieved from https://www.noisebridge.net/wiki/passport.

hackerspaces.org. (2016). Design Patterns. Retrieved from https://wiki.hacker-spaces.org/Design_Patterns.

Hagerdoorn, J. (1993). Understanding the rationale of strategic technology part-nering: Interorganizational modes of cooperation and sectoral differences. *Strategic Management Journal, 14*(5), 371–386.

Hall, B. H. & Lerner, J. (2010). The Financing of R&D and Innovation. In B. H. Hall & N. Rosenberg (Eds.), *Handbook of the Economics of Innovation* (Vol. 2, pp. 609–639): Elsevier.

Han, L. (2015). Anatomy of an Anarchist Hackerspace. *New Worker Magazine.* Retrieved from http://newworker.co/mag/anatomy-anarchist-hackerspace/.

Hardin, G. (1968). The tragedy of the commons. *Science, 162*(3859), 1243–1248.

Harper, D. A. (2008). Towards a theory of entrepreneurial teams. *Journal of Business Venturing, 23*(6), 613–626.

Harrod, R. F. (1939). An essay in dynamic theory. *The EconomicJjournal, 49*(193), 14–33.

Hart, O. & Moore, J. (1990). Property rights and the nature of the firm. *Journal of Political Economy, 98*(6), 1119–1158.

Harwick, C. (2016). Cryptocurrency and the problem of intermediation. *The Independent Review, 20*(4), 569.

Hatch, M. (2013). *The Maker Movement Manifesto: Rules for Innovation in the New World of Crafters, Hackers, and Tinkerers.* US: McGraw Hill Professional.

Hayek, F. A. (1937). Economics and knowledge. *Economica, 4*(13), 33–54.

Hayek, F. A. (1945). The use of knowledge in society. *The American Economic Review, 35*(4), 519–530.

Hayek, F. A. (1948). *Individualism and Economic Order.* US: University of Chicago Press.

Hayek, F. A. (1973). *Law, Legislation and Liberty, Volume 1: Rules and Order*. Chicago: University of Chicago Press.

Hayek, F. A. (1989). The pretence of knowledge. *The American Economic Review, 79*(6), 3–7.

Hayek, F. A. (2011). *The Fatal Conceit: The Errors of Socialism*. US: University of Chicago Press.

Hébert, R. F. & Link, A. N. (1988). *The Entrepreneur: Mainstream Views & Radical Critiques*. New York: Praeger Publishers.

Heller, M. A. (1998). The tragedy of the anticommons: Property in the transition from Marx to markets. *Harvard Law Review, 11*(3), 621–688.

Herzberg, R. Q. (2015). Governing their commons: Elinor and Vincent Ostrom and the Bloomington School. *Public Choice, 163*(1–2), 95–109.

Hess, C. (2008). *Mapping the New Commons*. Paper presented at the The Twelfth Biennial Conference of the International Association for the Study of the Commons, Cheltenham, UK.

Hess, C. & Ostrom, E. (2003). Ideas, artifacts, and facilities: Information as a common-pool resource. *Law and Contemporary Problems, 66*(1–2), 111–145.

High, J. (2009). Entrepreneurship and economic growth: The theory of emergent institutions. *Quarterly Journal of Austrian Economics, 12*(3), 3–36.

Hobbes, T. (2006 [1651]). *Leviathan*: A&C Black.

Hodgson, G. M. (1993). Institutional economics: Surveying the 'old' and the 'new'. *Metroeconomica, 44*(1), 1–28.

Holcombe, R. G. (1998). Entrepreneurship and economic growth. *Quarterly Journal of Austrian Economics, 1*(2), 45–62.

Holmstrom, B. (1989). Agency costs and innovation. *Journal of Economic Behavior & Organization, 12*(3), 305–327.

Hölmstrom, B. (1979). Moral hazard and observability. *The Bell Journal of Economics, 10*(1), 74–91.

Horwitz, S. (1994). Subjectivism. In P. J. Boettke (Ed.), *The Elgar Companion to Austrian economics* (pp. 17–22). Massachusetts, US: Edward Elgar.

Hurwicz, L. (1973). The design of mechanisms for resource allocation. *The American Economic Review, 63*(2), 1–30.

IFP. (2013). Hackerspaces a Breeding Ground for Start-ups, Entrepreneurs. *Entrepreneurs*. Retrieved from https://newsroom.intel.com/editorials/hackerspaces-a-breeding-ground-for-start-ups-entrepreneurs/.

Ioannides, S. (1999). Towards an Austrian perspective on the firm. *The Review of Austrian Economics, 11*(1), 77–97.

Jakee, K. & Spong, H. (2003a). Praxeology, entrepreneurship and the market process: A review of Kirzner's contribution. *Journal of the History of Economic Thought, 25*(4), 461–486.

Jakee, K. & Spong, H. (2003b). Uncertainty, Institutional Structure and the Entrepreneurial Process. In J. S. Metcalfe & U. Cantner (Eds.), *Change,*

Transformation and Development (pp. 125–144): Springer Science and Business Media.

Jomo, K. S. & Reinert, E. S. (2005). *Origins of Development Economics: How Schools of Economic Thought Addressed Development.* London, UK: Zed Books.

Jones, C. I. & Williams, J. C. (1998). Measuring the social return to R&D. *Quarterly Journal of Economics, 113*(4), 1119–1135.

Juma, C. (2016). *Innovation and Its Enemies: Why People Resist New Technologies.* Oxford, UK: Oxford University Press.

Kaish, S. & Gilad, B. (1991). Characteristics of opportunities search of entrepreneurs versus executives: Sources, interests, general alertness. *Journal of Business Venturing, 6*(1), 45–61.

Kasper, W. & Streit, M. E. (1998). *Institutional Economics: Social Order and Public Policy.* Cheltenham, UK: Edward Elgar.

Kastelle, T., Potts, J., & Dodgson, M. (2009). *The Evolution of Innovation Sysytems.* Paper presented at the Compenhagen Business School Summer Conference.

Katz, M. L. & Shapiro, C. (1985). Network externalities, competition, and compatibility. *The American Economic Review, 75*(3), 424–440.

Kealey, T. & Nelson, R. R. (1996). *The Economic Laws of Scientific Research.* London, UK: Palgrave Macmillan.

Kealey, T. & Ricketts, M. (2014). Modelling science as a contribution good. *Research Policy, 43*(6), 1014–1024.

Kera, D. (2012). Hackerspaces and DIYbio in Asia: Connecting science and community with open data, kits and protocols. *Journal of Peer Production, 1*(2), 1–8.

Kirzner, I. (2013). Uncertainty, discovery, and human action: A study of the entrepreneurial profile in the Misesian system. *MISES: Interdisciplinary Journal of Philosophy, Law and Economics, 1*(2), 305–323.

Kirzner, I. M. (1978a). *Competition and Entrepreneurship.* US: University of Chicago Press.

Kirzner, I. M. (1978b). The entrepreneurial role in Menger's system. *Atlantic Economic Journal, 6*(3), 31–45.

Kirzner, I. M. (1982). *Method, Process, and Austrian Economics: Essays in Honour of Ludwig von Mises.* Toronto, Canada: Lexington Books.

Kirzner, I. M. (1994). Entrepreneurship. In P. J. Boettke (Ed.), *The Elgar Companion to Austrian Economics* (pp. 103–110): Edward Elgar.

Kirzner, I. M. (1997). Entrepreneurial discovery and the competitive market process: An Austrian approach. *Journal of Economic Literature, 35*(1), 60–85.

Kirzner, I. M. (1999). Creativity and/or alertness: A reconsideration of the Schumpeterian entrepreneur. *The Review of Austrian Economics, 11*(1), 5–17.

Kirzner, I. M. (2009). The alert and creative entrepreneur: A clarification. *Small Business Economics, 32*(2), 145–152.

Klein, B., Crawford, R. G., & Alchian, A. A. (1978). Vertical integration, appropriable rents and the competitive contracting process. *The Journal of Law & Economics, 21*(2), 297–326.

Klein, P. G. (1998). New Institutional Economics. In B. Bouckeart & G. De Geest (Eds.), *Encyclopedia of Law and Economics*: Edward Elgar.

Klepper, S. (1996). Entry, exit, growth, and innovation over the product life cycle. *The American Economic Review, 86*(3), 562–583.

Klepper, S. (1997). Industry life cycles. *Industrial and Corporate Change, 6*(1), 145–182.

Knight, F. H. (1921). *Risk, Uncertainty and Profit*. Boston, MA, USA: Hart, Schaffner & Marx.

Koppl, R. (2014). Introduction to 'Entangled Political Economy'. In S. Horwitz & R. Koppl (Eds.), *Entangled Political Economy* (pp. 1–13): Emerald Group Publishing Limited.

Koppl, R., Kauffman, S., Felin, T., & Longo, G. (2015). Economics for a creative world. *Journal of Institutional Economics, 11*(1), 1–31.

Korsgaard, S., Berglund, H., Thrane, C., & Blenker, P. (2015). A tale of two Kirzners: Time, uncertainty, and the 'nature' of opportunities. *Entrepreneurship Theory and Practice, 40*(4), 867–889.

Kostakis, V., Niaros, V., & Giotitsas, C. (2014). Production and governance in hackerspaces: A manifestation of commons-based peer production in the physical realm? *International Journal of Cultural Studies, 18*(5), 555–573.

Krueger, A. O. (1974). The political economy of the rent-seeking society. *The American Economic Review, 64*(3), 291–303.

Kuchař, P. (2016). Entrepreneurship and institutional change. *Journal of Evolutionary Economics, 26*(2), 349–379.

Kuchař, P. & Dekker, E. (2017). Emergent orders of worth: Must we agree on more than a price? *Cosmos and Taxis: Studies in Emergent Order and Organization, 4*(1), 23–34.

La Porta, R., Lopez-de-Silanes, F., & Shleifer, A. (2008). The economic consequences of legal origins. *Journal of Economic Literature, 46*(2), 285–332.

Lachmann, L. M. (1956). *Capital and Its Structure*. US: Ludwig von Mises Institute.

Lachmann, L. M. (1976). From Mises to Shackle: An essay on Austrian economics and the Kaleidic society. *Journal of Economic Literature, 14*(1), 54–62.

Lachmann, L. M. (1990). GLS Shackle's Place in the History of Subjectivist Thought. In F. S. F (Ed.), *Unknowledge and Choice in Economics* (Vol. 14, pp. 54–62): Springer.

Laffont, J.-J., & Tirole, J. (1991). The politics of government decision-making: A theory of regulatory capture. *The Quarterly Journal of Economics, 106*(4), 1089–1127.

Landes, D. S. (1969). *The Unbound Prometheus: Technological Change and Industrial Development in Western Europe from 1750 to the Present.* Cambridge, UK: Cambridge University Press.

Langlois, R. N. (1994). Risk and Uncertainty. In P. J. Boettke (Ed.), *The Elgar Companion to Austrian Economics* (pp. 118-122). Cheltemham, UK: Edward Elgar.

Langlois, R. N. (2003). Schumpeter and the Obsolescence of the Entrepreneur. In R. Koppl, J. Birner, & P. Kurrild-Klitgaard (Eds.), *Advances in Austrian Economics* (Vol. 6, pp. 283–298). UK: Emerald Group Publishing Limited.

Langlois, R. N. (2007). The entrepreneurial theory of the firm and the theory of the entrepreneurial firm. *Journal of Management Studies, 44*(7), 1107–1124.

Langlois, R. N. & Foss, N. J. (1997). Capabilities and governance: The rebirth of production in the theory of economic organization. *Kyklos, 52*(2), 201–218.

Langlois, R. N. & Robertson, P. L. (2002). *Firms, Markets and Economic Change: A Dynamic Theory of Business Institutions.* London, UK: Routledge.

Lash, B. (2007). Memoir of a Homebrew Computer Club Member. Published Online. Available at: http://www.bambi.net/bob/homebrew.html.

Lavoie, D. (1991). The Discovery and Interpretation of Profit Opportunities: Culture and the Kirznerian Entrepreneur. In L. E. Grube & V. H. Storr (Eds.), *Culture and Economic Action* (pp. 48–67). Cheltenham, UK: Edward Elgar.

Lazzarotti, V. & Manzini, R. (2009). Different modes of open innovation: A Theoretical framework and an empirical study. *International Journal of Innovation Management, 13*(4), 615–636.

Leca, B., Battilana, J., & Boxenbaum, E. (2008). *Agency and institutions: A review of institutional entrepreneurship.* HBS Working Paper Series. Harvard Business School.

Lederman, O. (2015). *Hacking Innovation-group Dynamics in Innovation Teams.* (Master of Science in Media Arts and Sciences). Massachusetts Institute of Technology, USA.

Leeson, P. T. (2004). Cooperation and conflict: Evidence on self-enforcing arrangements and heterogeneous groups. *The American Journal of Economics and Sociology, 65*(4), 891–908.

Leeson, P. T. (2007a). An-arrgh-chy: The law and economics of pirate organization. *Journal of political economy, 115*(6), 1049–1094.

Leeson, P. T. (2007b). Efficient anarchy. *Public Choice, 130*(1–2), 41–53.

Leeson, P. T. (2009). *The Invisible Hook: The Hidden Economics of Pirates.* USA: Princeton University Press.

Leeson, P. T. (2010). Anarchy Unbound: How Much Order Can Spontaneous Order Create? In P. J. Boettke (Ed.), *Handbook on Contemporary Austrian Economics* (pp. 136). Cheltenham, UK: Edward Elgar.

Leeson, P. T. (2014). *Anarchy unbound: Why self-governance works better than you think*: Cambridge University Press.

Leeson, P. T. & Boettke, P. J. (2009). Two-tiered Entrepreneurship and Economic Development. *International Review of Law and Economics, 29*(3), 252–259.

Leeson, P. T. & Skarbek, D. B. (2010). Criminal Constitutions. *Global Crime, 11*(3), 279–297.

Leeson, P. T. & Subrick, J. R. (2006). Robust political economy. *The Review of Austrian Economics, 19*(2–3), 107–111.

Leeson, P. T. & Williamson, C. R. (2009). Anarchy and development: An application of the theory of second best. *The Law and Development Review, 2*(1), 77–96.

Leff, N. H. (1979). Entrepreneurship and economic development: The Problem revisited. *Journal of Economic Literature, 17*(1), 46–64.

Levy, S. (2001). *Hackers: Heroes of the Computer Revolution* (Vol. 4). New York: Penguin Books.

Liebowitz, S. J. & Margolis, S. E. (1995). Path dependence, lock-in, and history. *Journal of Law, Economics & Organization, 11*(1), 205–226.

Lindtner, S. (2012). *Remaking Creativity & Innovation: China's Nascent DIY Maker & Hackerspace Community*. Paper presented at the New Media and Cultural Transformation: Film, TV, Game, and Digital Communication, New York University Shanghai Centre.

Lindtner, S., Hertz, G. D., & Dourish, P. (2014). *Emerging Sites of HCI Innovation: Hackerspaces, Hardware Startups & Incubators*. Paper presented at the Proceedings of the SIGCHI Conference on Human Factors in Computing Systems, Toronto, Canada.

Lindtner, S. & Li, D. (2012). Created in China: The makings of China's hackerspace Community. *Interactions, 19*(6), 18–22.

Link, A. N. (1977). On the efficiency of federal R&D spending: A public choice approach. *Public Choice, 31*(1), 129–133.

Loasby, B. J. (2002). The Organizational Tasis of Cognition and the Cognitive basis of Prganization. In M. Augier & J. G. March (Eds.), *The Economics of Choice, Change and Organization, Essays in Memory of Richard M. Cyert*. Cheltenham, UK: Edward Elgar.

Lokshin, I. M. (2015). Total Factor Productivity and the Institutional Possibility Frontier: An Outline of a Link between Two Theoretical Perspectives on Institutions, Culture and Long Run Growth. *Higher School of Economics Research Paper No. WP BRP, 30*.

López, E. & Leighton, W. (2012). *Madmen, Intellectuals, and Academic Scribblers: The Economic Engine of Political Change.* US: Stanford University Press.

Lucas, R. E. (2009). Ideas and Growth. *Economica, 76*(301), 1–19.

Lucchi, N. (2013). Understanding genetic information as a commons: From bioprospecting to personalized medicine. *International Journal of the Commons, 7*(2), 313–338.

Lundvall, B.-Å. (1992). *National Systems of Innovation.* London, UK: Pinter.

Lutter, M. (2016). *Three Essays on Proprietary Cities.* (PhD Economics). George Mason University.

Lyons, J. (2013). *The Society for Useful Knowledge: How Benjamin Franklin and Friends Brought the Enlightenment to America.* US: Bloomsbury Publishing.

MacDonald, T. J. (2019). *The Political Economy of Non-Territorial Exit*: Edward Elgar Publishing.

MacDonald, T. J., Allen, D. W. E., & Potts, J. (2016). Blockchains and the Boundaries of Self-Organized Economies: Predictions for the Future of Banking. In P. Tasca, T. Aste, L. Pelizzon, & N. Perony (Eds.), *Banking Beyond Banks and Money: A Guide to Banking Services in the Twenty-First Century* (pp. 279–296). Cham: Springer International Publishing.

Madison, M. J., Frischmann, B. M., & Strandburg, K. J. (2010). Constructing Commons in the cultural environment. *Cornell Law Review, 95*(4), 657–710.

Manion, M. & Goodrum, A. (2000). Terrorism or civil disobedience: Toward a hacktivist ethic. *ACM SIGCAS Computers and Society, 30*(2), 14–19.

Manish, G. P. & Powell, B. (2015). From Subsistence to Advanced Material Production: Austrian Development Economics. In C. J. Coyne & P. J. Boettke (Eds.), *The Oxford Handbook of Austrian Economics* (pp. 698–712). UK: Oxford University Press.

Manne, R. (2015). *Cypherpunk Revolutionary: On Julian Assange* (Vol. 9): Black Inc.

Marengo, L. & Dosi, G. (2005). Division of labor, organizational coordination and market mechanisms in collective problem-solving. *Journal of Economic Behavior & Organization, 58*(2), 303–326.

Marshall, A. (1890). *Principles of Economics.* London, UK: Macmillan and Co.

Martin, B. R. (2016). R&D policy instruments—A critical review of what we do and don't know. *Industry and Innovation, 23*(2), 157–176.

Martin, S. & Scott, J. T. (2000). The nature of innovation market failure and the design of public support for private innovation. *Research Policy, 29*(4), 437–447.

Masten, S. (1996). *Case Studies in Contracting and Organization.* New York, US: Oxford University Press.

Matsuyama, K. (1997). Economic Development as Coordination Problems. In M. Aoki, H. Kim, & O. Masahiro (Eds.), *The Role of Government in East Asian Economic Development* (pp. 134–160): Oxford University Press.

Mattila, J. (2016). *The Blockchain Phenomenon: The Disruptive Potential of Distributed Consensus Architectures*. Berkley Roundtable on the International Economic (BRIE) Working Paper 2016-1. University of California, Berkley. Retrieved from https://brie.berkeley.edu/sites/default/files/juri-mattila-.pdf.

Maxigas. (2014). Hacklabs and hackerspaces—Tracing two geneologies. *Journal of Peer Production, 2*.

McCaffrey, M. (2014). On the theory of entrepreneurial incentives and alertness. *Entrepreneurship Theory and Practice, 38*(4), 891–911.

McCloskey, D. N. (1981). The Industrial Revolution 1780–1860: A Survey. In R. M. Flour & D. N. McCloskey (Eds.), *The Economic History of Great Britain Since 1700* (Vol. 1, pp. 103–127).

McCloskey, D. N. (2010). *Bourgeois Dignity: Why Economics Can't Explain the Modern World*. UK: University of Chicago Press.

McCloskey, D. N. (2016). *Bourgeois Equality: How Ideas, Not Capital or Institutions, Enriched the World*. US: University of Chicago Press.

McGinnis, M. & Ostrom, E. (1992). *Design Principles for Local and Global Commons*. Paper presented at the Linking Local and Global Commons, Harvard Center for International Affairs, Cambridge, MA.

McGinnis, M. D. (2005). Beyond individualism and spontaneity: Comments on Peter Boettke and Christopher Coyne. *Journal of Economic Behavior & Organization, 57*(2), 167–172.

McGinnis, M. D. & Ostrom, E. (2012). Reflections on Vincent Ostrom, public administration, and polycentricity. *Public Administration Review, 72*(1), 15–25.

Ménard, C. (2004). The economics of hybrid organizations. *Journal of Institutional and Theoretical Economics, 160*(3), 345–376.

Ménard, C. (Ed.) (2000). *Institutions, Contracts and Organizations*. London, UK: Edward Elgar.

Ménard, C. & Shirley, M. M. (2014). The future of new institutional economics: From early intuitions to a new paradigm? *Journal of Institutional Economics, 10*(4), 541–565.

Menger, C. (1871). *Principles of Economics*. London, UK: Macmillan.

Metcalfe, J. S. (2004). The entrepreneur and the style of modern economics. *Journal of Evolutionary Economics, 14*(2), 157–175.

Meyer, P. B. (2014). An Inventive Commons: Shared Sources of he Airplane and Its Industry. In B. M. Frischmann, M. J. Madison, & K. J. Strandburg (Eds.), *Governing Knowledge Commons* (pp. 341–364). New York, US: Oxford University Press.

Mises, L. v. (1949). *Human Action: A Treatise on Economics*. Auburn, Alabama: The Ludwig von Mises Institute.

Mitchell, M. & Boettke, P. J. (2017). *Applied Mainline Economics: Bridging the Gap between Theory and Public Policy*. Arlington, VA: Mercatus Center at George Mason University.

Mitchell, W. C. (1988). Virginia, Rochester, and Bloomington: Twenty-five years of public choice and political science. *Public Choice, 56*(2), 101–119.

Mnookin, R. H. & Kornhauser, L. (1979). Bargaining in the shadow of the law: The case of divorce. *The Yale Law Journal, 88*(5), 950–997.

Moberg, L. (2015). The political economy of special economic zones. *Journal of Institutional Economics, 11*(1), 167–190.

Mohnen, P. & Röller, L.-H. (2005). Complementarities in innovation policy. *European Economic Review, 49*(6), 1431–1450.

Moilanen, J. (2012). *Emerging Hackerspaces—Peer-production Generation*. Paper presented at the Open Source Systems: Long-Term Sustainability, 8th IFIP WG 2.13 International Conference, Hammamet, Tunisia.

Moilanen, J., Daly, A., Lobato, R., & Allen, D. W. E. (2014). Cultures of sharing in 3D printing: What can we learn from the licence choices of thingiverse users? *Journal of Peer Production, 6*. Retrieved from http://peerproduction. net/issues/issue-6-disruption-and-the-law/peer-reviewed-articles/cultures-of-sharing-in-thingiverse-what-can-we-learn-from-the-licence-choices-of-thingiverse-users/.

Mokyr, J. (2009). *The Enlightened Economy: An Economic History of Britain 1700–1850*. US: Yale University Press.

Mokyr, J. (2016). *A Culture of Growth: The Origins of the Modern Economy*. US: Princeton University Press.

Monteverde, K. & Teece, D. J. (1982). Appropriable rents and quasi-vertical integration. *Journal of Law and Economics, 25*, 321–328.

Mougayar, W. (2016). *The Business Blockchain: Promise, Practice, and Application of the Next Internet Technology* (1 ed.). New Jersey, US: Wiley.

Murphy, K. M., Shleifer, A., & Vishny, R. W. (1989). Industrialization and the big push. *The Journal of Political Economy, 97*(5), 1003–1026.

Myerson, R. B. (1979). Incentive compatibility and the bargaining problem. *Econometrica, 47*(1), 61–73.

Nabli, M. K. & Nugent, J. B. (1989). The new institutional economics and its applicability to development. *World Development, 17*(9), 1333–1347.

Nakamoto, S. (2008). *Bitcoin: A Peer-to-peer Electronic Cash System*. Retrieved from https://bitcoin.org/bitcoin.pdf.

Nandi, A. & Mandernach, M. (2016). *Hackathons as an Informal Learning Platform*. Paper presented at the SIGCSE '16 Proceedings of the 47th ACM Technical Symposium on Computing Science Education, Tennessee, USA.

Nelson, R. R. (1959). The simple economics of basic scientific research. *Journal of political economy, 67*(3), 297–306.

Nelson, R. R. (1993). *National Innovation Systems: A Comparative Analysis.* New York, US: Oxford University Press.

Nelson, R. R. (1995). Recent evolutionary theorizing about economic change. *Journal of Economic Literature, 33*(1), 48–90.

Nelson, R. R. & Winter, S. G. (2009). *An Evolutionary Theory of Economic Change*: Harvard University Press.

North, D. C. (1990). *Institutions, Institutional Change and Economic Performance.* US: Cambridge University Press.

North, D. C. (1993). *Five Propositions About Institutional Change.* Economics Working Paper Archive at WUSTL.

Nowak, M. A. (2006). Five rules for the evolution of cooperation. *Science, 314*(5805), 1560–1563.

Nowak, M. A. & Sigmund, K. (1998). Evolution of indirect reciprocity by image scoring. *Nature, 393*(6685), 573–577.

Nowak, M. A. & Sigmund, K. (2005). Evolution of indirect reciprocity. *Nature, 437*(7063), 1291–1298.

O'Driscoll, G. P., Rizzo, M. J., & Garrison, R. W. (1996). *The Economics of Time and Ignorance.* London, UK: Routledge.

Ohlig, J. & Weiler, L. (2007). *Building a Hackerspace.* Paper presented at the 24th Chaos Communication Congress, Berlin, Germany. https://events.ccc.de/congress/2007/Fahrplan/attachments/1003_Building%20a%20Hacker%20Space.pdf.

Olson, M. (2008). *The Rise and Decline of Nations: Economic Growth, Stagflation, and Social Rigidities.* US: Yale University Press.

Ostrom, E. (1990). *Governing the Commons: The Evolution of Institutions for Collective Action.* Cambridge: Cambridge university press.

Ostrom, E. (2005). *Understanding Institutional Diversity.* Princeton, NJ, US: Princeton University Press.

Ostrom, E. (2007). A diagnostic approach for going beyond panaceas. *Proceedings of the national Academy of Sciences, 104*(39), 15181–15187.

Ostrom, E. (2010). Beyond markets and states: Polycentric governance of complex economic systems. *The American Economic Review, 100*(3), 641–672.

Ostrom, E., Dietz, T., Dolšak, N., Stern, P. C., Stonich, S., & Weber, E. U. (2002). *The Drama of the Commons.* Washington, DC, US: The National Academy Press.

Ostrom, E. & Hess, C. (2007). A Framework for Analyzing the Knowledge Commons: a chapter from Understanding Knowledge as a Commons: from Theory to Practice. In C. Hess & E. Ostrom (Eds.), *Understanding Knowledge as a Commons: From Theory to Practice* (pp. 41–82). Cambridge, MA, US: The MIT Press.

Ostrom, E., Janssen, M. A., & Anderies, J. M. (2007). *Going Beyond Panaceas.* Paper presented at the Proceedings of the national Academy of sciences.

Ostrom, V., Tiebout, C. M., & Warren, R. (1961). The organization of government in metropolitan areas: A theoretical inquiry. *American Political Science Review, 55*(4), 831–842.

Pagenelli, M. (2014). Adam Smith and Entangled Political Economy. In S. Horwitz & R. Koppl (Eds.), *Advances in Austrian Economics* (Vol. 168, pp. 37–54). Bingley, UK.

Pasour Jr., E. (1978). Cost and choice-Austrian vs. conventional views. *Journal of Libertarian Studies, 2*(4), 327–336.

Peltzman, S. (1976). *Toward a More General Theory of Regulation.* NBER Working Paper 133. National Bureau of Economic Research Cambridge, Mass., US.

Pennington, M. (2010). *Robust Political Economy: Classical Liberalism and the Future of Public Policy*: Edward Elgar.

Pennington, M. (2011). Robust political economy. *Policy: A Journal of Public Policy and Ideas, 27*(4), 8.

Penrose, E. T. (1959). *The Theory of the Growth of the Firm.* US: Oxford University Press.

Phelan, S. E. (2014). Austrian theories of entrepreneurship: Insights from complexity theory. *The Review of Austrian Economics, 29*(3), 277–297.

Pisano, G. P. (1991). The governance of innovation: Vertical integration and collaborative arrangements in the biotechnology industry. *Research Policy, 20*(3), 237–249.

Popper, N. (2015). Digital Gold: Bitcoin and the Inside Story of the Misfits and Millionaires Trying to Reinvent Money. In. New York, US: Harper Collins.

Poteete, A. R., Janssen, M. A., & Ostrom, E. (2010). *Working together: collective action, the commons, and multiple methods in practice*: Princeton University Press.

Potts, J. (2014). Innovation is a Spontaneous Order. *Cosmos and Taxis: Studies in Emergent Order and Organization, 2*(1), 1–10.

Potts, J. (2018). Governing the innovation commons. *Journal of Institutional Economics, 14*(6), 1025–1047.

Potts, J. (2019). *Innovation Commons: The Origin of Economic Growth*: Oxford University Press.

Powell, W. W., Koput, K. W., & Smith-Doerr, L. (1996). Interorganizational collaboration and the locus of innovation: Networks of learning in biotechnology. *Administrative Science Quarterly, 41*(1), 116–145.

Quesnay, F. (1888). *Oeuvres économiques et philosophiques.* Francfort: Baer.

Rajagopalan, S. & Tabarrok, A. T. (2014). *Lessons from Gurgaon, India's Private City.* GMU Working Paper in Economics. Department of Economics. George Mason University. Available at SSRN 2514652.

Ratto, M. (2011). Critical making: Conceptual and material studies in technology and social life. *The Information Society, 27*(4), 252–260.

Raymond, E. (1999). The Cathedral and the Bazaar. *Knowledge, Technology & Policy, 12*(3), 23–49.

Reutzel, B. (2016). Why the Blockchain Hackathon Economy is Booming. *Coindesk*. Retrieved from http://www.coindesk.com/blockchain-hackathon-economy-booming/.

Ricardo, D. (1821). *Principles of Political Economy and Taxation*. London, UK: John Murray.

Richardson, G. B. (1972). The organisation of industry. *The Economic Journal, 82*(327), 883–896.

Robbins, L. (1932). *An Essay on the Nature and Significance of Economic Science*. London, UK: Macmillan.

Robertson, E. D. (2010). *Hacker Spaces: User-Led Innovation and Economic Development*. Georgia Institute of Technology, School of City and Regional Planning Award-Winning Research.

Robertson, P. L. & Langlois, R. N. (1995). Innovation, networks, and vertical integration. *Research Policy, 24*(4), 543–562.

Rodger, W. (2001). Cypherpunks RIP: List Dead and Burried' founder Says. *The Register*. Retrieved from http://www.theregister.co.uk/2001/11/30/cypherpunks_rip/.

Rodrik, D. (2008). *The New Development Economics: We Shall Experiment, But How Shall We Learn?* Harvard Kennedy School Working Paper Series. Harvard Kennedy School.

Romano, R. E. (1989). Aspects of R&D subsidization. *The Quarterly Journal of Economics, 104*(4), 863–873.

Romer, P. M. (1986). Increasing returns and long-run growth. *Journal of Political Economy, 94*(5), 1002–1037.

Romer, P. M. (1990). Endogenous technological change. *The Journal of Political Economy, 98*(5), S71–S102.

Rosenstein-Rodan, P. N. (1943). Problems of industrialisation of Eastern and South-Eastern Europe. *The Economic Journal, 53*(210/211), 202–211.

Rosenstein-Rodan, P. N. (1961). Notes on the Theory of the 'Big Push'. In *Economic Development for Latin America* (pp. 57–81). UK: Palgrave Macmillan.

Rosser, B. J. & Rosser, M. V. (2008). A critique of the new comparative economics. *The Review of Austrian Economics, 21*(1), 81–97.

Rostow, W. W. (1990). *The Stages of Economic Growth: A Non-Communist Manifesto*. New York, US: Cambridge University Press.

Rothbard, M. N. (1985). Professor Hébert on entrepreneurship. *Journal of Libertarian Studies, 7*(2), 281–286.

Rumelt, R. P. (2005). Theory, Strategy, and Entrepreneurship. In S. A. Alvarez, R. Agarwal, & O. Sorenson (Eds.), *Handbook of Entrepreneurship Research* (pp. 11–32): Springer.

Sachs, J. (2005). *The End of Poverty: How we can Make it Happen in our Lifetime.* UK: Penguin.

Salerno, J. T. (2008). The entrepreneur: Real and imagined. *The Quarterly Journal of Austrian Economics, 11*(3-4), 188–207.

Say, J. B. (1832). *A Treatise on Political Economy: Or the Production, Distribution, and Consumption of Wealth.* Philadelphia, US: Grigg & Elliot.

Schlesinger, J., Islam, M. M., & MacNeill, K. (2010). *Founding a Hackerspace.* (Bachelor of Science). Worcester Polytechnic Institute.

Schumpeter, J. A. (1934). *The Theory of Economic Development: An Inquiry into Profits, Capital, Credit, Interest, and the Business Cycle* (Vol. 55). New Jersey, US: Transaction Publishers.

Schumpeter, J. A. (1942). *Capitalism, Socialism and Democracy.* New York and London: Harper & Brothers Publishers.

Schweik, C. M. (2007). Free/open-source Software as a Framework for Establishing Commons in Science. In C. Hess & E. Ostrom (Eds.), *Understanding Knowledge as a Commons: From Theory to Practice* (pp. 277–309). Cambridge, MA: The MIT Press.

Schweik, C. M. (2014). Toward the Comparison of Open Source Commons Institutions. In B. M. Frischmann, M. J. Madison, & K. J. Strandburg (Eds.), *Governing Knowledge Commons* (pp. 255–279). New York: Oxford University Press.

Schweik, C. M. & English, R. C. (2012). *Internet Success: A Study of Open-source Software Commons.* Cambridge, US: MIT Press.

Scotchmer, S. (1991). Standing on the shoulders of giants: Cumulative research and the patent law. *The Journal of Economic Perspectives, 5*(1), 29–41.

Scott, A. (1955). The fishery: The objectives of sole ownership. *Journal of Political Economy, 63*(2), 116–124.

Scott, J. C. (2014). *The Art of Not Being Governed: An Anarchist History of Upland Southeast Asia.* US: Yale University Press.

Seckinger, N., Park, B., & Gerhard, D. (2012). "Hackerpsaces and Meta-Creativity: A Response to 'Moving Saskatchewan's Creative Industries Forward-Building a LongTerm Strategy'", CrashBangLabs Inc.

Seravalli, A. (2011). *Democratizing Production: Challenges in Co-designing Enabling Platforms for Social Innovation.* Paper presented at the The Tao of Sustainability, International Conference on Sustainable Design Strategies in a Globalization Context, Bejing, China.

Shackle, G. L. S. (1983). The Bounds of Unknowledge. In J. Wiseman (Ed.), *Beyond Positive Economics* (pp. 28–37). London, UK: Macmillan.

Shackle, G. L. S. (1992). *Epistemics and economics*: Transaction Publishers.

Shane, S. A. (2000). Prior knowledge and the discovery of entrepreneurial opportunities. *Organization science, 11*(4), 448–469.

Shane, S. A. & Eckhardt, J. T. (2003). Opportunities and entrepreneurship. *Journal of Management, 29*(3), 333–349.

Shane, S. A. & Venkataraman, S. (2000). The promise of entrepreneurship as a field of research. *Academy of Management Review, 25*(1), 217–226.

Shapiro, C. (2001). Navigating the Patent Thicket: Cross Licenses, Patent Pools, and Standard Setting. In A. Jaffe, J. Lerner, & S. Stern (Eds.), *Innovation Policy and the Economy* (pp. 119–150). Cambridge, US: MIT press.

Shelanski, H. A. & Klein, P. G. (1995). Empirical research in transaction cost economics: A review and assessment. *Journal of Law, Economics, & Organization, 11*(2), 335–361.

Shleifer, A. (2005). Understanding regulation. *European Financial Management, 11*(4), 439–451.

Simon, H. A. (1957). *Models of Man: Social and Rational*. New York, US: John Wiley and Sons, Inc.

Skarbek, D. (2011). Governance and prison gangs. *American Political Science Review, 105*(04), 702–716.

Skarbek, D. (2012). Prison gangs, norms, and organizations. *Journal of Economic Behavior & Organization, 82*(1), 96–109.

Skarbek, D. (2014). *The Social Order of the Underworld: How Prison Gangs Govern the American Penal System*: Oxford University Press.

Smith, A. (1976 [1776]). *An Inquiry into the Nature and Causes of the Wealth of Nations*. Chicago, US: University of Chicago Press.

Smith, A., Wagner, R. E., & Yandle, B. (2011). A theory of entangled political economy, with application to TARP and NRA. *Public Choice, 148*(1–2), 45–66.

Soete, L., Verspagen, B., & Ter Weel, B. (2010). Systems of Innovation. In B. H. Hall & N. Rosenberg (Eds.), *Handbook of the Economics of Innovation* (Vol. 2, pp. 1159–1180).

Somin, I. (2013). *Democracy and Political Ignorance: Why Smaller Government is Smarter*. US: Stanford University Press.

Spence, M. (1973). Job market signaling. *The Quarterly Journal of Economics, 87*(3), 355–374.

Stern, P. (2011). Design principles for global commons: Natural resources and emerging technologies. *International Journal of the Commons, 5*(2), 213–232.

Stigler, G. J. (1961). The economics of information. *The Journal of Political Economy, 69*(3), 213–225.

Stigler, G. J. (1971). The theory of economic regulation. *The Bell Journal of Economics and Management Science, 2*(1), 3–21.

Stringham, E. P. (2010). Economic Value and Cost Are Subjective. In P. J. Boettke (Ed.), *Edward Elgar Publishing* (pp. 43–66). Cheltenham, UK: Edward Elgar.

Stringham, E. P. (2015). *Private Governance: Creating Order in Economic and Social Life.* UK: Oxford University Press.

Swan, T. W. (1956). Economic growth and capital accumulation. *Economic record, 32*(2), 334–361.

Tadelis, S. & Williamson, O. (2010). Transaction Cost Economics. In R. Gibbons (Ed.), *The Handbook of Organizational Economics* (Vol. 14, pp. 159–190). US: Princeton University Press.

Tarko, V. (2015a). *Polycentric Governance: A Theoretical and Empirical Exploration.* George Mason University.

Tarko, V. (2015b). The role of ideas in political economy. *The Review of Austrian Economics, 28*(1), 17–39.

Tarko, V. (2016). *Elinor Ostrom: An Intellectual Biography.* London, UK: Rowman & Littlefield International.

Taylor, P. A. (2005). From hackers to hacktivists: Speed bumps on the global superhighway? *New Media & Society, 7*(5), 625–646.

Teece, D. & Pisano, G. (1994). The dynamic capabilities of firms: An introduction. *Industrial and Corporate Change, 3*(3), 537–556.

Teece, D. J. (1986). Transactions cost economics and the multinational enterprise an assessment. *Journal of Economic Behavior & Organization, 7*(1), 21–45.

Teece, D. J. (1996). Firm organization, industrial structure, and technological innovation. *Journal of Economic Behavior & Organization, 31*(2), 193–224.

Teece, D. J., Pisano, G., & Shuen, A. (1997). Dynamic capabilities and strategic management. *Strategic Management Journal, 18*(7), 509–533.

Thierer, A. (2016). Innovation Arbitrage, Technological Civil Disobedience & Spontaneous Deregulation. *The Technology Liberation Front.* Retrieved from https://techliberation.com/2016/12/05/innovation-arbitrage-technological-civil-disobedience-spontaneous-deregulation/.

Thierer, A. D. (2014). *Permissionless Innovation: The Continuing Case for Comprehensive Technological Freedom.* Arlington, Virginia, US: Mercatus Center at George Mason University.

Tirole, J. (1999). Incomplete contracts: Where do we stand? *Econometrica, 67*(4), 741–781.

Trainer, E. H., Kalyanasundaram, A., Chaihirunkarn, C., & Herbsleb, J. D. (2016). *How to Hackathon: Socio-technical Tradeoffs in Brief, Intensive Collocation.* Paper presented at the Conference on Computer-supported Cooperative Work & Social Computing, San Francisco, US. https://herbsleb. org/web-pubs/pdfs/trainer-howto-2016.pdf.

Tweney, D. (2009, 29 March). DIY Freaks Flock to 'Hacker Spaces' Worldwide. *Wired, 13.* Retrieved from http://www.wired.com/2009/03/hackerspaces.

Usher, D. (1964). The welfare economcis of innovation. *Econometrica, 31*(123), 279–287.

van Holm, E. J. (2015a). Makerspaces and contributions to entrepreneurship. *Procedia-Social and Behavioral Sciences, 195,* 24–31.

van Holm, E. J. (2015b). *What are Makerspaces, Hackerspaces, and Fab Labs?*

Vaughn, K. I. (1998). *Austrian Economics in America: The Migration of a Tradition.* Cambridge, UK: Cambridge University Press.

Venkataraman, S. (1997). The distinctive domain of entrepreneurship research. *Advances in Entrepreneurship, Firm Emergence and Growth, 3*(1), 119–138.

von Hippel, E. (1986). Lead users: A source of novel product concepts. *Management Science, 32*(7), 791–805.

von Hippel, E. & von Krogh, G. (2003). Open Source Software and the "Private-collective" Innovation Model: Issues for Organization Science. *Organization Science, 14*(2), 209–223.

von Krogh, G., Haefliger, S., Spaeth, S., & Wallin, M. W. (2012). Carrots and rainbows: Motivation and social practice in open source software development. *MIS Quarterly, 36*(2), 649–676.

Wagner, R. E. (2006). Retrogressive regime drift within a theory of emergent order. *The Review of Austrian Economics, 19*(2), 113–123.

Wagner, R. E. (2014). Entangled Political Economy: A Keynote Address. In R. Koppl & S. Horwitz (Eds.), *Advances in Austrian Economics* (Vol. 18, pp. 15–36): Emerald Group Publishing Limited.

Wagner, R. E. (2016a). *The Peculiar Business of Politics.* GMU Working Paper in Economics No. 16–27.

Wagner, R. E. (2016b). *Politics as a Peculiar Business: Insights from a Theory of Entangled Political Economy.* Cheltenham, UK: Edward Elgar.

Whitford, A. & Lee, S.-Y. (2012). Disorder, dictatorship and government effectiveness: Cross-national evidence. *Journal of Public Policy, 32*(1), 5–31.

Wieser, F. v. (1914). Theorie der gesellschaftlichen Wirtschaft. In K. Bücher, J. A. Schumpeter, & F. v. Wieser (Eds.), *Grundriss der Sozialökonomik* (Vol. 1, pp. 125–444): Grundlagen der Wirtschaft: Wirtschaft und Wirtschaftswissenschaft, Tübingen: Mohr.

Williams, A., Gibb, A., & Weekly, D. (2012). Research with a hacker Ethos: What DIY means for tangible interaction research. *Interactions, 19*(2), 14–19.

Williams, M. R. & Hall, J. C. (2015). Hackerspaces: A case study in the creation and management of a common pool resource. *Journal of Institutional Economics, 11*(4), 1–13.

Williamson, O. E. (1975). *Markets and Hierarchies: Analysis and Antitrust Implications: A Study in the Economics of Interal Organization.* New York, US: Free Press.

Williamson, O. E. (1979). Transaction-cost economics: The governance of contractual relations. *Journal of Law and Economics, 22*(2), 233–261.

Williamson, O. E. (1983). Credible commitments: Using hostages to support exchange. *The American Economic Review, 73*(4), 519–540.

Williamson, O. E. (1985a). *The Economic Institutions of Capitalism: Firms, Markets, Relational Contracting.* New York, US: The Free Press.

Williamson, O. E. (1985b). Employee ownership and internal governance: A perspective. *Journal of Economic Behavior & Organization, 6*(3), 243–245.

Williamson, O. E. (1991). Comparative economic organization: The analysis of discrete structural alternatives. *Administrative Science Quarterly, 36*(2), 269–296.

Williamson, O. E. (1996). *The Mechanisms of Governance.* New York, US: Oxford University Press.

Williamson, O. E. (1998). Transaction cost economics: How it works; where it is headed. *De economist, 146*(1), 23–58.

Williamson, O. E. (2000). The new institutional economics: Taking stock, looking ahead. *Journal of Economic Literature, 38*(3), 595–613.

Williamson, O. E. (2002a). The lens of contract: Private ordering. *American Economic Review, 92*(2), 438–443.

Williamson, O. E. (2002b). The theory of the firm as governance structure: From choice to contract. *The Journal of Economic Perspectives, 16*(3), 171–195.

Williamson, O. E. (2005). The economics of governance. *American Economic Review, 95*(2), 1–18.

Williamson, O. E. (2007). Transaction cost economics: An introduction. *Economics Discussion Paper* (2007–3).

Wilson, D. S., Ostrom, E., & Cox, M. E. (2013). Generalizing the core design principles for the efficacy of groups. *Journal of Economic Behavior & Organization, 90*, S21–S32.

Winter, S. G. (2003). Understanding dynamic capabilities. *Strategic Management Journal, 24*(10), 991–995.

Witt, U. (1999). Do entrepreneurs need firms? A contribution to a missing chapter in austrian economics. *The Review of Austrian Economics, 11*(1), 99–109.

Woolthuis, R. K., Lankhuizen, M., & Gilsing, V. (2005). A system failure framework for innovation policy design. *Technovation, 25*(6), 609–619.

Wu, T. (2006). Intellectual property, innovation, and decentralized decisions. *Virginia Law Review, 92*(1), 123–147.

Wykretowicz, D. (2013). *Vanguard of the 3D Printed Future: Peer Production with The Use of 3D Printing at Hackerspaces.* (Master of Arts). Central European University.

Yeager, L. (1987). Why subjectivism? *The Review of Austrian Economics, 1*(1), 5–31.

Ziman, J. (Ed.) (2000). *Technological Innovation as an Evolutionary Process.* Cambridge: Cambridge University Press.

Index

Printed in the United States
by Baker & Taylor Publisher Services